Pro Core Data for iOS

Data Access and Persistence Engine for iPhone, iPad, and iPod touch

Michael Privat
and Rob Warner

APress®

Pro Core Data for iOS: Data Access and Persistence Engine for iPhone, iPad, and iPod touch

ISBN-13 (pbk): 978-1-4302-3355-8

ISBN-13 (electronic): 978-1-4302-3356-5

Printed and bound in the United States of America 9 8 7 6 5 4 3 2 1

President and Publisher: Paul Manning
Lead Editor: Steve Anglin
Development Editor: Douglas Pundick
Technical Reviewer: Robert Hamilton
Editorial Board: Steve Anglin, Mark Beckner, Ewan Buckingham, Gary Cornell, Jonathan Gennick,
    Jonathan Hassell, Michelle Lowman, Matthew Moodie, Duncan Parkes, Jeffrey Pepper,
    Douglas Pundick, Ben Renow-Clarke, Dominic Shakeshaft, Matt Wade, Tom Welsh
Coordinating Editor: Jennifer L. Blackwell
Copy Editor: Kim Wimpsett
Indexer: BIM Indexing & Proofreading Services
Compositor: Richard Ables
Artist: April Milne
Cover Designer: Anna Ishchenko

Distributed to the book trade worldwide by Springer Science+Business Media, LLC., 233 Spring Street, 6th Floor, New York, NY 10013. Phone 1-800-SPRINGER, fax (201) 348-4505, e-mail orders-ny@springer-sbm.com, or visit www.springeronline.com.

For information on translations, please e-mail rights@apress.com, or visit www.apress.com.

Apress and friends of ED books may be purchased in bulk for academic, corporate, or promotional use. eBook versions and licenses are also available for most titles. For more information, reference our Special Bulk Sales–eBook Licensing web page at www.apress.com/info/bulksales.

The source code for this book is availale to readers at www.apress.com.

To my loving wife, Kelly, and our children, Matthieu and Chloé.

—Michael Privat

To my beautiful wife Sherry and our wonderful children: Tyson, Jacob, Mallory, Camie, and Leila.

—Rob Warner

...

Contents at a Glance

Contents

About the Authors

 **Michael Privat is** the president and CEO of Majorspot, Inc., developer of several iPhone and iPad apps:

- Ghostwriter Notes
- My Spending
- iBudget
- Chess Puzzle Challenge

He is also an expert developer and technical lead for Availity, LLC, based in Jacksonville, Florida. He earned his master's degree in computer science from the University of Nice in Nice, France. He moved to the United States to develop software in artificial intelligence at the Massachusetts Institute of Technology. He now lives in Jacksonville, Florida, with his wife, Kelly, and their two children.

 **Rob Warner** is a senior technical staff member for Availity, LLC, based in Jacksonville, Florida, where he works with various teams and technologies to deliver solutions in the healthcare sector. He coauthored *The Definitive Guide to SWT and JFace* (Apress, 2004), and he blogs at www.grailbox.com. He earned his bachelor's degree in English from Brigham Young University in Provo, Utah. He lives in Jacksonville, Florida, with his wife, Sherry, and their five children.

About the Technical Reviewer

Robert Hamilton is a seasoned information technology director for Blue Cross Blue Shield of Florida (BCBSF). He is experienced in developing apps for iPhone and iPad, most recently, Ghostwriter Notes.

Before entering his leadership role at BCBSF, Robert excelled as an application developer, having envisioned and created the first claims status application used by its providers through Avality.

A native of Atlantic Beach, Florida, Robert received his bachelor's of science degree in information systems from the University of North Florida. He supports the First Tee of Jacksonville and the Cystic Fibrosis Foundation. He is the proud father of two daughters.

Acknowledgments

There is no telling how many books never had a chance to be written because the potential authors had other family obligations to fulfill. I thank my wife, Kelly, and my children, Matthieu and Chloé, for allowing me to focus my time on this book for a few months and accomplish this challenge. Without the unconditional support and encouragement they gave me, I would not have been able to contribute to the creation of this book.

Working on this book with Rob Warner has also been enlightening. I have learned a lot from him through this effort. His dedication to getting the job done right carried me when I was tired. His technical skills got me unstuck a few times when I was clueless. His gift for writing so elegantly and his patience have made my engineer jargon sound like nineteenth-century prose.
I also thank the friendly and savvy Apress team who made the whole process work like a well-oiled machine. Jennifer Blackwell challenged us throughout the project with seemingly unreasonable deadlines that we always managed to meet. Douglas Pundick shared his editorial wisdom to keep this work readable, well organized, and understandable; Steve Anglin, Kim Wimpsett, and the rest of the Apress folks were always around for us to lean on.

Finally, I thank the incredibly talented people of Availity who were supportive of this book from the very first day and make this company a great place to work at. I thank Trent Gavazzi, Geoff Packwood, Ben Van Maanen, Taryn Tresca, Herve Devos, and all the others for their friendship and encouragement.

—Michael Privat

Thank you to my wife, Sherry, for her support and to my children for their patience. This book represents sacrifice from all of them. May one of them, one day, be bit by the programming bug.
Working with Michael Privat on this project has been an amazing experience. He is, indeed, tireless and brilliant, and this book couldn't have happened without him.

Apress is a terrific publisher to work with, and I thank them for the opportunity to write again. Publishing a book requires a team of folks, and I thank Steve Anglin, who brought such great energy and ideas; Jennifer Blackwell, who always kept us on task; Douglas Pundick, who had great insight and understanding; Kim Wimpsett, who clarified and corrected; and the rest of the Apress team. Robert Hamilton kept us technically correct throughout, and I'm glad we had him on board.

I have the opportunity to work with some amazing people in my day job at Availity—far too many to name—and I thank all of them for their support and friendships. Trent Gavazzi, Jon McBride, Mary Anne Orenchuk, and the rest of the senior leadership team were extremely supportive as we embarked on this project, and so many others offered kind words and encouragement. I also thank Geoff Packwood for helping me rekindle my passion and find my way.

Finally, I thank my parents for the love of learning they instilled in me. They pre-ordered this book despite their inability to decipher a word of it. They are great people.

—Rob Warner

Introduction

Once you've learned the basics of iOS development and you're ready to dig deeper into how to write great iOS applications, *Pro Core Data for iOS* leads you through the important topic of data persistence. Storing and retrieving customers' data is a task you must pull off flawlessly for your application to survive and be used. Introductory texts give you introductory-level understanding of the Core Data framework, which is fine for introductory-level applications but not for applications that cross the chasm from toys to real-life, frequently used applications. This book provides you with the deeper levels of information and understanding necessary for developing killer apps that store and retrieve data with the performance, precision, and reliability customers expect and require.

What to Expect from This Book

This book starts by setting a clear foundation for what Core Data is and how it works and then takes you step-by-step through how to extract the results you need from this powerful framework. You'll learn what the components of Core Data are and how they interact, how to design your data model, how to filter your results, how to tune performance, how to migrate your data across data model versions, and many other topics around and between these that will separate your apps from the crowd.

This book combines theory and code to teach its subject matter. Although you can take the book to your Barcalounger and read it cover to cover, you'll find the book is more effective if you're in front of a computer, typing in and understanding the code it explains. We also hope that, after you read the book and work through its exercises, you'll keep it handy as a reference, turning to it often for answers and clarification.

How This Book Is Organized

We've tried to arrange the material so that it grows in complexity, at least in a general sense, as the book progresses. The topics tend to build on each other, so you'll likely benefit most by working through the book front to back, rather than skipping around. If you're looking for guidance on a specific topic—

versioning and migrating data, say, or tuning performance and memory usage—skip ahead to that chapter. Most chapters focus on a single topic, indicated by that chapter's title. The final chapter covers an array of advanced topics that didn't fit neatly anywhere else.

Source Code and Errata

You can (and should!) download the source code from the Apress web site at www.apress.com. Feel free to use it in your own applications, whether personal or commercial. We tried to keep the text and code error-free, but some bug or typos might be unveiled over time. Corrections to both text and code can be found in this book's errata section on the Apress web site.

How to Contact Us

We'd love to hear from you. Please send any questions or comments regarding this book or its accompanying source code to the authors. You can find them here:

Michael Privat:
E-mail: mprivat@mac.com
Twitter: @michaelprivat
Blog: http://michaelprivat.com

Rob Warner:
E-mail: rwarner@grailbox.com
Twitter: @hoop33
Blog: http://grailbox.com

Chapter 1

Getting Started

If you misread this book's title, thought it discussed and deciphered core dumps, and hope it will help you debug a nasty application crash, you got the wrong book. Get a debugger, memory tools, and an appointment with the optometrist. Otherwise, you bought, borrowed, burglarized, or acquired this book somehow because you want to better understand and implement Core Data in your iOS applications. You got the right book.

You might read these words from a paper book, stout and sturdy and smelling faintly of binding glue. You might digitally flip through these pages on a nook, iPad, Kindle, Sony Reader, Kobo eReader, or some other electronic book reader. You might stare at a computer screen, whether on laptop, netbook, or monitor, reading a few words at a time while telling yourself to ignore your Twitter feed rolling CNN-like along the screen's edge. Regardless, as you read, you know that not only can you stop at any time but that you can resume at any time. These words persist on paper and digital page and, with proper care and timely transformation to future media, can survive your grandchildren's grandchildren. Any time you want to read this book, you pick up book, electronic reader, or keyboard, and if you marked the spot where you were last reading, you can even start from where you last stopped. We take this for granted with books.

Users take it for granted with applications.

Users expect to find their data each time they launch their applications. Apple's Core Data framework helps you ensure that they will. This chapter introduces you to Core Data, explaining what it is, how it came to be, and how to build simple Core Data–based applications for iOS. This book walks through the simpleness and complexities of Core Data. Use the information in the book to create applications that store and retrieve data reliably and efficiently so that users can depend on their data. Code carefully, though— you don't want to write buggy code and have to deal with nasty application crashes.

What Is Core Data?

When people use computers, they expect to preserve any progress they make toward completing their tasks. Saving progress, essential to office software, code editors, and games involving small plumbers, is what programmers call *persistence*. Most software requires persistence, or the ability to store and retrieve data, to be useful so that users don't have to reenter all their data each time they use the applications. Some software can survive without any data storage or retrieval; calculators, carpenter's levels, and apps that make annoying or obscene sounds spring to mind. Most useful applications, however, preserve some state, whether configuration-oriented data, progress toward achieving some goal, or mounds of related data that users create and care about. Understanding how to persist data to iDevices is critical to most useful iOS development.

Apple's Core Data provides a versatile persistence framework. Core Data isn't the only data storage option, nor is it necessarily the best option in all scenarios, but it fits well with the rest of the Cocoa Touch development framework and maps well to objects. Core Data hides most of the complexities of data storage and allows you to focus on what makes your application fun, unique, or usable.

Although Core Data can store data in a relational database (such as SQLite), it is not a database engine. It doesn't even have to use a relational database to store its data. Though Core Data provides an entity-relationship diagramming tool, it is not a data modeler. It isn't a data access layer like Hibernate, though it provides much of the same object-relational mapping functionality. Instead, Core Data wraps the best of all these tools into a data management framework that allows you to work with entities, attributes, and relationships in a way that resembles the object graphs you're used to working with in normal object-oriented programming.

Early iPhone programmers didn't have the power of the Core Data framework to store and retrieve data. The next section shows you the history behind persistence in iOS.

History of Persistence in iOS

Core Data evolved from a NeXT technology called Enterprise Objects Framework (EOF) by way of WebObjects, another NeXT technology that still powers parts of Apple's web site. It debuted in 2005 as part of Mac OS X 10.4 ("Tiger"), but didn't appear on iPhones until version 3.0 of the SDK, released in June 2009. Before Core Data, iPhone developers had a few persistence options:

- Use property lists, which contain nested lists of key/value pairs of various data types.

- Serialize objects to files using the SDK's NSCoding protocol.

- Take advantage of the iPhone's support for the relational database SQLite.

- Persist data to the Internet cloud.

Developers used all these mechanisms for data storage as they built the first wave of applications that flooded Apple's App Store. Each one of these storage options remains viable, and developers continue to employ them as they build newer applications using newer SDK versions.

None of these options, however, compares favorably to the power, ease of use, and Cocoa-fitness of Core Data. Despite the invention of frameworks like FMDatabase or ActiveRecord to make dealing with persistence on iOS easier in the pre–Core Data days, developers gratefully leapt to Core Data when it became available.

Although Core Data might not solve all persistence problems best and you might serve some of your persistence scenarios using other means like the options listed earlier, you'll turn to Core Data more often than not. As you work through this book and learn the problems that Core Data solves and how elegantly it solves them, you'll likely use Core Data any time you can. As new persistence opportunities arise, you won't ask yourself, "Should I use Core Data for this?" but rather, "Is there any reason *not* to use Core Data?"

The next section shows you how to build a basic Core Data application using Xcode's project templates. Even if you've already generated an Xcode Core Data project, though, and know all the buttons and check boxes to click, don't skip the next section. It explains the Core Data–related sections of code that the templates generate and forms a base of understanding on which the rest of the book builds.

Creating a Basic Core Data Application

The many facets, classes, and nuances of Core Data merit artful analysis and deep discussions to teach you all you need to know to gain mastery of Core Data's complexities. Building a practical foundation to support the theory, however, is just as essential to mastery. This section builds a simple Core Data–based application, using one of Xcode's built-in templates, and then dissects the most important parts of its Core Data–related code to show what they do and how they interact. At the end of this section, you will understand how this application interacts with Core Data to store and retrieve data.

Understanding the Core Data Components

Before building this section's basic Core Data application, you should have a high-level understanding of the components of Core Data. Figure 1-1 illustrates the key elements of the application we build in this section. Review this figure for a bird's-eye view of what this application accomplishes, where all its pieces fit, and why you need them.

As a user of Core Data, you should never interact directly with the underlying persistent store. One of the fundamental principles of Core Data is that the persistent store should be abstracted from the user. A key advantage of that is the ability to seamlessly change the backing store in the future without having to modify the rest of your code. You should try to picture Core Data as a framework that manages the persistence of objects rather than thinking about databases. Not surprisingly, the objects managed by the framework must extend `NSManagedObject` and are typically referred to as, well, managed objects. Don't think, though, that the lack of imagination in the naming conventions for the components of Core Data reveals an unimaginative or mundane framework. In fact, Core Data does an excellent job at keeping all the object graph interdependencies, optimizations, and caching in a predictable state so that you don't have to worry about it. If you have ever tried to build your own object management framework, you understand all the intricacies of the problem Core Data solves for you.

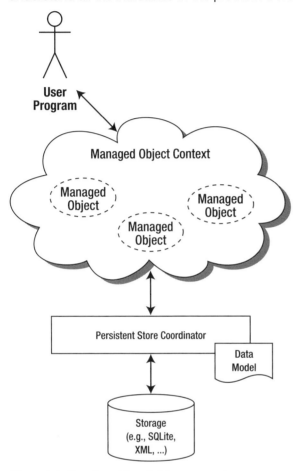

Figure 1-1. *Overview of Core Data's components*

Much like we need a livable environment to subsist, managed objects must live within an environment that's livable for them, usually referred to as a *managed object context*, or simply *context*. The context keeps track of the states of not only the object you are altering but also all the objects that depend on it or that it depends on. The NSManagedObjectContext object in your application provides the context and is the key property that your code must always be able to get a handle to. You typically accomplish exposing your NSManagedObjectContext object to your application by having your application delegate initialize it and expose it as one of its properties. Your application context often will give the NSManagedObjectContext object to the main view controller as well. Without the context, you will not be able to interact with Core Data.

Creating a New Project

To begin, launch Xcode, and create a new project by selecting **File ➤ New Project…** from the menu. Note that you can also create a new project by pressing ⇧+⌘+N. From the list of application templates, select the Application item under iPhone OS on the left, and pick Navigation-based Application on the right. Check Use Core Data for storage. See Figure 1-2. Click the Choose… button. On the ensuing screen, type **BasicApplication** in the Save As field, and change the parent directory for your project's directory as you see fit. See Figure 1-3. Click the Save button to set Xcode into motion. Xcode creates your project, generates the project's files, and opens its IDE window with all the files it generated, as Figure 1-4 shows.

Figure 1-2. *Creating a new project with Core Data*

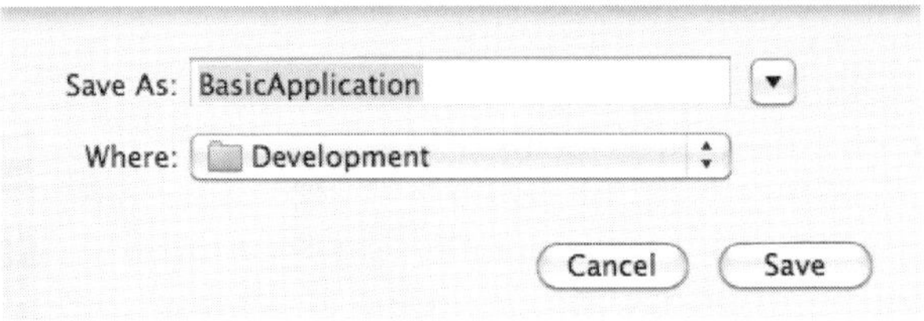

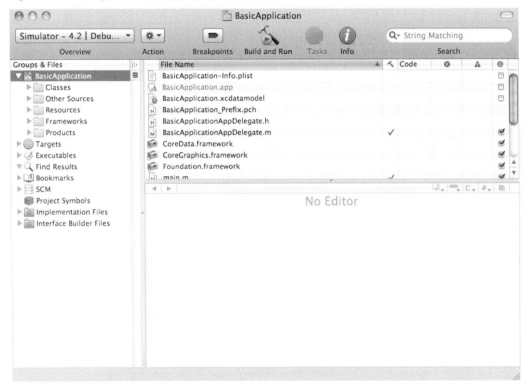

Figure 1-3. *Choosing where to save your project*

Figure 1-4. *Xcode showing your new project*

Running Your New Project

Before digging into the code, run it to see what it does. Launch the application by clicking the Build and Run button. The iPhone Simulator opens, and the application presents a navigation-based interface with a table view occupying the bulk of the screen, an Edit button in the top-left corner, and the conventional Add button, denoted by a plus sign, in the upper-right corner. The application's table shows an empty list indicating that the application isn't aware of any events. Create a new event stamped with the current time by clicking the plus button in the top-right corner of the application.

Now, stop the application by clicking the Tasks button in the Xcode IDE, which is the one to the right of the Build and Run button. If the application hadn't used persistence, it would have lost the event you just created as it exited. Maintaining a list of events with this application and no persistence would be a Sisyphean task—you'd have to re-create the events each time you launched the application. Because the application uses persistence, however, it stored the event you created using the Core Data framework. Relaunching the application shows that the event is still there, as Figure 1-5 demonstrates.

Figure 1-5. *The basic application with a persisted event*

Understanding the Application's Components

The anatomy of the application is relatively simple. It has a data model that describes the entities in the data store, a view controller that facilitates interactions between the view and the data store, and an application delegate that helps initialize and launch the application. Figure 1-6 shows the classes involved and how they relate to each other. Note how the RootViewController class, which is in charge of managing the user interface, has a handle to the managed object context so that it can interact with Core

Data. As we go through the code, we see that the RootViewController class obtained the managed object context from the application delegate's initialization.

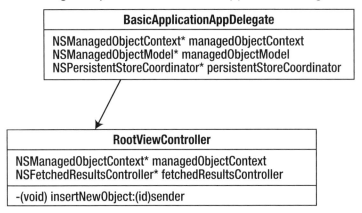

Figure 1-6. *Classes involved in the BasicApplication example*

The entry under the project's Resources group called BasicApplication.xcdatamodeld, which is actually a directory on the file system, contains the data model, BasicApplication.xcdatamodel. The data model is central to every Core Data application. This particular data model defines only one entity, named Event, for the application. Events are defined as entities that contain only one attribute named timeStamp of type Date, as shown in Figure 1-7.

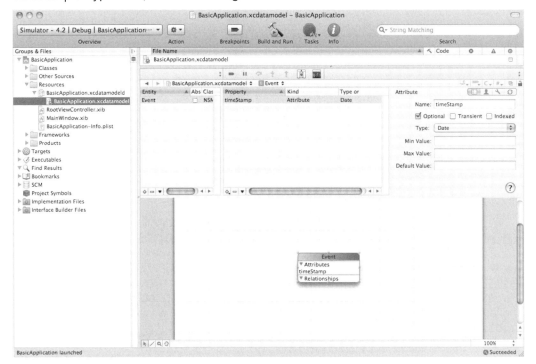

Figure 1-7. *The Xcode-generated data model*

Note also that the Event entity is of type NSManagedObject, which is the basic type for all entities managed by Core Data. Chapter 2 explains the NSManagedObject type in more detail.

Fetching Results

The next class of interest is the RootViewController. Opening its header file (RootViewController.h) reveals two properties:

```
@property (nonatomic, retain) NSManagedObjectContext *managedObjectContext;
@property (nonatomic, retain) NSFetchedResultsController➡
 *fetchedResultsController;
```

These properties are defined using the same syntax as the definitions of any Objective-C class properties. The NSFetchedResultsController is a type of controller provided by the Core Data framework that helps manage results from queries. NSManagedObjectContext is a handle to the application's persistent store that provides a context, or environment, for the managed objects to exist in.

The implementation of the RootViewController, found in RootViewController.m, shows how to interact with the Core Data framework to store and retrieve data. The RootViewController implementation provides an explicit getter for the fetchedResultsController property that preconfigures it to fetch data from the data store.

The first step in creating the fetch controller consists of creating a request that will retrieve Event entities, as shown in this code:

```
NSFetchRequest *fetchRequest = [[NSFetchRequest alloc] init];
NSEntityDescription *entity = [NSEntityDescription entityForName:@"Event"➡
 inManagedObjectContext:self.managedObjectContext];
[fetchRequest setEntity:entity];
```

The result of the request can be ordered using the sort descriptor from the Cocoa Foundation framework. The sort descriptor defines the field to use for sorting and whether the sort is ascending or descending. In this case, we sort by descending chronological order:

```
NSSortDescriptor *sortDescriptor = [[NSSortDescriptor alloc] initWithKey:➡
@"timeStamp" ascending:NO];
NSArray *sortDescriptors = [[NSArray alloc] initWithObjects:sortDescriptor, nil];
[fetchRequest setSortDescriptors:sortDescriptors];
```

Once we define the request, we can use it to construct the fetch controller. Because the RootViewController implements NSFetchedResultsControllerDelegate, it can be set as the NSFetchedResultsController's delegate so that it is automatically notified as the result set changes and so that it updates its view appropriately. We could get the same results by invoking the executeFetchRequest of the managed object context, but we would not benefit from the other advantages that come from using the NSFetchedResultsController such as the seamless integration with the UITableView, as we'll see later in this section and in Chapter 9. Here is the code that constructs the fetch controller:

```
NSFetchedResultsController *aFetchedResultsController = [[NSFetchedResultsController➥
 alloc] initWithFetchRequest:fetchRequest managedObjectContext:➥
self.managedObjectContext sectionNameKeyPath:nil cacheName:@"Root"];
aFetchedResultsController.delegate = self;
self.fetchedResultsController = aFetchedResultsController;
```

> **Note:** You may have noticed that the `initWithFetchRequest` shown earlier uses a parameter called `cacheName`. We could pass `nil` for the `cacheName` parameter to prevent caching, but naming a cache indicates to Core Data to check for a cache with a name matching the passed name and see whether it already contains the same fetch request definition. If it does find a match, it will reuse the cached results. If it finds a cache entry by that name but the request doesn't match, then it is deleted. If it doesn't find it at all, then the request is executed, and the cache entry is created for the next time. This is obviously an optimization that aims to prevent executing the same request over and over. Core Data manages its caches intelligently so that if the results are updated by another call, the cache is removed if impacted.

Finally, you tell the controller to execute its query to start retrieving results. To do this, use the `performFetch` method:

```
NSError *error = nil;
if (![fetchedResultsController_ performFetch:&error]) {
  NSLog(@"Unresolved error %@, %@", error, [error userInfo]);
  abort();
}
```

The entire getter method for fetchedResultsController looks like this:

```
- (NSFetchedResultsController *)fetchedResultsController {

  if (fetchedResultsController_ != nil) {
    return fetchedResultsController_;
  }

  /*
   Set up the fetched results controller.
   */
  // Create the fetch request for the entity.
  NSFetchRequest *fetchRequest = [[NSFetchRequest alloc] init];
  // Edit the entity name as appropriate.
  NSEntityDescription *entity = [NSEntityDescription entityForName:@"Event"➥
inManagedObjectContext:self.managedObjectContext];
  [fetchRequest setEntity:entity];

  // Set the batch size to a suitable number.
  [fetchRequest setFetchBatchSize:20];
```

```
  // Edit the sort key as appropriate.
  NSSortDescriptor *sortDescriptor = [[NSSortDescriptor alloc] initWithKey:➥
@"timeStamp" ascending:NO];
  NSArray *sortDescriptors = [[NSArray alloc] initWithObjects:sortDescriptor, nil];

  [fetchRequest setSortDescriptors:sortDescriptors];

  // Edit the section name key path and cache name if appropriate.
  // nil for section name key path means "no sections".
  NSFetchedResultsController *aFetchedResultsController = [[NSFetchedResultsController➥
 alloc] initWithFetchRequest:fetchRequest managedObjectContext:➥
self.managedObjectContext sectionNameKeyPath:nil cacheName:@"Root"];
  aFetchedResultsController.delegate = self;
  self.fetchedResultsController = aFetchedResultsController;

  [aFetchedResultsController release];
  [fetchRequest release];
  [sortDescriptor release];
  [sortDescriptors release];

  NSError *error = nil;
  if (![fetchedResultsController_ performFetch:&error]) {
    /*
     Replace this implementation with code to handle the error appropriately.

     abort() causes the application to generate a crash log and terminate. You should➥
not use this function in a shipping application, although it may be useful during➥
development. If it is not possible to recover from the error, display an alert panel➥
that instructs the user to quit the application by pressing the Home button.
     */
    NSLog(@"Unresolved error %@, %@", error, [error userInfo]);
    abort();
  }

  return fetchedResultsController_;
}
```

NSFetchedResultsController behaves as a collection of managed objects, similar to an NSArray, which makes it easy to use. In fact, it exposes a read-only property called fetchedObjects that is of type NSArray to make things even easier to access the objects it fetches. The RootViewController class, which also extends UITableViewController, demonstrates just how suited the NSFetchedResultsController is to manage the table's content.

Inserting New Objects

A quick glance at the insertNewObject method shows how new events (the managed objects) are created and added to the persistent store. Managed objects are defined by the entity description from the data model and can live only within a context. The first step is to get a hold of the current context as well as the entity definition. In this case, instead of explicitly naming the entity, we reuse the entity definitions that are attached to the fetched results controller:

```
NSManagedObjectContext *context = [fetchedResultsController managedObjectContext];
NSEntityDescription *entity = [[fetchedResultsController fetchRequest] entity];
```

Now that we've gathered all the elements needed to bring the new managed object to existence, we create the Event object and set its timeStamp value.

```
NSManagedObject *newManagedObject = [NSEntityDescription➡
 insertNewObjectForEntityForName:[entity name] inManagedObjectContext:context];
[newManagedObject setValue:[NSDate date] forKey:@"timeStamp"];
```

The last step of the process is to tell Core Data to save changes to its context. The obvious change is the object we just created, but keep in mind that calling the save method will also affect any other unsaved changes to the context.

```
NSError *error = nil;
if (![context save:&error]) {
  NSLog(@"Unresolved error %@, %@", error, [error userInfo]);
  abort();
}
```

The complete method for inserting the new Event object is as follows:

```
- (void)insertNewObject {

  // Create a new instance of the entity managed by the fetched results controller.
  NSManagedObjectContext *context = [self.fetchedResultsController➡
managedObjectContext];
  NSEntityDescription *entity = [[self.fetchedResultsController fetchRequest] entity];
  NSManagedObject *newManagedObject = [NSEntityDescription➡
insertNewObjectForEntityForName:[entity name] inManagedObjectContext:context];

  // If appropriate, configure the new managed object.
  [newManagedObject setValue:[NSDate date] forKey:@"timeStamp"];

  // Save the context.
  NSError *error = nil;
  if (![context save:&error]) {
    /*
     Replace this implementation with code to handle the error appropriately.

     abort() causes the application to generate a crash log and terminate. You should➡
not use this function in a shipping application, although it may be useful during➡
development. If it is not possible to recover from the error, display an alert panel➡
that instructs the user to quit the application by pressing the Home button.
     */
    NSLog(@"Unresolved error %@, %@", error, [error userInfo]);

    abort();
  }
}
```

Initializing the Managed Context

Obviously, none of this can happen without initializing the managed context first. This is the role of the application delegate. In a Core Data–enabled application, the delegate must expose three properties:

```
@property (nonatomic, retain, readonly) NSManagedObjectContext *managedObjectContext;
@property (nonatomic, retain, readonly) NSManagedObjectModel *managedObjectModel;
@property (nonatomic, retain, readonly) NSPersistentStoreCoordinator➥
 *persistentStoreCoordinator;
```

Note that they are all marked as read-only, which prevents any other component in the application from setting them directly. A closer look at BasicApplicationAppDelegate.m shows that all three properties have explicit getter methods.

First, the managed object model is derived from the data model (BasicApplication.xcdatamodel) and loaded:

```
- (NSManagedObjectModel *)managedObjectModel {

    if (managedObjectModel_ != nil) {
        return managedObjectModel_;
    }
    NSString *modelPath = [[NSBundle mainBundle] pathForResource:@"BasicApplication"➥
ofType:@"momd"];

    NSURL *modelURL = [NSURL fileURLWithPath:modelPath];
    managedObjectModel_ = [[NSManagedObjectModel alloc] initWithContentsOfURL:modelURL];
    return managedObjectModel_;
}
```

Then a persistent store is created to support the model. In this case, as well as in most Core Data scenarios, it is backed by a SQLite database. The managed object model is a logical representation of the data store, while the persistent store is the materialization of that data store.

```
- (NSPersistentStoreCoordinator *)persistentStoreCoordinator {

    if (persistentStoreCoordinator_ != nil) {
        return persistentStoreCoordinator_;
    }

    NSURL *storeURL = [[self applicationDocumentsDirectory]➥
URLByAppendingPathComponent:@"BasicApplication.sqlite"];

    NSError *error = nil;
    persistentStoreCoordinator_ = [[NSPersistentStoreCoordinator alloc]➥
initWithManagedObjectModel:[self managedObjectModel]];

    if (![persistentStoreCoordinator_ addPersistentStoreWithType:NSSQLiteStoreType➥
configuration:nil URL:storeURL options:nil error:&error]) {
        NSLog(@"Unresolved error %@, %@", error, [error userInfo]);
        abort();
    }
}
```

```
    return persistentStoreCoordinator_;
}
```

Finally, the managed object context is created:

```
- (NSManagedObjectContext *)managedObjectContext {
  if (managedObjectContext_ != nil) {
    return managedObjectContext_;
  }

  NSPersistentStoreCoordinator *coordinator = [self persistentStoreCoordinator];
  if (coordinator != nil) {
    managedObjectContext_ = [[NSManagedObjectContext alloc] init];
    [managedObjectContext_ setPersistentStoreCoordinator:coordinator];
  }
  return managedObjectContext_;
}
```

The context is used throughout the application as the single interface with the Core Data framework and the persistent store, as Figure 1-8 demonstrates.

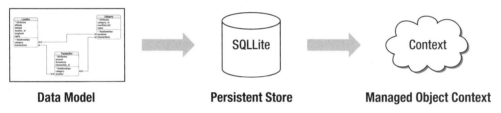

| **Data Model** | **Persistent Store** | **Managed Object Context** |

Figure 1-8. *Core Data initialization sequence*

Lastly, everything is put in motion when the application delegate's awakeFromNib method is called. The managed object context is created and given to the root view controller before its view is shown.

```
- (void)awakeFromNib {
  RootViewController *rootViewController = (RootViewController *)[navigationController⮞
topViewController];

  rootViewController.managedObjectContext = self.managedObjectContext;
}
```

The call to self.managedObjectContext starts a chain reaction by calling -(NSManagedObjectContext *)managedObjectContext, which calls -(NSPersistentStoreCoordinator *)persistentStoreCoordinator and then in turns calls -(NSManagedObjectModel *)managedObjectModel. The single call to self.managedObjectContext therefore initializes the entire Core Data stack and readies Core Data for use.

If you followed along with Xcode on your machine, you have a basic Core Data–based application, generated from Xcode's templates, that you can run to create, store, and retrieve event data. What if, however, you have an existing application to which you want to add the power of Core Data? The next section demonstrates how to add Core Data to an existing iOS application.

Adding Core Data to an Existing Project

Creating a new application and selecting the "Use Core Data for storage" check box, as shown in the previous section, isn't always possible. Frequently, developers start an application, write a lot of code, and only realize later that they need Core Data in their application. We've known developers who, instead of admitting that they should just add Core Data by hand to an existing application and fueled by their desire to prove that they can write their own better persistence layer rather than try to understand how to use the framework, embarked in convoluted programming that led to less than adequate results. Around the time they gave up, they probably realized they had confused persistence with obstinacy. In the spirit of making the jump easier, this section explains the steps involved with retrofitting an application in order to make it aware of and use Core Data.

Enabling an application to leverage Core Data is a three-step process:

1. Add the Core Data framework.

2. Create a data model.

3. Initialize the managed object context.

The next three sections walk you through these three steps so you can add Core Data support to any existing iOS application.

Adding the Core Data Framework

In the Objective-C world, libraries are referred to as *frameworks*. Expanding the Frameworks groups in the Xcode source tree shows that the project is aware of only a handful of frameworks. Typical iOS applications will at least have UIKit (the user interface framework for iOS), Foundation, and Core Graphics. The first step to add Core Data to an existing application consists of making the application aware of the Core Data framework by adding it to the project. To do this, Ctrl+click the Frameworks group, and select **Add ➤ Existing Frameworks…** from the menu. A dialog listing available frameworks displays, from which you can select CoreData.framework and then click Add, as shown in Figure 1-9.

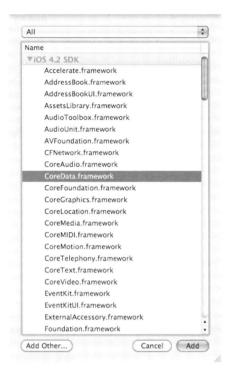

Figure 1-9. *Viewing the active frameworks*

Expand the Frameworks group to see that CoreData.framework is now listed. Now that the application is aware of the Core Data framework, the classes specific to that framework can be used without creating compilation errors.

Creating the Data Model

No Core Data application is complete without a data model. The data model describes all the entities that will be managed by the framework. For the sake of simplicity, the model created in this section contains a single class with a single attribute. The data model can be created in Xcode by selecting **File ➤ New File…** in the menu and picking the type Data Model from the iPhone OS Resource templates, as shown in Figure 1-10. Click Next, name the data model (e.g., MyModel.xcdatamodel, as shown in Figure 1-11), and click Next. A dialog allows you to add existing classes to your data model, as shown in Figure 1-12. You can ignore this for now and click Finish. This generates your new data model and opens it in Xcode. See Figure 1-13.

Figure 1-10. *Adding a data model*

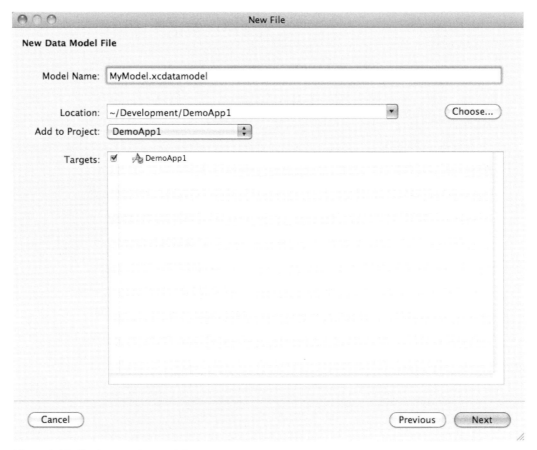

Figure 1-11. *Naming your data model*

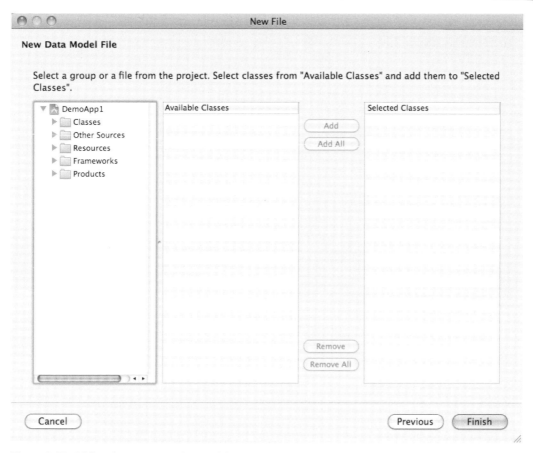

Figure 1-12. *Adding classes to your data model*

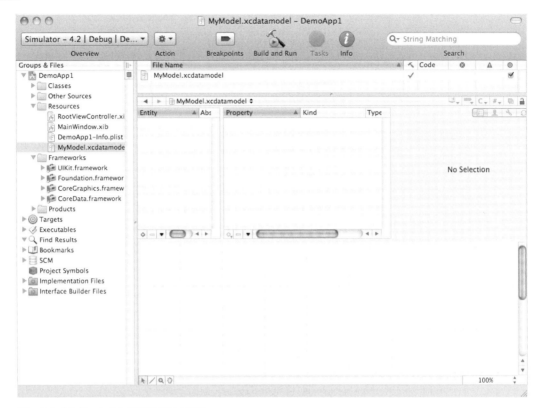

Figure 1-13. *Your new, empty data model*

Once the data model opens, you can add entities by clicking the plus button under the Entity section. You can add properties to entities by selecting the newly created entity and clicking the plus button under the Property section. In this example, we create a single entity called MyData with a single attribute called myAttribute of type String, as Figure 1-14 shows.

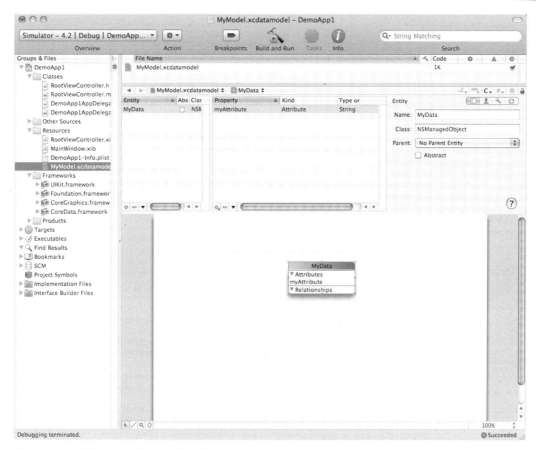

Figure 1-14. *Adding an entity and attribute*

Initializing the Managed Object Context

The last step consists of initializing the managed object context, the persistent data store, and the object model. For convenience, these components are typically defined as properties in the application delegate, so we add the following properties to the application delegate header file (DemoApp1AppDelegate.h):

```
#import <UIKit/UIKit.h>
#import <CoreData/CoreData.h>

@interface DemoApp1AppDelegate : NSObject <UIApplicationDelegate> {
    UIWindow *window;
    UINavigationController *navigationController;

@private
    NSManagedObjectContext *managedObjectContext_;
    NSManagedObjectModel *managedObjectModel_;
    NSPersistentStoreCoordinator *persistentStoreCoordinator_;
}
```

```
@property (nonatomic, retain) IBOutlet UIWindow *window;
@property (nonatomic, retain) IBOutlet UINavigationController *navigationController;

@property (nonatomic, retain, readonly) NSManagedObjectContext *managedObjectContext;
@property (nonatomic, retain, readonly) NSManagedObjectModel *managedObjectModel;
@property (nonatomic, retain, readonly) NSPersistentStoreCoordinator➥
 *persistentStoreCoordinator;

@end
```

The previous section showed that the context is created from a physical data store, which is in turn created from the data model. The initialization sequence remains the same and starts with loading the object model from the model we just defined:

```
- (NSManagedObjectModel *)managedObjectModel {
  if (managedObjectModel_ != nil) {
    return managedObjectModel_;
  }
  managedObjectModel_ = [[NSManagedObjectModel mergedModelFromBundles:nil] retain];
  return managedObjectModel_;
}
```

Note that, unlike with the generated code in the BasicApplication project, we don't specify the model we created specifically; mergedModelFromBundles will find and load all model files in the project. Either way will work, but this way is simpler.

Now that we've loaded the object model, we can leverage it in order to create the persistent store handler. This example uses NSSQLiteStoreType in order to indicate that the storage mechanism should rely on a SQLite database, as shown here:

```
- (NSPersistentStoreCoordinator *)persistentStoreCoordinator {
  if (persistentStoreCoordinator_ != nil) {
    return persistentStoreCoordinator_;
  }

  NSString* dir = [NSSearchPathForDirectoriesInDomains(NSDocumentDirectory,➥
NSUserDomainMask, YES) lastObject];
  NSURL *storeURL = [NSURL fileURLWithPath: [dir stringByAppendingPathComponent:➥
@"DemoApp1.sqlite"]];

  NSError *error = nil;
  persistentStoreCoordinator_ = [[NSPersistentStoreCoordinator alloc]➥
initWithManagedObjectModel:[self managedObjectModel]];
  if (![persistentStoreCoordinator_ addPersistentStoreWithType:NSSQLiteStoreType➥
configuration:nil URL:storeURL options:nil error:&error]) {
    NSLog(@"Unresolved error %@, %@", error, [error userInfo]);
    abort();
  }

  return persistentStoreCoordinator_;
}
```

Again, this code deviates slightly from the generated code in the BasicApplication project, using an approach for finding the user's document directory that doesn't rely on a helper method ((NSURL *)applicationDocumentsDirectory). Either approach will work, however.

Finally, we initialize the context from the persistent store that we just defined:

```
- (NSManagedObjectContext *)managedObjectContext {
  if (managedObjectContext_ != nil) {
    return managedObjectContext_;
  }

  NSPersistentStoreCoordinator *coordinator = [self persistentStoreCoordinator];
  if (coordinator != nil) {
    managedObjectContext_ = [[NSManagedObjectContext alloc] init];
    [managedObjectContext_ setPersistentStoreCoordinator:coordinator];
  }
  return managedObjectContext_;
}
```

The application can now use the managed object context to store and retrieve entities. We use a simple example in which the application persists and displays the number of times it was launched in order to illustrate this process.

In the application delegate implementation file, DemoApp1AppDelegate.m, edit the didFinishLaunchingWithOptions: method, and add code to retrieve the previous launches and add a new launch event.

> **Note:** Adding the code directly to the application delegate is only done here for convenience and simplicity. In a real application, this kind of code would most likely belong to a controller.

The code to retrieve the previous launches grabs the context and executes a request to fetch entities of type MyData:

```
NSManagedObjectContext *context = [self managedObjectContext];
NSFetchRequest *request = [[NSFetchRequest alloc] init];
NSEntityDescription *entity = [NSEntityDescription entityForName:@"MyData"
 inManagedObjectContext:context];
[request setEntity:entity];
NSArray* results = [context executeFetchRequest:request error:nil];
```

We can then iterate through the array of results in order to display the previous launches:

```
NSEnumerator *e = [results objectEnumerator];
NSManagedObject* object;
while (object = [e nextObject]) {
  NSLog(@"Found object %@", [object valueForKey:@"myAttribute"]);
}
```

> **Note:** One way to interact with the managed object's properties is to use the key/value pair generic accessor methods. `[object valueForKey:@"myAttribute"]` will retrieve the value of `myAttribute`, while `[object setValue:@"theValue" forKey:@"myAttribute"]` will set the value of `myAttribute`.

Lastly, we add a new entry to the context before letting the application continue its normal execution:

```
NSString* launchTitle = [NSString stringWithFormat:@"launch %d", [results count]];
object = [NSEntityDescription insertNewObjectForEntityForName:[entity name]➥
 inManagedObjectContext:context];
[object setValue:launchTitle forKey:@"myAttribute"];
NSLog(@"Added: %@", launchTitle);

NSError *error = nil;
if (![context save:&error]) {
  NSLog(@"Unresolved error %@, %@", error, [error userInfo]);
  abort();
}
```

Launching the application for the first time yields this output:

```
[Session started at 2010-12-06 17:14:40 -0500.]
2010-12-06 17:14:41.816 DemoApp1[79441:207] Added: launch 0
```

And launching it a second time displays the previous launch:

```
[Session started at 2010-12-06 17:16:06 -0500.]
2010-12-06 17:16:08.227 DemoApp1[79446:207] Found object launch 0
2010-12-06 17:16:08.229 DemoApp1[79446:207] Added: launch 1
```

The following is the complete method from the application delegate implementation file:

```
- (BOOL)application:(UIApplication *)application➥
 didFinishLaunchingWithOptions:(NSDictionary *)launchOptions {

  // Override point for customization after application launch.

  NSManagedObjectContext *context = [self managedObjectContext];
  NSFetchRequest *request = [[NSFetchRequest alloc] init];
  NSEntityDescription *entity = [NSEntityDescription entityForName:@"MyData"➥
 inManagedObjectContext:context];
  [request setEntity:entity];
  NSArray* results = [context executeFetchRequest:request error:nil];

  NSEnumerator *e = [results objectEnumerator];
  NSManagedObject* object;
  while (object = [e nextObject]) {
    NSLog(@"Found object %@", [object valueForKey:@"myAttribute"]);
  }
```

```
  NSString* launchTitle = [NSString stringWithFormat:@"launch %d", [results count]];
  object = [NSEntityDescription insertNewObjectForEntityForName:[entity name]➥
inManagedObjectContext:context];
  [object setValue:launchTitle forKey:@"myAttribute"];
  NSLog(@"Added: %@", launchTitle);

  NSError *error = nil;
  if (![context save:&error]) {
    NSLog(@"Unresolved error %@, %@", error, [error userInfo]);
    abort();
  }


  // Add the view controller's view to the window and display.
  [window addSubview:viewController.view];
  [window makeKeyAndVisible];

  return YES;
}
```

The existing application that used to be oblivious to Core Data has been outfitted with the powerful data storage management framework with a minimum amount of work. Follow these steps to add the power of Core Data to any of your existing applications.

Summary

Whether starting to build an iOS application from scratch or wanting to add persistence to an existing iOS application, you should strongly consider turning to Apple's Core Data framework. Using Xcode's templates and code generation gives you a jump start on starting down the Core Data path, or you can simply add Core Data by hand. Either way, you have in Core Data a persistence layer that abstracts most of the complexity of data storage and retrieval and allows you to work with data reliably as an object graph.

This chapter gave you an overview of Core Data's classes and how they work together, from the context to the managed objects to the persistent store and its coordinator. You caught a glimpse of fetch results controllers and how they work, but you saw only simple examples. The next chapter dives deeper into the Core Data framework, laying bare the classes and their interworkings so you know precisely how to use Core Data to persist your users' data.

Chapter 2

Understanding Core Data

Many developers, upon first seeing Core Data, deem Core Data and its classes a tangled mess of classes that impede, rather than enhance, data access. Perhaps they're Rails developers, used to making up method names to create dynamic finders and letting convention over configuration take care of the dirty work of data access. Maybe they're Java developers who have been annotating their Enterprise JavaBeans (EJBs) or hibernating their Plain Old Java Objects (POJOs). Whatever their backgrounds, many developers don't take naturally to the Core Data framework or its way of dealing with data, just as many developers squirm when first presented with Interface Builder and the live objects it creates when building user interfaces. We counsel you with patience and an open mind and assure you that the Core Data framework is no Rube Goldberg. The classes in the framework work together like Larry Bird's 1980s Boston Celtics in the half-court set, and when you understand them, you see their beauty and precision.

This chapter explains the classes in the Core Data framework, both individually and how they work together. Take the time to read about each class, to trace how they work together, and to type in and understand the examples.

Core Data Framework Classes

Chapter 1 guided you through the simple steps needed to get an application outfitted with Core Data. You saw bits of code, learned which classes to use, and discovered which methods and parameters to call and pass to make Core Data work. You've faithfully, and perhaps somewhat blindly, followed Chapter 1's advice while perhaps wondering what was behind all the code, classes, methods, and parameters. Most developers reading the previous chapter probably wondered what would happen if they substituted a parameter value for another. A few of them probably even tried it. A small percentage of those who tried got something other than an explosion, and a percentage of them actually got what they thought they would get.

Edward Dijkstra, renowned computer scientist and recipient of the 1972 Turing Award for his work developing programming languages, spoke of elegance as a quality that decides between success and failure instead of being a dispensable luxury. Core Data not only solves the problem of object persistence but solves it elegantly. To achieve elegance in your code, you should understand Core Data and not just guess at how it works. After reading this chapter, you will understand in detail not only the structure of the Core Data framework but also that the framework solves a complicated problem with only a small set of classes, making the solution simple, clear, and elegant.

Throughout the chapter, we build the class diagram that shows the classes involved in the framework and how they interact. We also see that some classes belong to the Core Data framework and others are imported from other Cocoa frameworks such as the Foundation framework. In parallel with building the class diagram, we build a small application in Xcode that deals with a fictitious company's organizational chart.

To follow along with this chapter, set up a blank iPhone application using the View-based Application template, as Figure 2-1 shows, and call it **OrgChart**.

Figure 2-1. *Create a new application in Xcode.*

Add the Core Data framework to the project, as shown in the "Adding Core Data to an Existing Project" section of Chapter 1. Your Xcode project should look like Figure 2-2. You can launch the app and make sure it starts without crashing. It doesn't do anything

other than display a gray screen, but that blank screen means you are set to continue
building the rest of the Core Data–based application.

Figure 2-2. *Xcode with a blank project*

Figure 2-3 depicts the classes of Core Data that you typically interact with. Chapter 1
talked about the managed object context, which is materialized by the
NSManagedObjectContext class and contains references to managed objects of type
NSManagedObject.

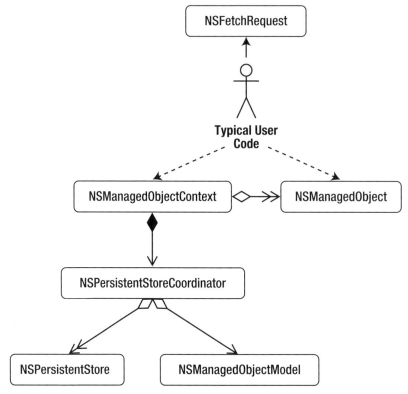

Figure 2-3. *High-level overview*

Your code stores data by adding managed objects to the context and retrieves data by using fetch requests implemented by the NSFetchRequest class. As shown in Chapter 1, the context is initialized using the persistent store coordinator, implemented by the NSPersistentStoreCoordinator class, and is defined by the data model, implemented by the NSManagedObjectModel class. The remainder of this chapter deals with how these classes are created, how they interact, and how to use them.

The Model Definition Classes

As explained in the previous chapter, all Core Data applications require an object model. The model defines the entities to be persisted and their properties. Entities have three kinds of properties:

- Attributes
- Relationships
- Fetched properties

Table 2-1 shows the different classes and brief descriptions of their roles. Enumerating through the classes to better understand how the mechanics behind model instantiation work is an interesting exercise, but in practice creating the model in Xcode is typically done graphically without having to type a single line of code.

Table 2-1. *The Classes Involved in Defining a Model*

Class Name	Role
NSManagedObjectModel	The data model itself
NSEntityDescription	An entity in the model
NSPropertyDescription	An abstract definition of an entity's property
NSAttributeDescription	An attribute of an entity
NSRelationshipDescription	A reference from an entity to another entity
NSFetchedPropertyDescription	The definition of a subset of entity instances based on a criteria

Figure 2-4 shows the relationships among the classes involved in defining a model. NSManagedObjectModel has references to zero or more NSEntityDescription objects. Each NSEntityDescription has references to zero or more NSPropertyDescription objects. NSPropertyDescription is an abstract class with three concrete implementations:

- NSAttributeDescription
- NSRelationshipDescription
- NSFetchedPropertyDescription

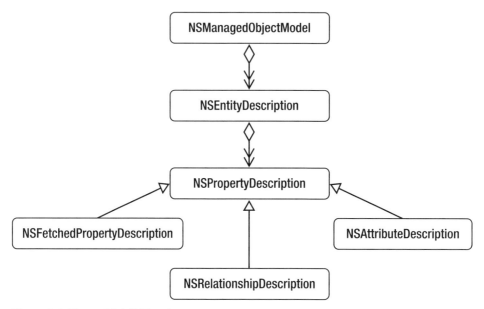

Figure 2-4. *The model definition classes*

This small set of classes is enough to define any object model you will use when working on your Core Data projects. As explained in more detail in Chapter 1, you create the data model in Xcode by selecting **File ➤ New File...** in the menu and picking the type Data Model from the iOS Resource templates. In this section, we create a model that represents a company's organizational chart. In Xcode, create your model in the Resources group. Call it OrgChart. In this data model, an organization has one person as the leader (the chief executive officer, or CEO). That leader has direct reports, which may or may not have direct reports of their own. For simplicity, we say that a person has two attributes: a unique employee identifier and a name. We are finally ready to start defining the data model in Xcode.

Open the data model file, and add a new Organization entity. Like a person, an organization is defined by a unique identifier and a name, so add two attributes to the Organization entity. Attributes are scalar properties of an entity, which means that they are simple data holders that can contain a single value. The attribute types are defined in the NSAttributeType structure, and each type enforces certain data constraints over the entity. For instance, if the type of the attribute is integer, an error will occur if you try to put an alphanumeric value in that field. Table 2-2 lists the different types and their meanings.

Table 2-2. *The Attribute Types*

Xcode Attribute Type	Objective-C Attribute Type	Objective-C Data	Description
Integer 16	NSInteger16AttributeType	NSNumber	A 16-bit integer
Integer 32	NSInteger32AttributeType	NSNumber	A 32-bit integer
Integer 64	NSInteger64AttributeType	NSNumber	A 64-bit integer
Decimal	NSDecimalAttributeType	NSDecimalNumber	A base-10 subclass of NSNumber
Double	NSDoubleAttributeType	NSNumber	An object wrapper for double
Float	NSFloatAttributeType	NSNumber	An object wrapper for float
String	NSStringAttributeType	NSString	A character string
Boolean	NSBooleanAttributeType	BOOL	A 16-bit integer
Date	NSDateAttributeType	NSDate	An object wrapper for a boolean value
Binary data	NSBinaryDataAttributeType	NSData	Unstructured binary data
Transformable	NSTransformableAttributeType	Any nonstandard type	Any type transformed into a supported type

Note: Chapter 5 expands on the Transformable type and how to use it. Transformable attributes are a way to tell Core Data that you want to use a nonsupported data type in your managed object and that you will help Core Data by providing code to transform the attribute data at persist time into a supported type.

Name the first attribute id and the second name. By default, the type of new attributes is set to Undefined, which purposely prevents the code from compiling in order to force you to set the type for each attribute. Organization identifiers are always going to be simple numbers, so use the type Integer 16 for the id attribute. Use the type String for the name attribute. At this point, your project should look like Figure 2-5.

Figure 2-5. *The project with the* `Organization` *entity*

At this point, if the data model were to be loaded by a running program, it would be represented by the object graph shown in Figure 2-6.

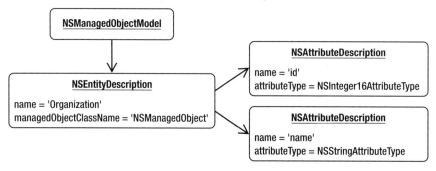

Figure 2-6. *The organization model as objects*

The graph shows that the managed object model, which is of type NSManagedObjectModel, points to an entity description, represented by an NSEntityDescription instance named Organization that uses an NSManagedObject for its managedObjectClassName property. This entity description has two attribute descriptions (type NSAttributeDescription). Each attribute description has two properties: name and attributeType. The first attribute description has the values id and

NSInteger16AttributeType for its name and attributeType properties, respectively, while the second has the values name and NSStringAttributeType.

In the same manner that you created the Organization entity, create another entity named Person with two attributes: id and name. We can link the organization to its leader by creating a relationship from the Organization entity to the Person entity and call it leader. Once the two entities exist in Xcode, creating a relationship is as simple as selecting the source entity, clicking the + button in the Property section, and selecting Add Relationship in the menu. Name the new relationship leader, and set Person as its destination. Now, add a relationship from Person to Person (yes, a relationship from the Person entity back to itself), and call it employees. This defines the relationship from a person to the person's subordinates. By default, Xcode creates one-to-one relationships, which means that a relationship left at the default links one source to one destination. Since one leader can manage many subordinates, the relationship between Person and Person should be a one-to-many relationship. You correct the relationship in Xcode by changing the relationship's property, as shown in Figure 2-7.

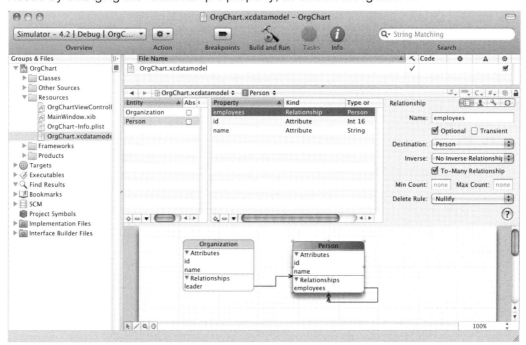

Figure 2-7. *One-to-many relationship*

Note: In this chapter, we want to show you how a data model designed using the model editor is interpreted into Core Data classes. We have purposely taken shortcuts when creating the model. For more detailed information on how to create object models, please refer to Chapter 4.

Note: You may notice that Xcode complains about the two relationships you've created, warning you of a consistency error and a misconfigured property. Xcode complains about Core Data relationships without inverses, but this shouldn't be an issue in this application. The only impact the lack of the inverse relationships has is that you can't navigate the inverse relationships. You can safely ignore these warnings for the time being.

The current data model is illustrated in Figure 2-8, while Figure 2-9 shows how the data model definition would be loading into live objects by Core Data.

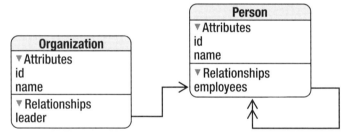

Figure 2-8. *The data model*

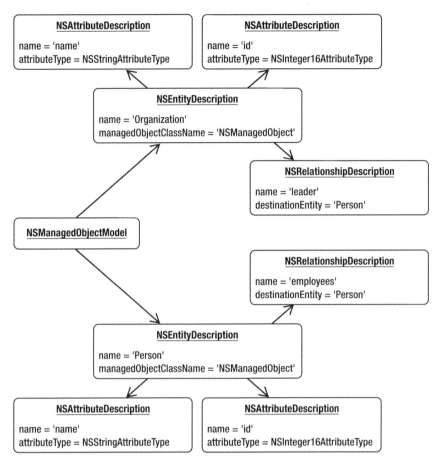

Figure 2-9. *The organization model with* `Person`

Note that the object graph depicted in Figure 2-9 is not showing the object graph that Core Data stores. Instead, it is an illustration of how Core Data interprets the data model you created graphically as objects it can use to create the data store schema. The typical way of making Core Data load and interpret a data model into an `NSManagedObjectModel` is done by calling `[NSManagedObjectModel mergedModelFromBundles:nil]`, which will find the models in your application bundle and create the object model description in memory.

Knowing how models are represented as objects inside Core Data is generally not very useful unless you are interested in creating custom data stores or want to generate the data model programmatically at runtime. This would be analogous to programmatically creating `UIViews` rather than using Xcode's built-in user interface editor, Interface Builder. Having a deep understanding of how Core Data works, however, allows you to anticipate and avoid complex issues, troubleshoot bugs, or solve problems creatively and elegantly.

You have seen how the data model is represented as Core Data classes, but you have also seen that unless you get into really advanced uses of the framework, you will hardly ever need to interact directly with these classes. All the classes discussed so far in this chapter deal with describing the model. The remainder of the chapter deals exclusively with classes that represent either the data itself or the accessors to the data.

The Data Access Classes

You learned in Chapter 1 that the initialization of Core Data starts with loading the data model into the NSManagedObjectModel object. The previous section runs through an example of how NSManagedObjectModel represents that model as NSEntityDescription and NSPropertyDescription objects. The second step of the initialization sequence is to create and bind to the persistent store through the NSPersistentStoreCoordinator. Finally, the third step in the initialization sequence creates the NSManagedObjectContext that your code interacts with in order to store and retrieve data. To make things a bit clearer, Figure 2-10 shows the class diagram involved in representing the context and the underlying persistent store.

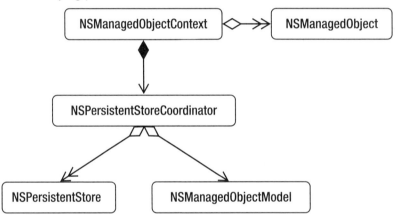

Figure 2-10. *The managed object context object graph*

Notice where the NSManagedObjectModel object sits in the class diagram in Figure 2-10. It is loaded and given to the persistent store coordinator (NSPersistentStoreCoordinator) so that the persistent store coordinator can figure out how to represent the data in the persistent stores. The persistent store coordinator acts as a mediator between the managed object context and the actual persistent stores where the data is written. Among other tasks, it manages the data migrations from one store to the other, through the migratePersistentStore: method.

The NSPersistentStoreCoordinator is initialized using the NSManagedObjectModel class. Once the coordinator object is allocated, it can load and register all the persistent stores. The following code demonstrates the initialization of the persistent store coordinator. It receives the managed object model in its initWithManagedObjectModel: method and then registers the persistent store by calling its addPersistentStoreWithType: method.

```
NSString* dir = [NSSearchPathForDirectoriesInDomains(NSDocumentDirectory,➡
NSUserDomainMask, YES) lastObject];
```

```
NSURL *storeURL = [NSURL fileURLWithPath:[dir➡
stringByAppendingPathComponent:@"OrgChart.sqlite"]];

NSError *error = nil;
persistentStoreCoordinator_ = [[NSPersistentStoreCoordinator alloc]➡
initWithManagedObjectModel:[self managedObjectModel]];
if (![persistentStoreCoordinator_ addPersistentStoreWithType:NSSQLiteStoreType➡
configuration:nil URL:storeURL options:nil error:&error]) {
  NSLog(@"Unresolved error %@, %@", error, [error userInfo]);
  abort();
}
```

iOS offers three types of persistent stores by default, as shown in Table 2-3.

Table 2-3. *The Default Persistent Store Types on iOS*

Store Type	Description
NSSQLiteStoreType	SQLite database
NSBinaryStoreType	Binary file
NSInMemoryStoreType	In-memory storage

Note: Core Data on Mac OS X offers a fourth type (NSXMLStoreType) that uses XML files as the storage mechanism. This fourth type isn't available on iOS, presumably because of iDevices' slower processors and the processor-intensive nature of parsing XML. Parsing XML is possible on iDevices, however, as the existence of several iOS XML parsing libraries proves. Apple seems to have issued no official explanation for the absence of the XML store type on iOS.

Typical users will find themselves using the SQLite type, which stores the data into a SQLite database running on your iDevice, most often or even exclusively. You should be aware of and understand the other types, however, because different circumstances may warrant using the other types. As useless as an in-memory "persistent" store may sound, a classic use of the in-memory storage is to cache information fetched from a remote server and create a local copy of the data to limit bandwidth usage and the associated latencies. The data remains persistent on the remote server and can always be fetched again.

Once the persistent store coordinator is created, the managed object context can be initialized as an NSManagedObjectContext instance. The managed object context is responsible for coordinating what goes in and what comes out of the persistent store. This may sound like a trivial task, but consider the following challenges:

- If two threads ask for the same object, they must obtain a pointer to the same instance.

- If the same object is asked for several times, the context must be intelligent enough to not go hit the persistent store but instead return the object from its cache.

- The context should be able to keep changes to the persistent store to itself until a commit operation is requested.

Note: Apple strongly, and rightfully, discourages subclassing the NSManagedObjectContext because of the complexity of what it does and the opportunities for putting the context and the objects it manages into an unpredictable state.

Table 2-4 lists some methods used to retrieve, create, or delete data objects. Updating data is done on the data object by changing its properties directly. The context keeps track of every object it pulls out of the data store and is aware of any change you make so that changes can be persisted to the backing store.

Table 2-4. *Some Useful Methods for Retrieving and Creating Data Objects*

Method Name	Description
-executeFetchRequest:error:	Executes a request to retrieve objects
-objectWithID:	Retrieves a specific object given its unique identifier
-insertObject:	Adds a new object to the context
-deleteObject:	Removes an object from the context

Keep in mind that NSManagedObjectContext orchestrates data transfers both into and out of the persistent store and guarantees the consistency of the data objects. You should carefully think about the impacts of deleting managed objects. When deleting a managed object that has a relationship to other managed objects, Core Data has to decide what to do with the related objects. One of the properties of a relationship is the "Delete rule," which is one of the four types of delete rules explained in Table 2-5. Table 2-5 calls the object being deleted the *parent object* and the objects that are at the end of a relationship the *related objects*.

Table 2-5. *The Relationship Rules*

Rule	Effect
No action	Does nothing and lets the related objects think the parent object still exists
Nullify	For each related object, sets the parent object property to null
Cascade	Deletes each related object
Deny	Prevents the parent object from being deleted if there is at least one related object

In addition to controlling access to and from the persistent store, the managed object context allows undo and redo operations using the same paradigm used in user interface design. Table 2-6 lists the important methods used in dealing with undo and redo operations.

Table 2-6. *Life-Cycle Operations in* NSManagedObjectContext

Method Name	Description
-undoManager	Returns the NSUndoManager controlling undo in the context.
-setUndoManager:	Specifies a new undo manager to use.
-undo	Sends an undo message to the NSUndoManager.
-redo	Sends a redo message to the NSUndoManager.
-reset	Forces the context to lose all references to the managed objects it retrieved.
-rollback	Sends undo messages to the NSUndoManager until there is nothing left to undo.
-save:	Sends all current changes in the context to the persistent store. Think of this as the "commit" action. Any changes in the context that have not been saved are lost if your application crashes.
-hasChanges	Returns true if the context contains changes that have not yet been committed to the persistent store.

Chapter 5 discusses undoing and redoing Core Data operations.

The NSManagedObjectContext is the gateway into the persistent stores that all data objects must go through. To be able to keep track of the data, Core Data forces all data objects to inherit from the NSManagedObject class. We saw earlier in this chapter that NSEntityDescription instances define the data objects. NSManagedObject instances are the data objects. Core Data uses their entity descriptions to know what properties to access and what types to expect.

Managed objects support key-value coding, or name-value pairs, in order to give generic accessors to the data they contain. The simplest way of accessing data is through the valueForKey: method. Data can be put into the objects using the setValue:forKey: method. The key parameter is the name of the attribute from the data model.

```
- (id)valueForKey:(NSString *)key
- (void)setValue:(id)value forKey:(NSString *)key
```

Notice that the valueForKey: method returns an instance of id, which is a generic type. The actual data type is dictated again by the data model and the type of attribute you specified. Refer to Table 2-2 for a list of these types.

NSManagedObject also provides several methods to help the NSManagedObjectContext determine whether anything has changed in the object. When the time comes to commit any changes, the context can ask the managed objects it keeps track of if they have changed. Apple strongly discourages you from overriding these methods in order to prevent interference with the commit sequence.

> **Note:** Each instance of NSManagedObject keeps a reference to the context to which it belongs. This can also be an inexpensive way of keeping a reference to the context without having to pass it around all the time. As long as you have one of the managed objects, you can get back to the context.

To create a new NSManagedObject instance, you first create an appropriate NSEntityDescription instance from the entity name and the managed object context that knows about that entity. The NSEntityDescription instance provides the definition, or description, for the new NSManagedObject instance. You then send a message to the NSEntityDescription instance you just created to insert a new managed object into the context and return it to you. The code looks like this:

```
NSEntityDescription *entity = [NSEntityDescription entityForName:@"Organization"➥
inManagedObjectContext:managedObjectContext];
NSManagedObject *org = [NSEntityDescription insertNewObjectForEntityForName:[entity➥
name] inManagedObjectContext:managedObjectContext];
```

Once you create the managed object in the context, you can set its values. To set the name property of the NSManagedObject instance called org that the previous code creates, invoke the following code:

```
[org setValue:@"MyCompany, Inc." forKey:@"name"];
```

Key-Value Observing

You can take responsibility for discovering any changes made to managed objects by querying them. This approach is useful in cases when some event prompts a controller to do something with the managed objects. In many cases, however, having the managed objects themselves take responsibility to notify you when they change allows more efficiency and elegance in your design. To provide this notification service, the NSManagedObject class supports key-value observation to send notifications immediately before and after a value changes for a key. Key-value observation isn't a pattern specific to Core Data but is used throughout the Cocoa frameworks.

The two main methods involved in the notifications related to key-value observation are willChangeValueForKey: and didChangeValueForKey:. The first method is invoked immediately before the change and the latter immediately after the change. For an object observerObject to receive notifications from changes to the value of property theProperty occurring in a managed object managedObject, however, the observer object must first register with that object using code like this:

```
[managedObject addObserver:observerObject forKeyPath:@"theProperty"
options:(NSKeyValueObservingOptionNew | NSKeyValueObservingOptionOld) context:nil];
```

After registering, the observer will start receiving instant change notifications to the properties to which it is listening. This is an extremely useful mechanism to use when trying to keep a user interface in sync with the data it displays.

The Query Classes

So far in this chapter, you have seen how to initialize the Core Data infrastructure and how to interact with the objects it creates. This section deals with the basics of retrieving data by sending fetch requests. Fetch requests are, not surprisingly, instances of NSFetchRequest. What might be a little more surprising to you is that it is almost the only class in the class structure related to retrieving data that is a member of the Core Data framework. Most of the other classes involved in formulating a request to fetch data belong to the Foundation Cocoa framework, also used by all other Cocoa frameworks. Figure 2-11 shows the class diagram derived from NSFetchRequest.

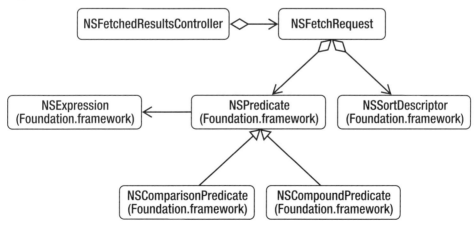

Figure 2-11. *The NSFetchRequest class diagram*

Fetch requests are composed of two main elements: an NSPredicate instance and an NSSortDescriptor instance. The NSPredicate helps filter the data by specifying constraints, and the NSSortDescriptor arranges the result set in a specific order. Both elements are optional, and if you don't specify them, your results aren't constrained if an NSPredicate isn't specified or aren't sorted if an NSSortDescriptor isn't specified.

Creating a simple request to retrieve all the organizations in our persistent store—unconstrained and unsorted—looks like this:

```
NSFetchRequest *fetchRequest = [[NSFetchRequest alloc] init];
NSEntityDescription *entity = [NSEntityDescription entityForName:@"Organization"➥
inManagedObjectContext:managedObjectContext];
[fetchRequest setEntity:entity];
NSArray* organizations = [managedObjectContext executeFetchRequest:fetchRequest➥
error:nil];
```

You first reserve the memory space for the request object. You then retrieve the entity description of the objects to retrieve from the context and set it into the request object. Finally, you execute the query in the managed object context by calling executeFetchRequest:.

Because you don't constrain the request with an NSPredicate instance, the organizations array contains instances of NSManagedObject that represent each of the organizations found in the persistent store. To filter the results and return only some of the organizations, use the NSPredicate class. To create a simple predicate that limits the results to organizations whose names contain the string "Inc.", you call NSPredicate's predicateWithFormat: method, passing the format string and the data that gets plugged into the format. You then add the predicate to the fetch request before executing the request in the managed object context. The code looks like this:

```
NSPredicate *predicate = [NSPredicate predicateWithFormat:@"name contains %@", @"Inc."];
[fetchRequest setPredicate:predicate];
```

To sort the result set alphabetically by the name of the organization, add a sort descriptor to the request prior to executing it:

```
NSSortDescriptor *sortByName = [[NSSortDescriptor alloc] initWithKey:@"name"➥
ascending:YES];
[fetchRequest setSortDescriptors:[NSArray arrayWithObject:sortByName]];
```

Chapter 6 goes much more in depth on how to use predicates for simple and complex queries and sort descriptors for sorting.

Figure 2-12 puts all the Core Data class diagrams you've seen in this chapter together into a single class diagram that shows you how all these classes fit in the framework.

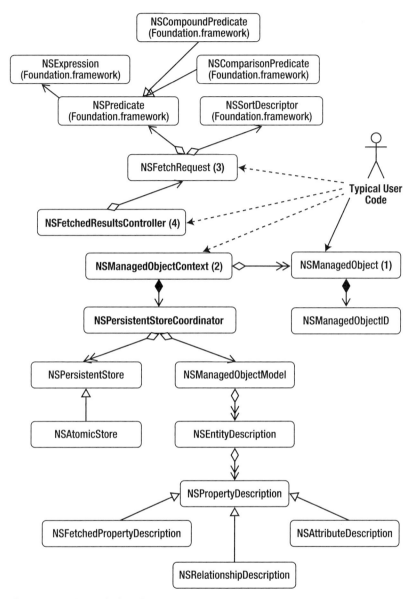

Figure 2-12. *The main Core Data classes*

Your user code, represented in the diagram by a stick figure, interacts chiefly with four classes:

- NSManagedObject (1)
- NSManagedObjectContext (2)
- NSFetchRequest (3)
- NSFetchedResultsController (4)

Find these four classes, numbered 1–4, in the diagram in Figure 2-12 and use them as anchor points, and you should recognize the individual class diagrams we've worked through in this chapter. The one exception is NSFetchedResultsController (4), which works closely with iOS table views. We cover NSFetchedResultsController in Chapter 9.

How the Classes Interact

You should now have a good understanding of the classes involved in interacting with Core Data and what is happening under the hood. This section expands on the OrgChart application created in the previous section to show some examples of interactions among Core Data classes. Like the previous section, this chapter maintains its focus at a relatively basic level. The goal for this chapter is to show how the classes play together. The rest of the book consists of chapters that take each concept (data manipulation, custom persistent store, performance enhancements, and so on) to much deeper levels.

The data model created in the previous section of this chapter should look like the one in Figure 2-13.

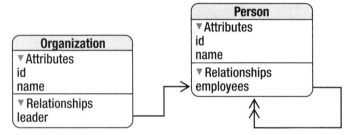

Figure 2-13. *The* Organization *data model*

Both the Organization and Person entities use an attribute of type Integer 16 to serve as unique identifiers for each entity. Most programmers reading this have probably already thought about autoincrement and have been clicking around the Xcode user interface to find out by themselves how to enable autoincrement for the identifier attributes. If you're one of these programmers and you're back to reading this chapter, you probably became frustrated and have given up looking. The reason you couldn't find autoincrement is because it's not there. Core Data manages an object graph using real object references. It has no need for a unique autoincrement identifier that can be used as a primary key in the same sense it would be used in a relational database. If the persistent store happens to be a relational database like SQLite, the framework will probably use some autoincrement identifiers as primary keys. Regardless, you, as a Core Data user, should not have to worry about that; it's an implementation detail. We have purposely introduced the notion of identifiers in this example for two reasons:

- To raise the question of autoincrement
- To show examples of how to manage numeric values with Core Data

The person identifier is similar in meaning to a Social Security number. It isn't meant to autoincrement because it is an identifier computed outside the data store. In the

Organization example, we simply derive the ID from an object hash. Although this doesn't guarantee uniqueness, it serves this application's purpose and is simple to implement.

> **Note:** As a programmer, you should be careful not to focus too much on what you already know about databases. Core Data isn't a database; it's an object graph persistence framework. Its behavior is closer to an object-oriented database than a traditional relational database.

Listing 2-1 shows the header file for the application delegate class, OrgChartAppDelegate.h. You can see declarations for the three Core Data–related properties:

- NSManagedObjectContext *managedObjectContext_
- NSManagedObjectModel *managedObjectModel_
- NSPersistentStoreCoordinator *persistentStoreCoordinator_

You also see the declaration for a method to return the application's document directory, which is where the persistent store will live. The implementation file, OrgChartAppDelegate.m, will define methods for each of these.

Listing 2-1. *OrgChartAppDelegate.h*

```objc
#import <UIKit/UIKit.h>
#import <CoreData/CoreData.h>

@class OrgChartViewController;

@interface OrgChartAppDelegate : NSObject <UIApplicationDelegate> {
  UIWindow *window;
  OrgChartViewController *viewController;

@private
  NSManagedObjectContext *managedObjectContext_;
  NSManagedObjectModel *managedObjectModel_;
  NSPersistentStoreCoordinator *persistentStoreCoordinator_;
}

@property (nonatomic, retain) IBOutlet UIWindow *window;
@property (nonatomic, retain) IBOutlet OrgChartViewController *viewController;

@property (nonatomic, retain, readonly) NSManagedObjectContext *managedObjectContext;
@property (nonatomic, retain, readonly) NSManagedObjectModel *managedObjectModel;
@property (nonatomic, retain, readonly) NSPersistentStoreCoordinator
*persistentStoreCoordinator;

@end
```

In OrgChartAppDelegate.m, add the accessors for the three properties you declared in OrgChartAppDelegate.h. Each accessor first determines whether the object it's responsible for has been created. If it has, the accessor returns the object. If not, the accessor creates the object using the appropriate Core Data formula, creating any of the

other member objects it requires, and returns it. The code to add to
OrgChartAppDelegate.m looks like this:

```
#pragma mark -
#pragma mark Core Data stack

/**
 Returns the managed object model for the application.
 If the model doesn't already exist, it is created from the application's model.
 */
- (NSManagedObjectModel *)managedObjectModel {

  if (managedObjectModel_ != nil) {
    return managedObjectModel_;
  }
  managedObjectModel_ = [[NSManagedObjectModel mergedModelFromBundles:nil] retain];
  return managedObjectModel_;
}

- (NSPersistentStoreCoordinator *)persistentStoreCoordinator {
  if (persistentStoreCoordinator_ != nil) {
    return persistentStoreCoordinator_;
  }

  NSString* dir = [NSSearchPathForDirectoriesInDomains(NSDocumentDirectory,➥
NSUserDomainMask, YES) lastObject];
  NSURL *storeURL = [NSURL fileURLWithPath:[dir➥
stringByAppendingPathComponent:@"OrgChart.sqlite"]];

  NSError *error = nil;
  persistentStoreCoordinator_ = [[NSPersistentStoreCoordinator alloc]➥
initWithManagedObjectModel:[self managedObjectModel]];
  if (![persistentStoreCoordinator_ addPersistentStoreWithType:NSSQLiteStoreType➥
configuration:nil URL:storeURL options:nil error:&error]) {
    NSLog(@"Unresolved error %@, %@", error, [error userInfo]);
    abort();
  }

  return persistentStoreCoordinator_;
}

- (NSManagedObjectContext *)managedObjectContext {
  if (managedObjectContext_ != nil) {
    return managedObjectContext_;
  }

  NSPersistentStoreCoordinator *coordinator = [self persistentStoreCoordinator];
  if (coordinator != nil) {
    managedObjectContext_ = [[NSManagedObjectContext alloc] init];
    [managedObjectContext_ setPersistentStoreCoordinator:coordinator];
  }
  return managedObjectContext_;
}
```

Since this chapter focuses on how Core Data works, not on user interface design and development, the OrgChart application can remain content with a blank, gray screen. All its work will happen in the didFinishLaunchingWithOptions: method, and we show you how to use external tools to verify that Core Data persisted the objects appropriately.

Before you can read any data from the persistent store, you have to put it there. Change the didFinishLaunchingWithOptions: method to call a new method called createData:, like this:

```
- (BOOL)application:(UIApplication *)application
didFinishLaunchingWithOptions:(NSDictionary *)launchOptions {
  [self createData];

  [window addSubview:viewController.view];
  [window makeKeyAndVisible];
  return YES;
}
```

In OrgChartAppDelegate.h, declare the createData: method like this:

```
- (void)createData;
```

Now define the createData: method in OrgChartAppDelegate.m like this:

```
- (void)createData {
}
```

Inside the createData: implementation, you create an organization and three employees. Start with the organization. Remember that the managed objects, as far as you're concerned, live in the managed object context. Don't worry about the persistent store; the managed object context takes care of managing the persistent store for you. You just create the managed object representing the organization and insert it into the managed object context using this code:

```
NSManagedObjectContext *context = [self managedObjectContext];
NSEntityDescription *orgEntity = [NSEntityDescription entityForName:@"Organization"➥
inManagedObjectContext:context];
NSManagedObject *organization = [NSEntityDescription
insertNewObjectForEntityForName:[orgEntity name] inManagedObjectContext:context];
```

You've now created an organization, but you've given it no name and no identifier. The name attribute is of type String, so set the name for the organization like this:

```
[organization setValue:@"MyCompany, Inc." forKey:@"name"];
```

The id attribute is of type Integer 16, which is a class. All Core Data attributes must have a class type, not a primitive type. To create the id attribute for the organization, create a primitive int from the hash of the organization object and then convert the primitive int into an NSNumber object, which can be used in the setValue:forKey: method. The code looks like this:

```
int orgId = [organization hash];
[organization setValue:[NSNumber numberWithInt:orgId] forKey:@"id"];
```

> **Note:** Core Data uses objects for attributes in order to comply with key-value coding requirements. Any primitive type should be converted into NSNumber to use the setValue:forKey: method.

The organization now has a name and an identifier, although the changes haven't yet been committed to the persistent store. The framework knows that you've altered an object that it's tracking and makes the necessary adjustments to the persistent store when the save: method is called to commit the context changes.

An organization without people accomplishes little, so create three people named John, Jane, and Bill using the same approach you used to create the organization: get the appropriate entity description from the managed object context, create a new managed object from that entity description, and set the name and identifier values. The code looks like this:

```
NSEntityDescription *personEntity = [NSEntityDescription entityForName:@"Person"
inManagedObjectContext:context];
NSManagedObject *john = [NSEntityDescription
insertNewObjectForEntityForName:[personEntity name] inManagedObjectContext:context];
[john setValue:[NSNumber numberWithInt:[john hash]] forKey:@"id"];
[john setValue:@"John" forKey:@"name"];
NSManagedObject *jane = [NSEntityDescription
insertNewObjectForEntityForName:[personEntity name] inManagedObjectContext:context];
[jane setValue:[NSNumber numberWithInt:[jane hash]] forKey:@"id"];
[jane setValue:@"Jane" forKey:@"name"];
NSManagedObject *bill = [NSEntityDescription
insertNewObjectForEntityForName:[personEntity name] inManagedObjectContext:context];
[bill setValue:[NSNumber numberWithInt:[bill hash]] forKey:@"id"];
[bill setValue:@"Bill" forKey:@"name"];
```

> **Note:** Because NSEntityDescription is a definition of a Core Data entity and because it doesn't change while the application is running, reusing the definition when creating multiple instances of the same entity saves memory and makes sense.

You now have one organization and three unrelated people. The organizational chart should have John as the leader of the company, while Jane and Bill should report to John. The OrgChart application's data model has two types of relationships. The leader is a one-to-one relationship from Organization to Person, while the employees are set through a one-to-many relationship between Person and itself. Setting the value of the one-to-one relationship is surprisingly simple:

```
[organization setValue:john forKey:@"leader"];
```

Core Data knows that you are assigning a relationship value because it knows the data model and knows that leader represents a one-to-one relationship. Your code would not run if you were to pass a managed object with the wrong entity type as the value.

To assign Jane and Bill as John's subordinates, you have to assign values to the "employees" one-to-many relationship. Core Data returns the "many" side of a one-to-many relationship as a set (NSSet), which is an unordered collection of unique objects. For John's "employees" relationship, Core Data returns the set of the existing employees working for John if you call the valueForKey: method. Since you want to add objects to the set, however, call the mutableSetValueForKey: method, because it returns an NSMutableSet, which you can add to and delete from, instead of an immutable NSSet. Adding a new Person managed object to the returned NSMutableSet adds a new employee to the relationship. The code looks like this:

```
NSMutableSet *johnsEmployees = [john mutableSetValueForKey:@"employees"];
[johnsEmployees addObject:jane];
[johnsEmployees addObject:bill];
```

Once again, since you've modified the object graph of objects tracked by Core Data, you don't have to do anything else in order to help it manage the dependencies between the different pieces of data. Everything behaves just like you would expect from regular objects. Once again, though, the changes aren't committed until you save the managed object context, which you do like this:

```
NSError *error = nil;
if (![context save:&error]) {
  NSLog(@"Unresolved error %@, %@", error, [error userInfo]);
  abort();
}
```

This ends the contents of the createData: method.

SQLite Primer

Since the OrgChart application uses SQLite for its persistent store and you just created the store and put some data into it, you can use any SQLite viewing tool such as SQLite Database Browser (http://sqlitebrowser.sourceforge.net/) or SQLite Manager (http://code.google.com/p/sqlite-manager/) to view it. Be aware, however, that poking around a SQLite database that Core Data owns can create problems if you change the database from an external tool. The way Core Data manages a SQLite database is an implementation detail that could change. Further, you can mangle the data in ways that prevent Core Data from reading the data or properly reconstructing the object graph. Consider yourself warned. While developing applications, however, you can recover from a damaged database by deleting it and allowing your application to re-create it, so don't hesitate to jump into the database using a tool to debug your applications.

Despite the availability of graphical browsing tools, we use the adequate command-line tool that's already installed on your Mac: sqlite3. On your Mac, open Terminal.app to get to the command prompt and change to the iPhone Simulator's deployment directory, like this:

```
cd ~/Library/Application\ Support/iPhone\ Simulator
```

To find the database file, named OrgChart.sqlite, use the find command:

```
find . -name "OrgChart.sqlite" -print
```

You should see output that looks something like this:

```
./4.2/Applications/2378DE7D-2034-4B46-B591-D34A7C3C6608/Documents/OrgChart.sqlite
```

The generated ID will differ from the previous example, and Apple has moved the relative path in the past and may do so again, so your path will vary from this. This is the relative path to your database file, so to open the database, pass that relative path to the `sqlite3` executable, like this:

```
sqlite3 ./4.2/Applications/2378DE7D-2034-4B46-B591-
D34A7C3C6608/Documents/OrgChart.sqlite
```

Running this command will put you inside the SQLite shell. You can run SQL commands from this point until you exit the shell.

```
SQLite version 3.6.18
Enter ".help" for instructions
Enter SQL statements terminated with a ";"
sqlite>
```

One interesting command is the `.schema` command, which will display the SQL schema Core Data created to support your object model:

```
sqlite> .schema
CREATE TABLE ZORGANIZATION ( Z_PK INTEGER PRIMARY KEY, Z_ENT INTEGER, Z_OPT INTEGER, ZID
INTEGER, ZLEADER INTEGER, ZNAME VARCHAR );
CREATE TABLE ZPERSON ( Z_PK INTEGER PRIMARY KEY, Z_ENT INTEGER, Z_OPT INTEGER, ZID
INTEGER, Z2EMPLOYEES INTEGER, ZNAME VARCHAR );
CREATE TABLE Z_METADATA (Z_VERSION INTEGER PRIMARY KEY, Z_UUID VARCHAR(255), Z_PLIST
BLOB);
CREATE TABLE Z_PRIMARYKEY (Z_ENT INTEGER PRIMARY KEY, Z_NAME VARCHAR, Z_SUPER INTEGER,
Z_MAX INTEGER);
CREATE INDEX ZORGANIZATION_ZLEADER_INDEX ON ZORGANIZATION (ZLEADER);
CREATE INDEX ZPERSON_Z2EMPLOYEES_INDEX ON ZPERSON (Z2EMPLOYEES);
sqlite>
```

The first things that jump out are that the tables are not named exactly like our entities, the tables have more columns than our entities have attributes, and the database has extra tables not found in the Core Data data model. You can also see that Core Data took care of creating integer columns to be used as primary keys, and it manages their uniqueness. If you know SQLite well, you know that any column defined as INTEGER PRIMARY KEY will autoincrement, but the point is that we don't have to know that or even care. Core Data handles the uniqueness.

You should be able to decipher Core Data's code for mapping entities to tables and recognize the two tables that support the entities: ZORGANIZATION and ZPERSON. You can query the tables after running the OrgChart application and validate that the data is in fact stored in the database:

```
sqlite> select Z_PK, ZID, ZLEADER, ZNAME from ZORGANIZATION;
1|622361088|1|MyCompany, Inc.

sqlite> select Z_PK, ZID, Z2EMPLOYEES, ZNAME from ZPERSON;
1|2090367488||John
```

```
2|-1852278272|1|Jane
3|2090367488|1|Bill
sqlite>
```

The rows are fairly easy to read. You see the single organization you created, and its leader (ZLEADER) is the person where Z_PK=1 (John). John has no boss, but Jane and Bill have the same boss (Z2EMPLOYEES), and his Z_PK is 1 (John again, as expected).

To exit the SQLite shell, type .quit and press Enter.

```
sqlite> .quit
```

Reading the Data Using Core Data

In this chapter, you wrote data to a SQLite database using Core Data, and you used the sqlite3 command-line tool to read the data and confirm that it had been correctly stored in the persistent store. You can also use Core Data to read the data from the persistent store. Go back to Xcode, and open the OrgChartAppDelegate.m file to add methods for reading the data using Core Data.

Since the "employees" relationship is recursive (that is, the same source and destination entity), use a recursive method to display a person and their subordinates. The recursive displayPerson: method shown next accepts two parameters—the person to display and an indentation level—and recurses through a person's employees to print them at appropriate indentation levels. The code looks like this:

```
-(void)displayPerson:(NSManagedObject*)person withIndentation:(NSString*)indentation {
    NSLog(@"%@Name: %@", indentation, [person valueForKey:@"name"]);

    // Increase the indentation for sub-levels
    indentation = [NSString stringWithFormat:@"%@   ", indentation];

    NSSet *employees = [person valueForKey:@"employees"];
    id employee;
    NSEnumerator *it = [employees objectEnumerator];
    while((employee = [it nextObject]) != nil) {
        [self displayPerson:employee withIndentation:indentation];
    }
}
```

Now write a method that retrieves all the organizations from the context and displays them along with their leaders and the leaders' employees. The code looks like this:

```
-(void)readData {
    NSManagedObjectContext *context = [self managedObjectContext];
    NSEntityDescription *orgEntity = [NSEntityDescription entityForName:@"Organization"
inManagedObjectContext:context];

    NSFetchRequest *fetchRequest = [[NSFetchRequest alloc] init];
        [fetchRequest setEntity:orgEntity];

    NSArray *organizations = [context executeFetchRequest:fetchRequest error:nil];

    id organization;
```

```
    NSEnumerator *it = [organizations objectEnumerator];
    while((organization = [it nextObject]) != nil) {
        NSLog(@"Organization: %@", [organization valueForKey:@"name"]);

        NSManagedObject *leader = [organization valueForKey:@"leader"];
        [self displayPerson:leader withIndentation:@"   "];
    }
}
```

Add the method declarations to OrgChartAppDelegate.h to silence the compiler warnings like this:

```
- (void)readData;
- (void)displayPerson:(NSManagedObject *)person withIndentation:(NSString *)indentation;
```

Finally, alter the didFinishLaunchingWithOptions: method to call [self readData] instead of [self createData]:

```
- (BOOL)application:(UIApplication *)application
didFinishLaunchingWithOptions:(NSDictionary *)launchOptions {
    //[self createData];
    [self readData];

    [window addSubview:viewController.view];
    [window makeKeyAndVisible];
    return YES;
}
```

Build and launch the application, and then look in the Debug log to see the following output, which shows the organization you created with John as it leader and also shows John's two subordinates:

```
2010-12-08 07:42:16.955 OrgChart[83470:207] Organization: MyCompany, Inc.
2010-12-08 07:42:16.959 OrgChart[83470:207]    Name: John
2010-12-08 07:42:16.960 OrgChart[83470:207]      Name: Bill
2010-12-08 07:42:16.961 OrgChart[83470:207]      Name: Jane
```

Feel free to experiment with the OrgChart application, altering the managed objects created in the createData: method and calling createData: to store your changes and readData: to verify your changes were written. You can delete the SQLite database file between runs and let the OrgChart application re-create it, or you can let multiple runs accumulate objects in the database. If you, for example, add a new person (Jack) as Jane's subordinate, then the OrgChart application's output would look like the following:

```
2010-12-08 07:42:16.955 OrgChart[83470:207] Organization: MyCompany, Inc.
2010-12-08 07:42:16.959 OrgChart[83470:207]    Name: John
2010-12-08 07:42:16.960 OrgChart[83470:207]      Name: Bill
2010-12-08 07:42:16.961 OrgChart[83470:207]      Name: Jane
2010-12-08 07:42:16.961 OrgChart[83470:207]        Name: Jack
```

Jack works for Jane. Both Jane and Bill work for John. John is the company's leader.

Summary

By now the Core Data framework should look a lot less overwhelming to you. In this chapter, we explored the main classes involved in efficiently managing the persistence of entire object graphs without having to expose the user to complex graph algorithms and grueling C APIs used to interact with certain databases. Using Core Data is comparable to driving a car without having to be a mechanic. The framework is able to represent object models and manage data object graphs with just about a dozen classes. The simplicity of the class structure is misleading. You have seen how powerful Core Data can be. This is only a beginning. As we dig deeper into the many configuration options, UI bindings, alternate persistent stores, and custom managed object classes, you will see how powerful and elegant Core Data is.

Chapter 3

Storing Data: SQLite and Other Options

Chapter 2 explains the classes that comprise the Core Data framework and the interdependencies and precision with which they work together. The following chapters explain and demonstrate the flexibility of the framework to get the desired results, but the framework flexes only so far. The framework imposes a structure, order, and rigidity for putting data into and taking data out of a persistent store. You must work within that order and structure, doing things the Core Data way, to store and retrieve data reliably. Core Data's shackles fall off, however, when defining what the persistent store looks like or how it works. Though people tend to think that data "belongs" in a database and Apple both provides and defaults to a SQLite database for Core Data's persistent store, you have other options, and your data can rest in whatever form you want. For most cases, you'll probably be happy with the default SQLite database, but this chapter discusses other options and where they may be useful.

In this chapter, we build a simple application with two tables and a one-to-many relationship between them. Imagine you've volunteered to run a youth soccer league, and you're trying to keep track of the teams. In your data model, you have a Team table that tracks the team name and the uniform color and a Player table that tracks the first name, last name, and e-mail address for each player. One team has many players, and each player belongs to only one team. We build this application first for SQLite and then port it to each of the other options for your persistent store: in-memory and atomic (or custom) stores. Follow along, and feel free to store your data in SQLite or any other persistent store you can imagine.

Using SQLite as the Persistent Store

In this section, we build a Core Data–based application that we use throughout this chapter to demonstrate different persistent store options. We start from Xcode's Core

Data template and build upon the generated code to create an application that stores a bunch of teams and a bunch of players and allows users to maintain them. Don't get caught up in the application code or the user interface; instead, focus on the backing persistent store and its many forms.

To begin, launch Xcode, and choose **File ➤ New Project**. Select Application under iPhone OS on the left of the ensuing dialog box, and select Navigation-based Application on the right. Select the Use Core Data for storage check box. Your dialog box should look like Figure 3-1. Click the Choose… button, and save the project as **League Manager**.

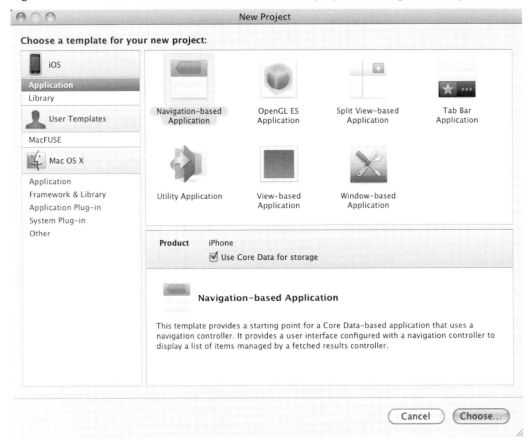

Figure 3-1. *Selecting the Navigation-based Application template*

The most interesting part of the League Manager application, at least for current purposes, is the data model. Understanding persistent stores depends on creating and understanding the proper data model, so step through this carefully and precisely. Open the data model in Xcode by expanding the Resources folder on the left and selecting League_Manager.xcdatamodel, which is below League_Manager.xcdatamodeld. The right side of Xcode displays the generated data model, which has a single entity called Event with a single attribute called timeStamp. Delete the Event entity by selecting it and pressing your Delete key, which should give you an empty data model, as in Figure 3-2.

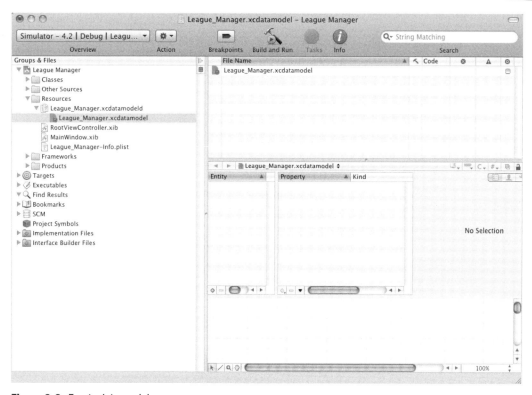

Figure 3-2. *Empty data model*

The League Manager data model calls for two entities: one to hold teams and one to hold players. For teams, we track two attributes: name and uniform color. For players, we track three: first name, last name, and e-mail address (so we can contact players about practices, games, and the schedule for orange-slice responsibilities). We also track which players play for a given team, as well as which team a given player plays for. Start by creating the Team entity; you click the + button below the Entity section in Xcode. Xcode creates a new entity called Entity, with the name conveniently highlighted so you can type **Team** and press Enter. Now click the + button below the Property section, select Add Attribute, type **name** to name the new attribute, and select String from the Type drop-down. Now create the second attribute, following the same steps, but name the attribute **uniformColor**, and select the String type. Your data model should look like Figure 3-3.

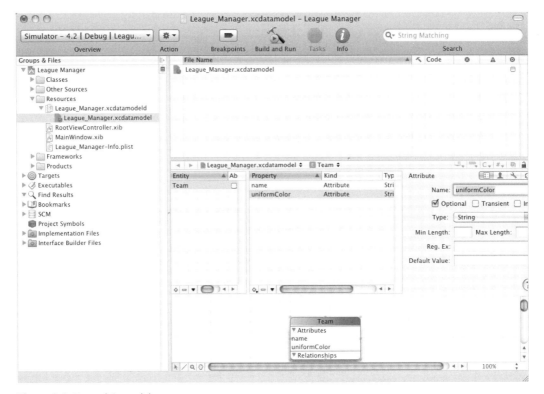

Figure 3-3. *Team data model*

Before you can create the one-to-many relationship between teams and players, you must have players for teams to relate to. Create another entity called `Player` with three attributes, all of type `String`: firstName, lastName, and email. Your data model should now look like Figure 3-4.

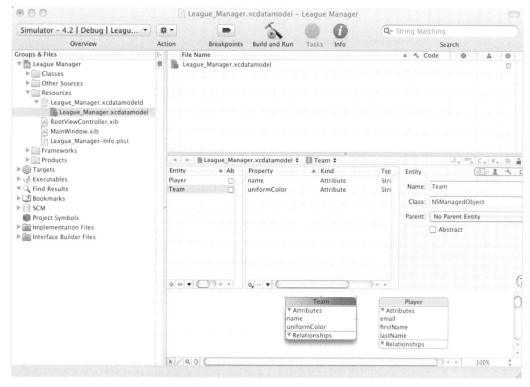

Figure 3-4. *Team and Player data model*

Configuring the One-to-Many Relationship

To create the one-to-many relationship between the Team entity and the Player entity, select the Team entity, and click the + button below the Property section. This time, however, select Add Relationship from the menu. Name this relationship **players**, and select Player from the Destination drop-down. Leave the Optional check box selected. Select the To-Many Relationship check box; one team can have many players. For Delete Rule, select Cascade from the drop-down so that deleting a team deletes all its players. We cannot yet select the inverse relationship in the Inverse drop-down because we haven't created the inverse relationship yet. The Relationship information section should look like Figure 3-5.

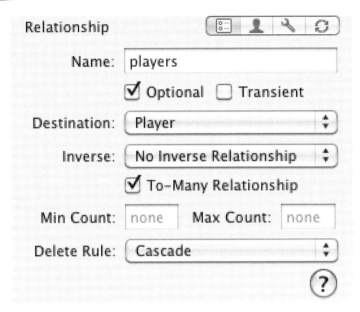

Figure 3-5. *Players relationship options*

Next, create the relationship back from the Player entity to the Team entity by selecting the Player entity, adding a relationship, and calling it **team**. Select Team from the Destination column and "players" from the Inverse column. Leave the relationship options as the default. You should now be able to select the Team entity and verify that the "players" relationship has an inverse: "team." Your Xcode window should look like Figure 3-6.

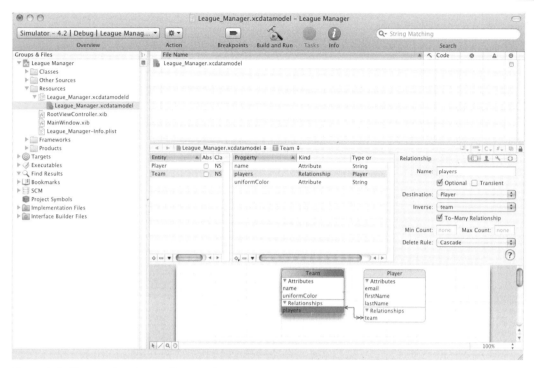

Figure 3-6. *The complete League Manager data model*

Building the User Interface

With the data model complete, League Manager now requires code to display the data. Xcode generated most of the code necessary to display the list of teams; the next task is to tweak the code, since it's prepared to show `Event` entities and the `Event` entity no longer exists in the data model. This code resides in `RootViewController.h` and `RootViewController.m`, so start by opening the `RootViewController.h` file. Notice that it has two members: an `NSManagedObjectContext` instance and an `NSFetchedResultsController` instance. We could move the `NSManagedObjectContext` instance, which you recognize as the object context for our application, to our application's delegate (`League_ManagerAppDelegate`), but we'll leave it here for this simple application. The `NSFetchedResultsController` instance works with the table view to show our teams.

We need a method to add a team, so add one called `insertTeamWithName:`, and declare it in `RootViewController.h`. Also, the generated code saves the context in a couple of places, so adhere to the Don't Repeat Yourself (DRY) principle and move it all to one method called `saveContext:`. The code for `RootViewController.h` now looks like this, with the new method declarations in bold:

```
#import <CoreData/CoreData.h>

@interface RootViewController : UITableViewController
<NSFetchedResultsControllerDelegate> {
  NSFetchedResultsController *fetchedResultsController;
  NSManagedObjectContext *managedObjectContext;
}
@property (nonatomic, retain) NSFetchedResultsController *fetchedResultsController;
@property (nonatomic, retain) NSManagedObjectContext *managedObjectContext;

- (void)insertTeamWithName:(NSString *)name uniformColor:(NSString *)uniformColor;
- (void)saveContext;

@end
```

Open the RootViewController.m file, and add a line to the viewDidLoad: method that sets the title for the application. That line looks like this:

```
self.title = @"League Manager";
```

Now define the insertTeamWithName: method in RootViewController.m. That method looks like this:

```
- (void)insertTeamWithName:(NSString *)name uniformColor:(NSString *)uniformColor {
  // Create a new instance of the entity managed by the fetched results controller.
  NSManagedObjectContext *context = [self.fetchedResultsController➥
managedObjectContext];

  NSEntityDescription *entity = [[self.fetchedResultsController fetchRequest] entity];
  NSManagedObject *newManagedObject = [NSEntityDescription➥
insertNewObjectForEntityForName:[entity name] inManagedObjectContext:context];


  // Configure the new team
  [newManagedObject setValue:name forKey:@"name"];
  [newManagedObject setValue:uniformColor forKey:@"uniformColor"];

  // Save the context
  [self saveContext];
}
```

This code gets the managed object context from the application's fetchedResultsController and then inserts a new NSManagedObject instance into that managed object context. Notice that it doesn't specify that the new entity we're trying to insert is named Team. The name gets defined in the accessor for fetchedResultsController. The generated code used the name Event, so find the line in fetchedResultsController that looks like this:

```
NSEntityDescription *entity = [NSEntityDescription entityForName:@"Event"➥
inManagedObjectContext:self.managedObjectContext];
```

and change it to this:

```
NSEntityDescription *entity = [NSEntityDescription entityForName:@"Team"➥
inManagedObjectContext:self.managedObjectContext];
```

Also, you'll notice another vestige of the generated model in the `fetchedResultsController` method: a reference to the attribute called `timeStamp`, used for sorting the fetched results (Chapter 6 discusses sorting and how it works). Change to sort on the team name, ascending, so that this line:

```
NSSortDescriptor *sortDescriptor = [[NSSortDescriptor alloc] initWithKey:@"timeStamp"➥
ascending:NO];
```

now looks like this:

```
NSSortDescriptor *sortDescriptor = [[NSSortDescriptor alloc] initWithKey:@"name"➥
ascending:YES];
```

After creating the managed object representing the new team, the code in the `insertTeamWithName:` method sets its name and uniform color using the parameters passed:

```
[newManagedObject setValue:name forKey:@"name"];
[newManagedObject setValue:uniformColor forKey:@"uniformColor"];
```

Finally, the `insertTeamWithName:` method saves the object graph, including the new team, by calling the `saveContext:` method that we declared but haven't yet defined. We define it by cutting and pasting that bit of code from the now-superfluous `insertNewObject:` method that Xcode generated. After snipping that bit, delete the `insertNewObject:` method and define `saveContext:` like this:

```
- (void)saveContext {
  NSManagedObjectContext *context = [self.fetchedResultsController➥
managedObjectContext];

  NSError *error = nil;
  if (![context save:&error]) {
    /*
    Replace this implementation with code to handle the error appropriately.

    abort() causes the application to generate a crash log and terminate. You should
not use this function in a shipping application, although it may be useful during
development. If it is not possible to recover from the error, display an alert panel
that instructs the user to quit the application by pressing the Home button.
    */
    NSLog(@"Unresolved error %@, %@", error, [error userInfo]);
    abort();
  }
}
```

Leave the generated comment there to remind you that calling `abort` represents a decidedly un-user-friendly way to handle errors. Chapter 9 talks about appropriate error handling. Since you now have a method that you can reuse to save the context, replace the other instance of that code, found in the `commitEditingStyle:` method, with the new `saveContext:` method.

Configuring the Table

The table cells are still configured to show Event entities instead of Team entities. We want to show two pieces of information for a team in each table cell: the team's name and its uniform color. To accomplish this, first change the style of the cells created, as well as the CellIdentifier used, in the cellForRowAtIndexPath: method. Change this line:

```
static NSString *CellIdentifier = @"Cell";
```

to this:

```
static NSString *CellIdentifier = @"TableCell";
```

and change the created table cells from style UITableViewCellStyleDefault to style UITableViewCellStyleValue1 so that this line:

```
cell = [[[UITableViewCell alloc] initWithStyle:UITableViewCellStyleDefault➡
reuseIdentifier:CellIdentifier] autorelease];
```

looks like this:

```
cell = [[[UITableViewCell alloc] initWithStyle:UITableViewCellStyleValue1➡
reuseIdentifier:CellIdentifier] autorelease];
```

The generated code has created a method called configureCell that's responsible for, well, configuring the cell. Change that method from configuring for Event entities to configuring for Team entities. We also want to be able to drill down from the team to see its players, so we add a detail disclosure button to each cell. The generated method looks like this:

```
- (void)configureCell:(UITableViewCell *)cell atIndexPath:(NSIndexPath *)indexPath {
    NSManagedObject *managedObject = [self.fetchedResultsController➡
objectAtIndexPath:indexPath];

    cell.textLabel.text = [[managedObject valueForKey:@"timeStamp"] description];
}
```

Change it to look like this:

```
- (void)configureCell:(UITableViewCell *)cell atIndexPath:(NSIndexPath *)indexPath {
    NSManagedObject *managedObject = [self.fetchedResultsController➡
objectAtIndexPath:indexPath];

    cell.textLabel.text = [[managedObject valueForKey:@"name"] description];
    cell.detailTextLabel.text = [[managedObject valueForKey:@"uniformColor"] description];
    cell.accessoryType = UITableViewCellAccessoryDetailDisclosureButton;
}
```

Creating a Team

The application doesn't do much yet. For example, you can't add a team or any players. This is a good time, though, to compile and run the application to make sure you're on track. If the application doesn't build or run at this point, go back and review your data model and your code, and make sure it matches the code shown previously before proceeding.

If you run the application and tap the + button to add a team, you notice that the application crashes. The + button is still wired to the `insertNewObject:` method that we deleted. You need to wire it to a method that will allow you to create a new team. The design for creating a new team calls for a modal window that allows you to enter the name and uniform color for the team. You reuse this modal window for editing an existing team as well, which users can do by tapping the team's cell. Create this modal window by selecting **File ➤ New File**… from the Xcode menu, and select Cocoa Touch Class under iOS on the left and UIViewController subclass on the right. Leave only the "With XIB for user interface" check box selected, as Figure 3-7 shows, and click the Next button.

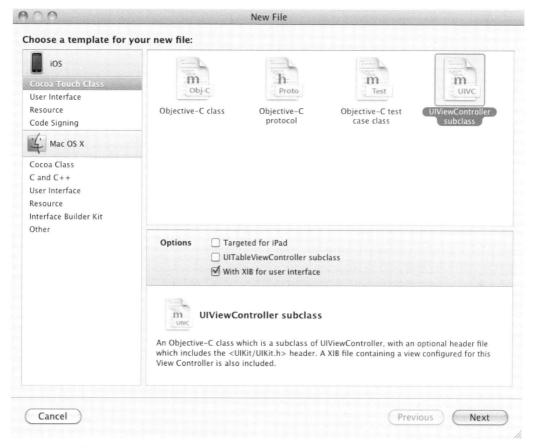

Figure 3-7. *Adding a view controller for the new team*

Save the new view controller as `TeamViewController.m`, and open the header file (`TeamViewController.h`). In League Manager, the `RootViewController` class controls the managed object context, so `TeamViewController` needs a reference to it and an accompanying initializer. Since you can use this controller to edit a team, as well as create a new one, you allow calling code to pass a team object to edit, and you store a property for that and add it to the initializer. The user interface has two text fields, one for the team name and one for the uniform color, so TeamViewController needs properties for those fields. The user interface also has two buttons, Save and Cancel, so TeamViewController must have methods to wire to those buttons. Add all that up, and you get the TeamViewController.h shown in Listing 3-1.

Listing 3-1. *TeamViewController.h*

```
#import <UIKit/UIKit.h>

@class RootViewController;

@interface TeamViewController : UIViewController {
  IBOutlet UITextField *name;
  IBOutlet UITextField *uniformColor;
  NSManagedObject *team;
  RootViewController *rootController;
}
@property (nonatomic, retain) UITextField *name;
@property (nonatomic, retain) UITextField *uniformColor;
@property (nonatomic, retain) NSManagedObject *team;
@property (nonatomic, retain) RootViewController *rootController;

- (IBAction)save:(id)sender;
- (IBAction)cancel:(id)sender;
- (id)initWithRootController:(RootViewController *)aRootController team:➥
(NSManagedObject *)aTeam;


@end
```

Now open TeamViewController.m; delete the commented-out generated methods; import RootViewController.h; add @synthesize lines for name, uniformColor, team, and rootController; and add release calls for team and rootController to the dealloc: method. Next, add a definition for the initWithRootController: method that looks like this:

```
- (id)initWithRootController:(RootViewController *)aRootController team:➥
(NSManagedObject *)aTeam {
  if ((self = [super init])) {
    self.rootController = aRootController;
    self.team = aTeam;
  }
  return self;
}
```

In the case in which users add a new team, the aTeam parameter will be nil, and the TeamViewController.m will own the responsibility to create it. In the case in which users edit an existing team, however, you must take the existing team's attribute values and put them into the appropriate text fields. Do that in the viewDidLoad: method, like this:

```
- (void)viewDidLoad {
  [super viewDidLoad];
```

```
  if (team != nil) {
    name.text = [team valueForKey:@"name"];
    uniformColor.text = [team valueForKey:@"uniformColor"];
  }
}
```

Finally, implement the save: and cancel: methods so that this controller can respond appropriately to when the user taps the Save or Cancel buttons. The save: method checks for a non-nil rootController instance and then determines whether to create a new team or edit an existing team by checking whether its team member is nil. If it's not nil, it updates the values for the existing team and asks the rootController member to save its context. If it is nil, it asks the rootViewController instance to create a new team in the managed object context, passing the user-entered values for team name and uniform color. Finally, it dismisses itself. The method implementation looks like this:

```
- (IBAction)save:(id)sender {
  if (rootController != nil) {
    if (team != nil) {
      [team setValue:name.text forKey:@"name"];
      [team setValue:uniformColor.text forKey:@"uniformColor"];
      [rootController saveContext];
    } else {
      [rootController insertTeamWithName:name.text uniformColor:uniformColor.text];
    }
  }
  [self dismissModalViewControllerAnimated:YES];
}
```

The cancel: method simply dismisses itself. The entire file should look like Listing 3-2.

Listing 3-2. *TeamViewController.m*

```
#import "TeamViewController.h"
#import "RootViewController.h"

@implementation TeamViewController

@synthesize name;
@synthesize uniformColor;
@synthesize team;
@synthesize rootController;

- (id)initWithRootController:(RootViewController *)aRootController team:➥
(NSManagedObject *)aTeam {
  if ((self = [super init])) {
    self.rootController = aRootController;
    self.team = aTeam;
  }
  return self;
}

- (void)viewDidLoad {
```

```objc
  [super viewDidLoad];
  if (team != nil) {
    name.text = [team valueForKey:@"name"];
    uniformColor.text = [team valueForKey:@"uniformColor"];
  }
}

- (IBAction)save:(id)sender {
  if (rootController != nil) {
    if (team != nil) {
      [team setValue:name.text forKey:@"name"];
      [team setValue:uniformColor.text forKey:@"uniformColor"];
      [rootController saveContext];
    } else {
      [rootController insertTeamWithName:name.text uniformColor:uniformColor.text];
    }
  }
  [self dismissModalViewControllerAnimated:YES];
}

- (IBAction)cancel:(id)sender {
  [self dismissModalViewControllerAnimated:YES];
}

- (void)didReceiveMemoryWarning {
  [super didReceiveMemoryWarning];
}

- (void)viewDidUnload {
  [super viewDidUnload];
}

- (void)dealloc {
  [super dealloc];
}

@end
```

With the code written to support the user interface, you're ready to build the labels, text fields, and buttons the users will interact with to create teams. Double-click TeamViewController.xib on the left side of Xcode to open it in Interface Builder, and then double-click the View icon to display the view, which is currently blank. Drag two Label instances onto the view, and change them to read **Team Name:** and **Uniform Color:**. Drag two Text Field instances onto the view, and align them to the right of the Labels. Drag two Round Rect Button instances below the Label and Text Field controls, and change the labels on them to **Save** and **Cancel**. Your view should look like Figure 3-8.

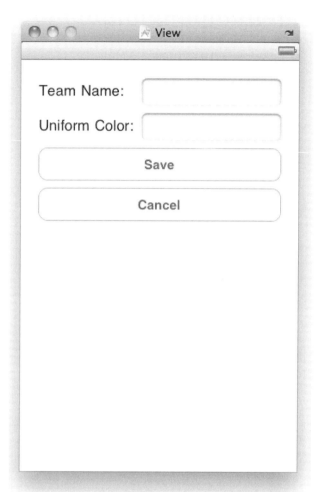

Figure 3-8. *Updated team view*

Bind the Text Field instances to the appropriate TeamViewController members, name and uniformColor, by Ctrl+dragging from the File's Owner icon to the respective Text Field instances and selecting name or uniformColor from the pop-up menu as appropriate. Wire the buttons to the save: and cancel: methods by Ctrl+dragging from each button, in turn, to the File's Owner icon and selecting the appropriate method from the pop-up menu.

Before building and running the application, you must go back to RootViewController and include code to display the team interface you just built. You display it in two scenarios: when users tap the + button to create a new team and when they tap the team in the table to edit it. Start by creating the method to respond to the + button tap. Declare a method called showTeamView: in RootViewController.h:

```
- (void)showTeamView;
```

Go to RootViewController.m, import TeamViewController.h, and add the definition for the showTeamView: method. This method creates a TeamViewController instance, initializing it with the RootViewController instance and a nil team, so that the TeamViewController knows to create a new team if the user taps Save. The method should look like this:

```
- (void)showTeamView {
  TeamViewController *teamViewController = [[TeamViewController alloc]➥
initWithRootController:self team:nil];

  [self presentModalViewController:teamViewController animated:YES];
  [teamViewController release];
}
```

Now you need to wire the + button to call this method. Go to the viewDidLoad: method, and change this line:

```
UIBarButtonItem *addButton = [[UIBarButtonItem alloc]
initWithBarButtonSystemItem:UIBarButtonSystemItemAdd target:self➥
action:@selector(insertNewObject)];
```

to this:

```
UIBarButtonItem *addButton = [[UIBarButtonItem alloc]
initWithBarButtonSystemItem:UIBarButtonSystemItemAdd target:self➥
action:@selector(showTeamView)];
```

The application should now be able to add teams, but before testing that, add the code to edit teams. This code should determine the tapped team by asking the fetchedResultsController which team was tapped, which it will determine using the indexPath passed to this method. This code then creates a TeamViewContoller instance and initializes it with the RootViewController and the tapped team. Find the didSelectRowAtIndexPath: method, and add the code to edit the tapped team, like this:

```
- (void)tableView:(UITableView *)tableView didSelectRowAtIndexPath:(NSIndexPath
*)indexPath {
  NSManagedObject *team = [[self fetchedResultsController] objectAtIndexPath:indexPath];
  TeamViewController *teamViewController = [[TeamViewController alloc]➥
initWithRootController:self team:team];

  [self presentModalViewController:teamViewController animated:YES];
  [teamViewController release];
}
```

Build the application and run it. The application looks like it did the last time you ran it, as Figure 3-9 shows.

Figure 3-9. *League Manager without any teams*

Now, however, if you tap the + button, you see the screen to create a new team, as Figure 3-10 shows.

Figure 3-10. *Adding a new team to League Manager*

Go ahead and add a few teams, edit some teams, and delete some teams. You can close and relaunch the application, and you'll find the teams as they were when you quit the application—they're all being added to your SQLite data store. You will notice that the teams are sorted alphabetically by team name. Figure 3-11 shows some sample teams, with name and uniform color.

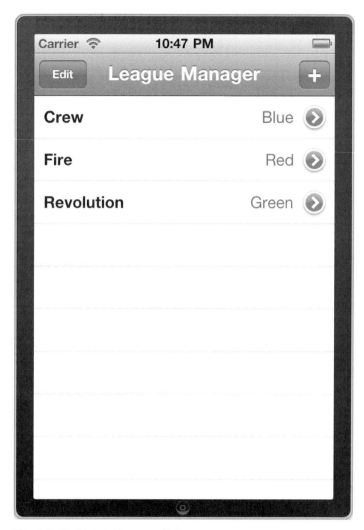

Figure 3-11. *League Manager with teams*

You might notice that you can create teams with blank names and uniform colors. If this were a real application, you would take steps to prevent users from creating teams with no name and perhaps with no uniform color. This chapter remains focused on the different persistent store options, however, so we've purposely left out any validation code. You'll notice that the player user interface created later in this chapter has no validation code either, so you can create blank players. Chapter 5 talks about how to validate data.

Go ahead and quit the application, feel accomplished for having gotten this far, and then realize that you've covered only the Team entity. You still must implement the Player user interface and entity to call the League Manager application complete.

The Player User Interface

To implement the Player user interface, you must have two views and their accompanying controllers: one to list the players for a team and one to add a new or edit an existing player. These controllers largely mirror the ones for Team, although they don't contain an NSFetchedResultsController or the rest of the Core Data classes that RootViewController does. Instead, they delegate the Core Data interaction to RootViewController.

Create the controller and view to list players for a team first. Add a new UIViewController subclass, making sure to select "UITableViewController subclass" and deselect "With XIB for user interface." Call it **PlayerListViewController**, and then turn your attention to the file PlayerListViewController.h. This class lists players for a team, so it needs a reference to Team entity for which it manages players. Also, since it defers Core Data interaction to the RootViewController class, it requires a reference to the RootViewController. This controller will have a + button for adding a new player, so declare a method to respond to taps on that button called showPlayerView:. Finally, since it doesn't use an NSFetchedResultsController instance to sort the players, it must implement sorting for the players. To accomplish all this, we end up with a PlayerListViewController.h file that looks like Listing 3-3.

Listing 3-3. *PlayerListViewController.h*

```
#import <UIKit/UIKit.h>

@class RootViewController;

@interface PlayerListViewController : UITableViewController {
  NSManagedObject *team;
  RootViewController *rootController;
}
@property (nonatomic, retain) NSManagedObject *team;
@property (nonatomic, retain) RootViewController *rootController;

- (id)initWithRootController:(RootViewController *)aRootController team:➡
(NSManagedObject *)aTeam;

- (void)showPlayerView;
- (NSArray *)sortPlayers;

@end
```

You'll recognize pieces of RootViewController.m in the PlayerListViewController.m file. Open the file, and add an import for RootViewController.h and @synthesize lines for the team and rootController properties. Add an initWithRootController: method that accepts those two properties and stores them that looks like this:

```
- (id)initWithRootController:(RootViewController *)aRootController team:➡
(NSManagedObject *)aTeam {
  if ((self = [super init])) {
    self.rootController = aRootController;
    self.team = aTeam;
```

```
    }
    return self;
}
```

Xcode generated a `viewDidLoad:` method for you but commented it out. Uncomment it, and change its contents to update the view title appropriately and to display a + button to add a player to the team. Since you haven't yet begun building the user interface for adding or editing a player, wire the + to the method called `showPlayerView:` that you leave blank for now. Those two methods look like this:

```
- (void)viewDidLoad {
    [super viewDidLoad];

    self.title = @"Players";

    UIBarButtonItem *addButton = [[UIBarButtonItem alloc]➥
initWithBarButtonSystemItem:UIBarButtonSystemItemAdd target:self➥
action:@selector(showPlayerView)];
    self.navigationItem.rightBarButtonItem = addButton;
    [addButton release];
}

- (void)showPlayerView {
}
```

Delete the rest of the commented-out generated methods, except for `viewWillAppear:`. In that method, instruct the controller's table view to reload its data, like this:

```
- (void)viewWillAppear:(BOOL)animated {
    [super viewWillAppear:animated];
    [self.tableView reloadData];
}
```

If you want the table view to reload its data, you must tell the table view what data to load and display. The player list will display all the players for a team, sorted alphabetically, in a single section. To get the players for a team, call the team's `valueForKey:@"players"` method, which uses the "players" relationship from the data model to pull all the `Player` entities from the SQLite persistent store and returns them as an `NSSet`. The code to set up the single section and the number of rows for the table looks like this:

```
- (NSInteger)numberOfSectionsInTableView:(UITableView *)tableView {
    return 1;
}

- (NSInteger)tableView:(UITableView *)tableView numberOfRowsInSection:(NSInteger)section
{
    return [(NSSet *)[team valueForKey:@"players"] count];
}
```

For the table cells, again use the `UITableViewCellStyleValue1` to display text on the left (the first and last names of the player) and text on the right (the e-mail address). Change the generated `cellForRowAtIndexPath:` to look like this:

```
- (UITableViewCell *)tableView:(UITableView *)tableView➥
cellForRowAtIndexPath:(NSIndexPath *)indexPath {
  static NSString *CellIdentifier = @"PlayerCell";

  UITableViewCell *cell = [tableView dequeueReusableCellWithIdentifier:CellIdentifier];
  if (cell == nil) {
    cell = [[[UITableViewCell alloc] initWithStyle:UITableViewCellStyleValue1➥
reuseIdentifier:CellIdentifier] autorelease];

  }

  NSManagedObject *player = [[self sortPlayers] objectAtIndex:indexPath.row];
  cell.textLabel.text = [NSString stringWithFormat:@"%@ %@", [[player➥
valueForKey:@"firstName"] description], [[player valueForKey:@"lastName"] description]];

  cell.detailTextLabel.text = [[player valueForKey:@"email"] description];
  return cell;
}
```

Here you see a call to sortPlayers:. Recall that the "players" relationship on the "team" instance returns an NSSet, which not only has no sorting but also isn't indexable, because it has no deterministic order. The cellForRowAtIndexPath: method demands a cell for a specific index into the backing data, so no NSSet method can perform the task you need here: to return the appropriate cell for the table at this index path. Instead, you convert the NSSet to an NSArray sorted by players' last names using this sortPlayers: method:

```
- (NSArray *)sortPlayers {
  NSSortDescriptor *sortLastNameDescriptor = [[[NSSortDescriptor alloc]➥
initWithKey:@"lastName" ascending:YES] autorelease];

  NSArray *sortDescriptors = [NSArray arrayWithObjects:sortLastNameDescriptor, nil];
  return [[(NSSet *)[team valueForKey:@"players"] allObjects]➥
sortedArrayUsingDescriptors:sortDescriptors];

}
```

Add releases for team and rootController to your dealloc: method to complete this phase of changes to PlayerListViewController.m. To display the player list view for a team, go back to RootViewController.m, and add a method to respond to taps on the detail disclosure buttons for teams. The method to implement is called accessoryButtonTappedForRowWithIndexPath:, and in this method you retrieve the tapped team from the fetched results controller, create a PlayerListViewController instance and initialize it with the root view controller and the tapped team, and show the controller. The code looks like this:

```
- (void)tableView:(UITableView *)tableView➥
accessoryButtonTappedForRowWithIndexPath:(NSIndexPath *)indexPath {
  NSManagedObject *team = [self.fetchedResultsController objectAtIndexPath:indexPath];
  PlayerListViewController *playerListViewController = [[PlayerListViewController➥
alloc] initWithRootController:self team:team];

  [self.navigationController pushViewController:playerListViewController animated:YES];
  [playerListViewController release];
}
```

Add an import for `PlayerListViewController.h` to the top of `RootViewController.m`, and you're ready to build and launch League Manager anew. You should see the teams you created before, but now when you tap the detail disclosure button for a team, you move to the Players list view, as in Figure 3-12. Since you as yet have no way to add players, the list is blank, and the + button does nothing.

Figure 3-12. *Team with no players*

Adding, Editing, and Deleting Players

The League Manager application is nearly complete; it lacks means only for adding, editing, and deleting players. To accomplish these tasks, create a new `UIViewController` subclass, deselect "UITableViewController subclass," and select "With XIB for user interface." Call this controller **PlayerViewController**. It looks similar to the `TeamViewController` class and interface but has three fields: `firstName`, `lastName`, and `email`. It also has a reference to the `RootViewController` instance so it can defer all Core Data storage and retrieval to that class. It has a member for the team this player belongs to, and it also has a reference to the player. If the player is `nil`, `PlayerViewController` knows to create a new player. Otherwise, it knows to edit the existing player object. Finally, the user interface has three buttons: one to save the player, one to cancel the operation (add or edit), and one to delete the player. See Listing 3-4 for what `PlayerViewController.h` should look like.

Listing 3-4. *PlayerViewController.h*

```
#import <UIKit/UIKit.h>

@class RootViewController;

@interface PlayerViewController : UIViewController <UIActionSheetDelegate> {
  IBOutlet UITextField *firstName;
  IBOutlet UITextField *lastName;
  IBOutlet UITextField *email;
  NSManagedObject *team;
  NSManagedObject *player;
  RootViewController *rootController;
}
@property (nonatomic, retain) UITextField *firstName;
@property (nonatomic, retain) UITextField *lastName;
@property (nonatomic, retain) UITextField *email;
@property (nonatomic, retain) NSManagedObject *team;
@property (nonatomic, retain) NSManagedObject *player;
@property (nonatomic, retain) RootViewController *rootController;

- (IBAction)save:(id)sender;
- (IBAction)cancel:(id)sender;
- (IBAction)confirmDelete:(id)sender;
- (id)initWithRootController:(RootViewController *)aRootController team:➥
(NSManagedObject *)aTeam player:(NSManagedObject *)aPlayer;


@end
```

Now, open the `PlayerViewController.m` file, import `RootViewController.h`, add `@synthesize` lines for the various properties, and add release calls to the `dealloc:` method. Add the `initWithRootController:` method declared in `PlayerViewController.h` to initialize this view controller with a `RootViewController` instance, a team, and a possibly-nil player. That method looks like this:

```
- (id)initWithRootController:(RootViewController *)aRootController team:➥
(NSManagedObject *)aTeam player:(NSManagedObject *)aPlayer {
  if ((self = [super init])) {
    self.rootController = aRootController;
    self.team = aTeam;
    self.player = aPlayer;
  }
  return self;
}
```

Use the `viewDidLoad:` method to take the values from the `player` managed object, if non-nil, and put them in the `firstName`, `lastName`, and `email` fields. That method looks like this:

```
- (void)viewDidLoad {
  [super viewDidLoad];
  if (player != nil) {
    firstName.text = [player valueForKey:@"firstName"];
    lastName.text = [player valueForKey:@"lastName"];
    email.text = [player valueForKey:@"email"];
  }
}
```

Your next step is to add methods to respond to the three buttons. The `save:` and `cancel:` methods mirror the ones created for the `TeamViewController` class; they look like this:

```
- (IBAction)save:(id)sender {
  if (rootController != nil) {
    if (player != nil) {
      [player setValue:firstName.text forKey:@"firstName"];
      [player setValue:lastName.text forKey:@"lastName"];
      [player setValue:email.text forKey:@"email"];
      [rootController saveContext];
    } else {
      [rootController insertPlayerWithTeam:team firstName:firstName.text➥
lastName:lastName.text email:email.text];

    }
  }
  [self dismissModalViewControllerAnimated:YES];
}

- (IBAction)cancel:(id)sender {
  [self dismissModalViewControllerAnimated:YES];
}
```

The `insertPlayerWithTeam:` method doesn't yet exist, so you'll create that in a moment. First, though, implement the `confirmDelete:` method for the Delete button in the user interface to call. This method doesn't delete the player right away but instead presents an action sheet requesting users to confirm their intentions. The implementation here first checks whether the player is not `nil`. In other words, you can delete only existing players. You really should show the Delete button only when editing a player, but in the interest of maintaining focus on Core Data, keep things simple and ignore Delete button presses when adding a player. The `confirmDelete:` method looks like this:

```
- (IBAction)confirmDelete:(id)sender {
  if (player != nil) {
    UIActionSheet *confirm = [[UIActionSheet alloc] initWithTitle:nil delegate:self➥
cancelButtonTitle:@"Cancel" destructiveButtonTitle:@"Delete Player"➥
otherButtonTitles:nil];

    confirm.actionSheetStyle = UIActionSheetStyleBlackTranslucent;
    [confirm showInView:self.view];
    [confirm release];
```

```
    }
}
```

Note that you pass `self` as the delegate to the `UIActionSheet`'s initialization method. The Cocoa framework will call the `clickedButtonAtIndex:` method of the delegate you pass, so implement that method. It checks to see whether the clicked button was the Delete button and then asks the root view controller to delete the player using a method, `deletePlayer:`, that you must create. The `clickedButtonAtIndex:` method looks like this:

```
- (void)actionSheet:(UIActionSheet *)actionSheet➥
clickedButtonAtIndex:(NSInteger)buttonIndex {
  if (buttonIndex == 0 && rootController != nil) {
    // The Delete button was clicked
    [rootController deletePlayer:player];
    [self dismissModalViewControllerAnimated:YES];
  }
}
```

Now, move back to RootViewController.h and declare the two methods, insertPlayerWithTeam: and deletePayer:, that PlayerViewController calls. Those declarations look like this:

```
- (void)insertPlayerWithTeam:(NSManagedObject *)team firstName:(NSString *)firstName➥
lastName:(NSString *)lastName email:(NSString *)email;
- (void)deletePlayer:(NSManagedObject *)player;
```

Open RootViewController.m, and define those two methods. The insertPlayerWithTeam: method looks similar to the insertTeamWithName: method, with some important differences. The insertTeamWithName: method takes advantage of the fetched results controller and its tie to Team entities, while Player entities have no tie to the fetched results controller. The insertPlayerWithTeam: method, then, creates a Player entity by explicitly passing the Player name to the insertNewObjectForEntityForName: method. It also must create the relationship to the appropriate Team entity by setting it as the value for the "team" key, which is what the relationship is called in the data model. The insertPlayerWithTeam: method looks like this:

```
- (void)insertPlayerWithTeam:(NSManagedObject *)team firstName:(NSString *)firstName
lastName:(NSString *)lastName email:(NSString *)email {
  // Create the player
  NSManagedObjectContext *context = [self.fetchedResultsController➥
managedObjectContext];

  NSManagedObject *player = [NSEntityDescription➥
insertNewObjectForEntityForName:@"Player" inManagedObjectContext:context];

  [player setValue:firstName forKey:@"firstName"];
  [player setValue:lastName forKey:@"lastName"];
  [player setValue:email forKey:@"email"];
  [player setValue:team forKey:@"team"];

  // Save the context.
  [self saveContext];
}
```

The deletePlayer: method simply retrieves the managed object context, calls its deleteObject: method, passing in the Player managed object, and saves the managed object context. It looks like this:

```
- (void)deletePlayer:(NSManagedObject *)player {
  NSManagedObjectContext *context = [self.fetchedResultsController➡
managedObjectContext];

  [context deleteObject:player];
  [self saveContext];
}
```

The final step is to create the user interface and display it when users want to add or edit a player. Select PlayerViewController.xib, select the View icon, and drag three Label instances and three Text Field instances onto the view. Call the labels **First Name:**, **Last Name:**, and **E-mail:**. Connect the text fields to the appropriate properties. Drag three Round Rect Button instances to the view and call them Save, Cancel, and Delete, and wire them to the appropriate methods. Your view should look the one in Figure 3-13.

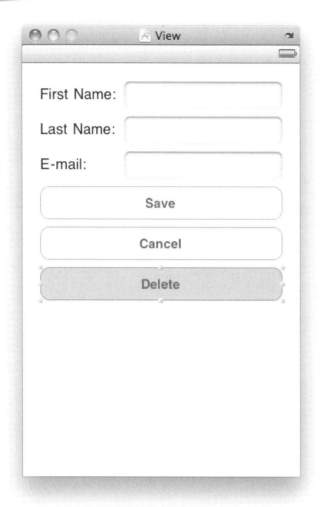

Figure 3-13. *Player view*

To display the Player view when users summon it, go to `PlayerListViewController.m`, import `PlayerViewController.h`, and find the empty `showPlayerView:` method you created earlier. In that method, you create a `PlayerViewController` instance; initialize it with the root view controller, the team, and a `nil` player so that the application will create a new player; and then show the view as a modal window. The code looks like this:

```
- (void)showPlayerView {
  PlayerViewController *playerViewController = [[PlayerViewController alloc]➥
initWithRootController:rootController team:team player:nil];

  [self presentModalViewController:playerViewController animated:YES];
  [playerViewController release];
}
```

You also must make the application respond to taps on a player's cell so that users can edit or delete the selected player. Find the generated didSelectRowAtIndexPath: method, still in PlayerListViewController.m, and gut it. Replace its contents with code to get the tapped player from the sorted players array, create the player view controller, initialize it as before but this time with the selected player, and show the view. The method now looks like this:

```
- (void)tableView:(UITableView *)tableView didSelectRowAtIndexPath:(NSIndexPath *)indexPath {
  NSManagedObject *player = [[self sortPlayers] objectAtIndex:indexPath.row];
  PlayerViewController *playerViewController = [[PlayerViewController alloc]
initWithRootController:rootController team:team player:player];
  [self presentModalViewController:playerViewController animated:YES];
  [playerViewController release];
}
```

That finishes the League Manager application. Build and run it. Any teams you've added should still be shown, thanks to the SQLite persistent store. Drill down into the teams and add some players, delete some players, and edit some players. Try deleting teams as well, and watch the players disappear.

Seeing the Data in the Persistent Store

Chapter 2 shows how to use the sqlite3 command-line tool to browse the data in the SQLite Core Data persistent store. To finish the section on SQLite persistent stores, find your SQLite database (League_Manager.sqlite3), and launch sqlite3, passing the database, with a command like this:

```
sqlite3 ./4.2/Applications/26ADDCEE-765A-48C1-A01D-➥
32FADF2859FD/Documents/League_Manager.sqlite
```

Keep the League Manager application running in the iPhone Simulator so that you can bounce between the application and sqlite3 tool to see the effects on the database.

Start by showing the tables using the .tables command. Your output should look like this:

```
sqlite> .tables
ZPLAYER        ZTEAM        Z_METADATA    Z_PRIMARYKEY
```

The ZPLAYER table holds the Player entities, and the ZTEAM table holds the Team entities. Create the three teams: Crew, with Blue uniforms; Fire, with Red uniforms, and Revolution, with Green uniforms. In the SQLite database, they look something like this, depending on how many teams you've created and deleted:

```
sqlite> select * from ZTEAM;
2|2|5|Crew|Blue
3|2|1|Fire|Red
4|2|1|Revolution|Green
```

The League Manager application has no players, as a quick check in the database shows:

```
sqlite> select * from ZPLAYER;
```

Drill into the Crew team, and add three players: Jordan Gordon, Pat Sprat, and Bailey Staley. Refer to Figure 3-14 to see how to enter a player. After adding the three players, you should see them all in a list on the Players screen, as in Figure 3-15.

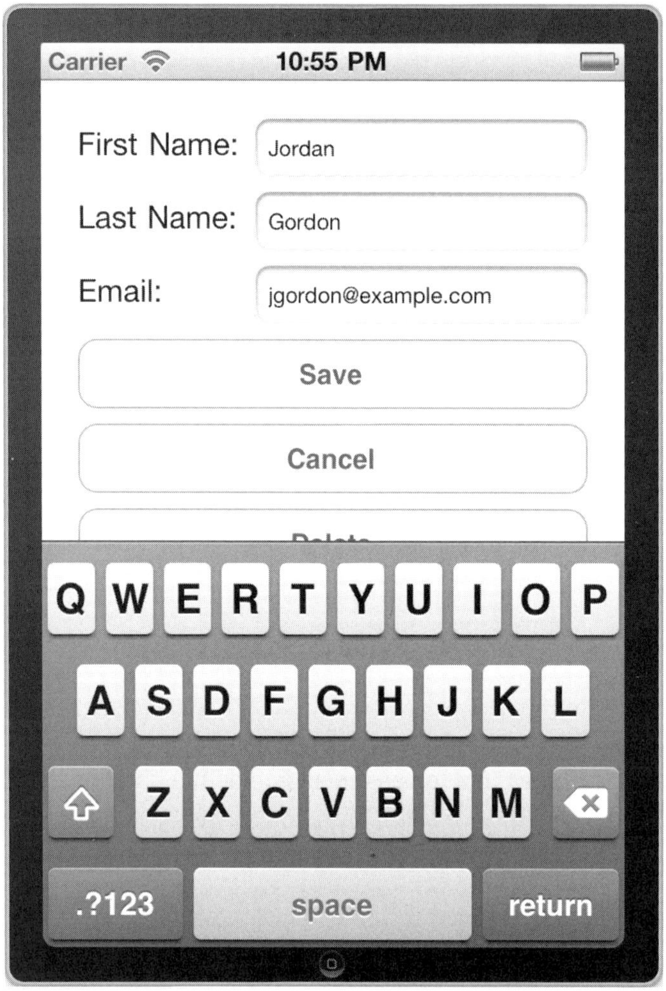

Figure 3-14 *Adding a player*

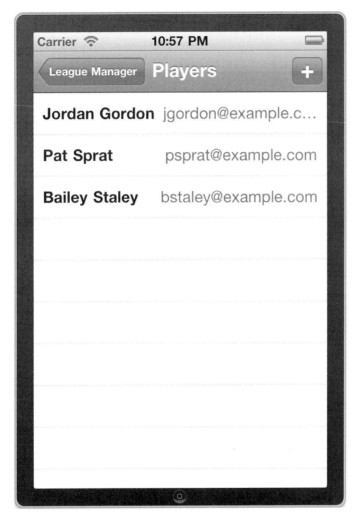

Figure 3-15. *Players*

Rerun the select command on the ZPLAYER table. The output should look something like this:

```
sqlite> select * from ZPLAYER;
3|1|1|2|Jordan|Gordon|jgordon@example.com
4|1|1|2|Pat|Sprat|psprat@example.com
5|1|1|2|Bailey|Staley|bstaley@example.com
```

Now add another player, but this time to the Fire team. Call this player Terry Gary. Now, run a command to show each team with the players on it, like this:

```
sqlite> select ZTEAM.ZNAME, ZPLAYER.ZFIRSTNAME, ZPLAYER.ZLASTNAME from ZTEAM, ZPLAYER
where ZTEAM.Z_PK = ZPLAYER.ZTEAM;
Crew|Jordan|Gordon
Crew|Pat|Sprat
```

```
Crew|Bailey|Staley
Fire|Terry|Gary
```

Now, delete Pat Sprat and rerun the same SQLite command, and you should see output like this:

```
sqlite> select ZTEAM.ZNAME, ZPLAYER.ZFIRSTNAME, ZPLAYER.ZLASTNAME from ZTEAM, ZPLAYER
where ZTEAM.Z_PK = ZPLAYER.ZTEAM;
Crew|Jordan|Gordon
Crew|Bailey|Staley
Fire|Terry|Gary
```

Finally, delete the Fire team, and verify that not only has the Fire team been deleted, but also its only player, Terry Gary:

```
sqlite> select ZTEAM.ZNAME, ZPLAYER.ZFIRSTNAME, ZPLAYER.ZLASTNAME from ZTEAM, ZPLAYER
where ZTEAM.Z_PK = ZPLAYER.ZTEAM;
Crew|Jordan|Gordon
Crew|Bailey|Staley
```

The SQLite database proves to work in ways you understand. Feel free, as you're developing iOS applications, to peek into the SQLite database to gain a better understanding and appreciation for how Core Data works. Most of your data-backed application will likely use SQLite databases, so understanding how they work with Core Data can help with troubleshooting issues or optimizing performance.

Using an In-Memory Persistent Store

In the previous section, you built a Core Data–based application that uses the default SQLite persistent store type. This section deals with an alternate type: the in-memory persistent store. Let's take a look at how to switch the store type before elaborating on why you would ever want to use this type of store.

Changing the store type Core Data uses for your application is as simple as specifying the new type when creating the persistent store coordinator in the application delegate. The code for the persistentStoreCoordinator: method in League_ManagerAppDelegate.m now looks like this, with the updated code in bold:

```
/**
 Returns the persistent store coordinator for the application.
 If the coordinator doesn't already exist, it is created, and the application's store is
added to it.
 */
- (NSPersistentStoreCoordinator *)persistentStoreCoordinator {

    if (persistentStoreCoordinator != nil) {
        return persistentStoreCoordinator;
    }

//    NSURL *storeUrl = [NSURL fileURLWithPath: [[self applicationDocumentsDirectory]
stringByAppendingPathComponent: @"League_Manager.sqlite"]];

    NSError *error = nil;
```

```
    persistentStoreCoordinator = [[NSPersistentStoreCoordinator alloc]
initWithManagedObjectModel:[self managedObjectModel]];
    if (![persistentStoreCoordinator addPersistentStoreWithType:NSInMemoryStoreType
configuration:nil URL:nil options:nil error:&error]) {

        /*
        Replace this implementation with code to handle the error appropriately.

        abort() causes the application to generate a crash log and terminate. You
should not use this function in a shipping application, although it may be useful during
development. If it is not possible to recover from the error, display an alert panel
that instructs the user to quit the application by pressing the Home button.

        Typical reasons for an error here include:
        * The persistent store is not accessible
        * The schema for the persistent store is incompatible with current managed
object model
        Check the error message to determine what the actual problem was.
        */
        NSLog(@"Unresolved error %@, %@", error, [error userInfo]);
        abort();
    }

    return persistentStoreCoordinator;
}
```

The data store has been switched to in-memory. The first thing to notice after launching the application again is that any data you previously had in your data store is gone. This is happening because we switched the data store and didn't try to migrate the data from the old store to the new one. Chapter 8 explains how to migrate data between two persistent stores.

The life cycle of the in-memory data store starts when the Core Data stack is initialized and ends when the application stops.

Note: Since iOS4 and the introduction of multitasking to the iDevices, switching to another application does not necessarily terminate the currently running application. Instead, it goes into the background. The in-memory persistent store survives when an application is sent to the background so that the data is still around when the application comes back to the foreground.

When working on a data management framework and thinking about the different types of persistent stores that it should provide by default, an in-memory store isn't the first idea that comes to mind. Trying to come up with a good reason to use an in-memory store can be a challenge, but some legitimate reasons exist. For example, local caching of remote data can benefit from in-memory persistent stores. Consider a case in which your application is fed data from a remote server. If your application executes a lot of queries, good software engineering practices would prescribe the use of efficient data transfer. The remote server may transfer the data in compressed packages to your client application, which can then uncompress that data and store it in an in-memory store so that it can be efficiently queried. In this situation, you would want the data to be refreshed every time the application starts, or even periodically while the application runs, so losing the in-memory data store would be acceptable.

Figure 3-16 illustrates the start-up sequence of an application that caches remote information locally in an in-memory store.

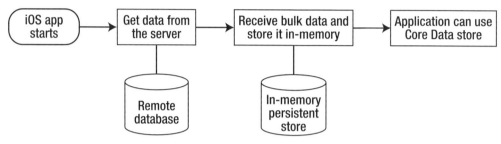

Figure 3-16. *Caching remote information locally*

As you develop your Core Data–backed iOS applications, consider using in-memory data stores when applications don't require data persistence across invocations. Traditional applications, however, which require that users' data doesn't disappear simply because the application stopped running, can't use this persistent store type.

Creating Your Own Custom Persistent Store

The principle of abstracting the persistent store implementation from the user forms the basis for the Core Data framework. This abstraction makes it possible to change the persistent store type among the different default types (NSSQLiteStoreType, NSInMemoryStoreType, NSBinaryStoreType) without changing more than a line of your code. In some cases, the default store types don't best accomplish what you are trying to achieve. The Core Data framework offers a hook for creating custom store types for these special cases. In this section, we create a new store type and use it with the League Manager application.

Before getting into the implementation itself, you should be aware that Core Data only allows you to create atomic store types. An atomic store is a store that writes its entire content all at once every time a save operation is executed. This effectively excludes the ability to create SQL-based store types that could be backed by a database other than SQLite where only the rows of data that are modified are affected in the database. In this section, we build a file-based custom store that will store its data in a comma-separated values (CSV) file except that we will use the pipe (|) symbol to separate values.

Custom data stores must extend the NSAtomicStore class (a subclass of NSPersistentStore), which provides the infrastructure necessary to hold the data. To get a better idea of how this works, you must picture two internal layers inside the Core Data framework, as shown on Figure 3-17. Users interact with the layer that contains NSManagedObjects and NSManagedObjectContext. The other layer performs the actual persistence and contains the persistent store coordinator and the persistent stores. In the case of custom stores, the persistence layer also contains NSAtomicStoreCacheNode, which contains objects that hold the data within this layer. The NSAtomicStoreCacheNode object is to the NSAtomicStore what the NSManagedObject is to the NSManagedObjectContext.

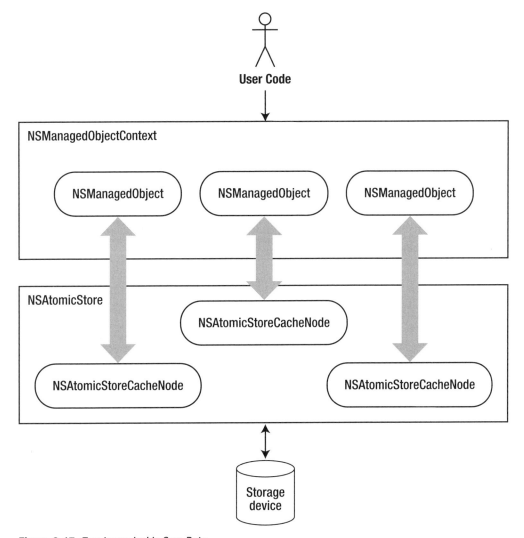

Figure 3-17. *Two layers inside Core Data*

Initializing the Custom Store

A new custom store is responsible for transferring data between the storage device and the NSAtomicStoreCacheNodes as well as transferring data between the NSManagedObjects and the NSAtomicStoreCacheNodes.

The first step to create a custom store is to add a class (or classes) to implement it. The custom store this section builds lives in one class called CustomStore. CustomStore.h starts out trivial: it extends NSAtomicStore as expected, as Listing 3-5 shows.

Listing 3-5. *CustomStore.h*

```
#import <Foundation/Foundation.h>

@interface CustomStore : NSAtomicStore {
}

@end
```

The implementation class must implement a few methods. It has accessors for its type and identifier, explained later in this section. It has an initializer that takes a persistent store coordinator and some other parameters. It also has a few other methods stubbed out that you'll implement as this section unfolds. See Listing 3-6.

Listing 3-6. *CustomStore.m*

```
#import "CustomStore.h"

@implementation CustomStore

#pragma mark -
#pragma mark NSPersistentStore

- (NSString *)type {
  return [[self metadata] objectForKey:NSStoreTypeKey];
}

- (NSString *)identifier {
  return [[self metadata] objectForKey:NSStoreUUIDKey];
}

- (id)initWithPersistentStoreCoordinator:(NSPersistentStoreCoordinator *)coordinator➡
configurationName:(NSString *)configurationName URL:(NSURL *)url options:(NSDictionary➡
*)options {

    self = [super initWithPersistentStoreCoordinator:coordinator➡
configurationName:configurationName URL:url options:options];

  return self;
}

+ (NSDictionary *)metadataForPersistentStoreWithURL:(NSURL *)url error:(NSError **)error
{
  return nil;
```

```objectivec
}

#pragma mark -
#pragma mark NSAtomicStore

- (BOOL)load:(NSError **)error {
  return YES;
}

- (id)newReferenceObjectForManagedObject:(NSManagedObject *)managedObject {
  return nil;
}

- (NSAtomicStoreCacheNode *)newCacheNodeForManagedObject:(NSManagedObject➥
*)managedObject {

  return nil;
}

- (BOOL)save:(NSError **)error {
  return YES;
}

-(void)updateCacheNode:(NSAtomicStoreCacheNode *)node fromManagedObject:➥
(NSManagedObject *)managedObject {

}

@end
```

All Core Data stores have supporting metadata that help the persistent store coordinator manage the different stores. The metadata is materialized in the NSPersistentStore class as an NSDictionary. Two data elements are of particular interest to a new data store: NSStoreTypeKey and NSStoreUUIDKey. The NSStoreTypeKey value must be a string that uniquely identifies the data store type, while the NSStoreUUIDKey must be a string that uniquely identifies the data store itself.

In this chapter's example, two data files support the custom store. The first file, which has a .txt extension, contains the data itself, and the second file, which has a .plist extension, contains the metadata. For the problem of loading and saving the metadata, add a method to save the metadata and complete the implementation of metadataForPersistentStoreWithURL:error: to load the metadata.

Data stores are initialized relative to a base URL. In the CustomStore example, the URL points to the data file (the .txt file), and the metadata file URL is derived from the base URL by swapping the .txt extension for a .plist extension.

To create unique identifiers, add a static utility method that creates and returns universally unique identifiers (UUIDs):

```objectivec
+ (NSString *)makeUUID {
  CFUUIDRef uuidRef = CFUUIDCreate(NULL);
  CFStringRef uuidStringRef = CFUUIDCreateString(NULL, uuidRef);
  CFRelease(uuidRef);
  NSString* uuid = [NSString stringWithString:(NSString *)uuidStringRef];
```

```
CFRelease(uuidStringRef);
  return uuid;
}
```

The writeMetadata:toURL: method takes the metadata NSDictionary and writes it to a file:

```
+ (void)writeMetadata:(NSDictionary*)metadata toURL:(NSURL*)url {
  NSString *path = [[url relativePath] stringByAppendingString:@".plist"];
  [metadata writeToFile:path atomically:YES];
}
```

Loading the metadata is slightly more complicated because if the data store is new and the metadata file does not exist, the metadata file must be created along with an empty data file. Core Data expects a store type, and a store UUID from the metadata helps the persistent store coordinator deal with the custom store, so set those values for the NSStoreTypeKey and NSStoreUUIDKey:

```
+ (NSDictionary *)metadataForPersistentStoreWithURL:(NSURL *)url error:(NSError **)error
{
  NSString *path = [[url relativePath] stringByAppendingString:@".plist"];

  if(! [[NSFileManager defaultManager] fileExistsAtPath:path]) {
    NSMutableDictionary *metadata = [NSMutableDictionary dictionary];
    [metadata setValue:@"CustomStore" forKey:NSStoreTypeKey];
    [metadata setValue:[CustomStore makeUUID] forKey:NSStoreUUIDKey];
    [CustomStore writeMetadata:metadata toURL:url];
    [@"" writeToURL:url atomically:YES encoding:[NSString defaultCStringEncoding]➥
error:nil];

    NSLog(@"Created new store at %@", path);
  }

  return [NSDictionary dictionaryWithContentsOfFile:path];
}
```

Armed with methods to retrieve the metadata and create a blank store, you can complete the initialization method:

```
- (id)initWithPersistentStoreCoordinator:(NSPersistentStoreCoordinator *)coordinator➥
configurationName:(NSString *)configurationName URL:(NSURL *)url options:(NSDictionary➥
*)options {
  self = [super initWithPersistentStoreCoordinator:coordinator➥
configurationName:configurationName URL:url options:options];

  NSDictionary *metadata = [CustomStore metadataForPersistentStoreWithURL:[self URL]➥
error:nil];

  [self setMetadata:metadata];

  return self;
}
```

Mapping Between NSManagedObject and NSAtomicStoreCacheNode

To make the custom store function properly, you must provide implementations for three additional utility methods. The first one creates a new reference object for a given managed object. Reference objects represent unique identifiers for each NSAtomicStoreCacheNode (similar to a database primary key). A Reference object is to an NSAtomicStoreCacheNode what an NSObjectID is to an NSManagedObject. Since the custom data store has to manage data transfer between NSManagedObjects and NSAtomicCacheNodes, it must be able to create a reference object for a newly created managed object. For this, we use the UUID again:

```
- (id)newReferenceObjectForManagedObject:(NSManagedObject *)managedObject {
    NSString *uuid = [CustomStore makeUUID];
    [uuid retain];
    return uuid;
}
```

The second method needed creates a new NSAtomicStoreCacheNode instance to match a newly created NSManagedObject. When a new NSManagedObject is added and needs to be persisted, the framework first gets a reference object using the newReferenceObjectForManagedObject: method. NSAtomicCache keeps track of the mapping between NSObjectIDs and reference objects. When Core Data persists a managed object into the persistent store, it calls the newCacheNodeForManagedObject: method, which, like its name indicates, creates a new NSAtomicStoreCacheNode that will serve as a peer to the NSManagedObject.

```
- (NSAtomicStoreCacheNode *)newCacheNodeForManagedObject:(NSManagedObject➡
*)managedObject {
  NSManagedObjectID *oid = [managedObject objectID];
  id referenceID = [self referenceObjectForObjectID:oid];

  NSAtomicStoreCacheNode* node = [self nodeForReferenceObject:referenceID➡
andObjectID:oid];

  [self updateCacheNode:node fromManagedObject:managedObject];
  return node;
}
```

The newCacheNodeForManagedObject: implementation looks up the reference object that was created for the managed object and creates a new cache node linked to that reference ID. Finally, the method copies the managed object's data into the node using the updateCacheNode:fromManagedObject: method. Our custom store also needs to provide an implementation for this third method:

```
- (void)updateCacheNode:(NSAtomicStoreCacheNode *)node➡
fromManagedObject:(NSManagedObject *)managedObject {
  NSEntityDescription *entity = managedObject.entity;

  NSDictionary *attributes = [entity attributesByName];
  for(NSString *name in [attributes allKeys]) {
    [node setValue:[managedObject valueForKey:name] forKey:name];
```

```
   }

NSDictionary *relationships = [entity relationshipsByName];
for(NSString *name in [relationships allKeys]) {
  id value = [managedObject valueForKey:name];
  if([[relationships objectForKey:name] isToMany]) {
    NSSet *set = (NSSet*)value;
    NSMutableSet *data = [NSMutableSet set];
    for(NSManagedObject *managedObject in set) {
      NSManagedObjectID *oid = [managedObject objectID];
      id referenceID = [self referenceObjectForObjectID:oid];
      NSAtomicStoreCacheNode* n = [self nodeForReferenceObject:referenceID➥
andObjectID:oid];

      [data addObject:n];
    }
    [node setValue:data forKey:name];
  }
  else {
    NSManagedObject *managedObject = (NSManagedObject*)value;
    NSManagedObjectID *oid = [managedObject objectID];
    id referenceID = [self referenceObjectForObjectID:oid];
    NSAtomicStoreCacheNode* n = [self nodeForReferenceObject:referenceID➥
andObjectID:oid];

    [node setValue:n forKey:name];
  }
 }
}
```

The implementation finds the entity description for the given managed object and uses it to iterate through attributes and relationships in order to copy their values into the node.

To keep track of cache nodes, create a utility method that, given a reference object, returns the matching NSAtomicStoreCacheNode if it exists or creates a new one.

```
- (NSAtomicStoreCacheNode *)nodeForReferenceObject:(id)reference➥
andObjectID:(NSManagedObjectID *)oid {
  NSAtomicStoreCacheNode *node = [nodeCacheRef objectForKey:reference];
  if(node == nil) {
    node = [[[NSAtomicStoreCacheNode alloc] initWithObjectID:oid] autorelease];
    [nodeCacheRef setObject:node forKey:reference];
  }
  return node;
}
```

The implementation of nodeForReferenceObject:andObjectID: uses a dictionary called nodeCacheRef, so declare it in the CustomStore.h header file, as Listing 3-7 shows.

Listing 3-7. CustomStore.h

```
#import <Foundation/Foundation.h>

@interface CustomStore : NSAtomicStore {
  NSMutableDictionary *nodeCacheRef;
}
```

```
@end
```

Initialize nodeCacheRef in the
initWithPersistentStoreCoordinator:configurationName:URL:options: method.

```
- (id)initWithPersistentStoreCoordinator:(NSPersistentStoreCoordinator *)coordinator
configurationName:(NSString *)configurationName URL:(NSURL *)url options:(NSDictionary
*)options {
  self = [super initWithPersistentStoreCoordinator:coordinator➥
configurationName:configurationName URL:url options:options];

  NSDictionary *metadata = [CustomStore metadataForPersistentStoreWithURL:[self URL]➥
error:nil];

  [self setMetadata:metadata];
  nodeCacheRef = [[NSMutableDictionary dictionary] retain];
  return self;
}
```

Serializing the Data

So far, all you've done is implement utility methods to deal with the metadata, initialize the data store, and perform the data transfer between NSManagedObject instances and NSAtomicStoreCacheNode instances. Until you implement the methods that read and write to the storage device, however, the custom store has no use. When extending NSAtomicStore, you are required to provide implementations for the load: and save: methods, which serve as the meat of the custom store implementation. In this example, start with the save: method. The code for the following save: method might seem overwhelming at first, but if you take time to follow the code, you will realize that it simply iterates through the cache nodes and writes attribute values into the file, followed by relationship values. Attribute values are converted into NSStrings and appended to the pipe-delimited file as key-value pairs in the form *attributeName=value*. Relationships work in a similar way except that the value written is not the destination node itself but its reference object as created by the newReferenceObjectForManagedObject: method. For one-to-many relationships, the code writes a comma-delimited list of reference objects. Here is the save: method:

```
- (BOOL)save:(NSError **)error {
  NSURL *url = [self URL];

  // First update the metadata
  [CustomStore writeMetadata:[self metadata] toURL:url];

  NSString* dataFile = @"";
  // Then write the actual data
  NSSet *nodes = [self cacheNodes];
  NSAtomicStoreCacheNode *node;
  NSEnumerator *enumerator = [nodes objectEnumerator];
  while((node = [enumerator nextObject]) != nil) {
    NSManagedObjectID *oid = [node objectID];
    id referenceID = [self referenceObjectForObjectID:oid];
```

```objc
      NSEntityDescription *entity = [oid entity];
      dataFile = [dataFile stringByAppendingFormat:@"%@|%@", entity.name, referenceID];

      {   // Attributes
        NSDictionary *attributes = [entity attributesByName];
        NSAttributeDescription *key = nil;
        NSEnumerator *enumerator = [attributes objectEnumerator];
        while((key = [enumerator nextObject]) != nil) {
          NSString *value = [node valueForKey:key.name];
          if(value == nil) value = @"(null)";
          dataFile = [dataFile stringByAppendingFormat:@"|%@=%@", key.name, value];
        }
      }

      {   // Relationships
        NSDictionary *relationships = [entity relationshipsByName];
        NSRelationshipDescription *key = nil;
        NSEnumerator *enumerator = [relationships objectEnumerator];
        while((key = [enumerator nextObject]) != nil) {
          id value = [node valueForKey:key.name];
          if(value == nil) {
            dataFile = [dataFile stringByAppendingFormat:@"|%@=%@", key.name, @"(null)"];
          }
          else if(![key isToMany]) {   // One-to-One
            NSManagedObjectID *oid = [(NSAtomicStoreCacheNode*)value objectID];
            id referenceID = [self referenceObjectForObjectID:oid];
            dataFile = [dataFile stringByAppendingFormat:@"|%@=%@", key.name,➡
referenceID];
          }
          else {   // One-to-Many
            NSSet* set = (NSSet*)value;
            if([set count] == 0) {
              dataFile = [dataFile stringByAppendingFormat:@"|%@=%@", key.name,➡
@"(null)"];
            }
            else {
              NSString *list = @"";
              for(NSAtomicStoreCacheNode *item in set) {
                id referenceID = [self referenceObjectForObjectID:[item objectID]];
                list = [list stringByAppendingFormat:@"%@,", referenceID];
              }
              list = [list substringToIndex:[list length]-1];
              dataFile = [dataFile stringByAppendingFormat:@"|%@=%@", key.name, list];
            }
          }
        }
      }
      dataFile = [dataFile stringByAppendingString:@"\n"];
    }
    NSString *path = [url relativePath];
    [dataFile writeToFile:path atomically:YES encoding:[NSString➡
defaultCStringEncoding] error:error];
    return YES;
```

```
}
```

Each data record in the text file, represented in code by an NSAtomicStoreCacheNode instance, follows this format:

```
Entity Name|Reference
Object|attribute1=value1|attribute2=value2|...|relationship1=ref1,ref2,ref3|relationship
2=ref4|...
```

The load: method follows the same steps as the save: method but in reverse. It reads the data file line by line and, for each line, uses the first element to find the entity description, uses the second element as the node's reference object, and then iterates through the remaining elements to load the attributes and relationships. It uses these elements to reconstruct the NSAtomicStoreCacheNode instances.

```
- (BOOL)load:(NSError **)error {
  NSURL* url = [self URL];
  NSMutableSet *nodes = [NSMutableSet set];
  NSString *path = [url relativePath];
  if(! [[NSFileManager defaultManager] fileExistsAtPath:path]) {
    [self addCacheNodes:nodes];
    return YES;
  }
  NSPersistentStoreCoordinator *coordinator = [self persistentStoreCoordinator];
  NSString *fileString = [NSString stringWithContentsOfFile:path encoding:[NSString➥
defaultCStringEncoding] error:error];

  NSArray *lines = [fileString componentsSeparatedByString:@"\n"];
  NSString *line;
  NSEnumerator *enumerator = [lines objectEnumerator];
  while( (line = [enumerator nextObject]) != nil) {
    NSArray *components = [line componentsSeparatedByString:@"|"];
    if([components count] < 2) continue;
    NSString *entityName = [components objectAtIndex:0];
    NSString *pkey = [components objectAtIndex:1];

    // Make the node
    NSEntityDescription *entity = [[[coordinator managedObjectModel] entitiesByName]➥
valueForKeyPath:entityName];

    if (entity != nil) {
      NSManagedObjectID *oid = [self objectIDForEntity:entity referenceObject:pkey];
      NSAtomicStoreCacheNode *node = [self nodeForReferenceObject:pkey andObjectID:oid];
      NSDictionary *attributes = [entity attributesByName];
      NSDictionary *relationships = [entity relationshipsByName];

      for(int i=2; i<[components count]; i++) {
        NSArray *entry = [[components objectAtIndex:i]➥
componentsSeparatedByString:@"="];

        NSString *key = [entry objectAtIndex:0];
        if([attributes objectForKey:key] != nil) {
          NSAttributeDescription *attributeDescription = [attributes objectForKey:key];
          NSAttributeType type = [attributeDescription attributeType];

          // Default value to type string
```

```objc
      id dataValue = [entry objectAtIndex:1];
      if([(NSString*)dataValue compare:@"(null)"] == NSOrderedSame) {
        continue;
      }


      if ((type == NSInteger16AttributeType) || (type == ➥
NSInteger32AttributeType) || (type == NSInteger64AttributeType)) {
        dataValue = [NSNumber numberWithInteger:[dataValue integerValue]];
      }
      else if (type == NSDecimalAttributeType) {
        dataValue = [NSDecimalNumber decimalNumberWithString:dataValue];
      }
      else if (type == NSDoubleAttributeType) {
        dataValue = [NSNumber numberWithDouble:[dataValue doubleValue]];
      }
      else if (type == NSFloatAttributeType) {
        dataValue = [NSNumber numberWithFloat:[dataValue floatValue]];
      }
      else if (type == NSBooleanAttributeType) {
        dataValue = [NSNumber numberWithBool:[dataValue intValue]];
      }
      else if (type == NSDateAttributeType) {
        NSDateFormatter *formatter = [[NSDateFormatter alloc] init];
        [formatter setDateFormat:@"yyyy-MM-dd HH:mm:ss ZZZ"];
        dataValue = [formatter dateFromString:dataValue];
        [formatter release];
      }
      else if (type == NSBinaryDataAttributeType) {
        NSLog(@"Binary type not supported");
      }
      [node setValue:dataValue forKey:key];
    }
    else if([relationships objectForKey:key] != nil) {  // See if it's a
relationship
      NSArray *ids = [[entry objectAtIndex:1] componentsSeparatedByString:@","];
      NSRelationshipDescription *relationship = [relationships objectForKey:key];
      if([relationship isToMany]) {
        NSMutableSet* set = [NSMutableSet set];
        for(NSString *fKey in ids) {
          if(fKey != nil && [fKey compare:@"(null)"] != NSOrderedSame) {
            NSManagedObjectID *oid = [self objectIDForEntity:[relationship➥
destinationEntity] referenceObject:fKey];

            NSAtomicStoreCacheNode *destinationNode = [self➥
nodeForReferenceObject:fKey andObjectID:oid];

            [set addObject:destinationNode];
          }
        }
        [node setValue:set forKey:key];
      }
      else {
        NSString* fKey = [ids count] > 0 ? [ids objectAtIndex:0] : nil;
        if(fKey != nil && [fKey compare:@"(null)"] != NSOrderedSame) {
```

```
                NSManagedObjectID *oid = [self objectIDForEntity:[relationship➡
destinationEntity] referenceObject:fKey];

                NSAtomicStoreCacheNode *destinationNode = [self➡
nodeForReferenceObject:fKey andObjectID:oid];

                [node setValue:destinationNode forKey:key];
            }
          }
        }
      }
      // Remember this node
      [nodes addObject:node];
    }
  }
  // Register all the nodes
  [self addCacheNodes:nodes];
  return YES;
}
```

Remember that although the text file stores the data as plain text, Core Data deals with objects. The code must check the data type of each attribute using the entity description and create the appropriate data object instance. For relationships, the code must use the store reference objects in order to either reuse existing nodes or create new ones if needed. To reuse existing nodes or create new ones, the load: method uses the previously implemented nodeForReferenceObject:andObjectID: method.

Before moving on from CustomStore.m, add declarations for the three utility methods you've created so the compiler won't complain. Because these methods aren't used outside the CustomStore class, we don't add them to the header file. The declarations look like this:

```
@interface CustomStore (private)

+ (void)writeMetadata:(NSDictionary*)metadata toURL:(NSURL*)url;
+ (NSString *)makeUUID;
- (NSAtomicStoreCacheNode*)nodeForReferenceObject:(id)reference➡
andObjectID:(NSManagedObjectID*)oid;

@end
```

Using the Custom Store

The last step required to use the custom store with the League Manager application is to register it and use it when initializing the persistent store coordinator. This is all done in the application delegate (League_ManagerAppDelegate.m). First, add an import at the top of the class so that the implementation is aware of the CustomStore class:

```
#import "CustomStore.h"
```

Modify the awakeFromNib: method to register the custom store when the application awakes:

```
- (void)awakeFromNib {
```

```
[NSPersistentStoreCoordinator registerStoreClass:[CustomStore class]➥
forStoreType:@"CustomStore"];

  NSLog(@"Registered types:  %@", [NSPersistentStoreCoordinator registeredStoreTypes] );

  RootViewController *rootViewController = (RootViewController *)[navigationController➥
topViewController];

  rootViewController.managedObjectContext = self.managedObjectContext;
}
```

Finally, alter the persistentStoreCoordinator: accessor to use the new custom store:

```
- (NSPersistentStoreCoordinator *)persistentStoreCoordinator {
  if (persistentStoreCoordinator_ != nil) {
    return persistentStoreCoordinator_;
  }

// NSURL *storeURL = [[self applicationDocumentsDirectory]➥
URLByAppendingPathComponent:@"League_Manager.sqlite"];

  NSURL *storeUrl = [[self applicationDocumentsDirectory]➥
URLByAppendingPathComponent: @"League_Manager.txt"];
  NSError *error = nil;
  persistentStoreCoordinator_ = [[NSPersistentStoreCoordinator alloc]➥
initWithManagedObjectModel:[self managedObjectModel]];

//    if (![persistentStoreCoordinator_ addPersistentStoreWithType:NSSQLiteStoreType
configuration:nil URL:storeUrl options:nil error:&error]) {
  if (![persistentStoreCoordinator_ addPersistentStoreWithType:@"CustomStore"
configuration:nil URL:storeUrl options:nil error:&error]) {
      /*
      Replace this implementation with code to handle the error appropriately.

      abort() causes the application to generate a crash log and terminate. You
should not use this function in a shipping application, although it may be useful during
development. If it is not possible to recover from the error, display an alert panel
that instructs the user to quit the application by pressing the Home button.

      Typical reasons for an error here include:
      * The persistent store is not accessible
      * The schema for the persistent store is incompatible with current managed
object model
      Check the error message to determine what the actual problem was.
      */
    NSLog(@"Unresolved error %@, %@", error, [error userInfo]);
    abort();
  }
  return persistentStoreCoordinator_;
}
```

At this point, you should be able to start the application, and it will use the new custom
store. A file called League_Manager.txt will be created in the same directory where the
League_Manager.sqlite database was when you first implemented it earlier in this
chapter. Take the application for a spin, add a few teams and players, and then go

check the League_Manager.txt data file using any text editor. Depending on the teams and players you create, the file will look something like this:

```
Player|697DA122-AD7E-4125-A1E3-
3CA2742670C1|email=kevin@boston.email|firstName=Kevin|lastName=Garnett|team=E70D529C-
CCBD-4BA5-B2BB-A9F8E151FAF4
Player|E4525745-553F-4381-9B23-
E361404CAA2A|email=ray@boston.email|firstName=Ray|lastName=Allen|team=E70D529C-CCBD-
4BA5-B2BB-A9F8E151FAF4
Player|00E87758-1149-4ACB-BFFE-
CC869E28366E|email=lebron@miami.email|firstName=LeBron|lastName=James|team=B1B6C951-
87D5-4717-A8D3-769C7DB2A5A5
Team|E70D529C-CCBD-4BA5-B2BB-A9F8E151FAF4|name=Boston
Celtics|uniformColor=Green|players=E4525745-553F-4381-9B23-E361404CAA2A,697DA122-AD7E-
4125-A1E3-3CA2742670C1
Team|B1B6C951-87D5-4717-A8D3-769C7DB2A5A5|name=Miami
Heat|uniformColor=Black|players=00E87758-1149-4ACB-BFFE-CC869E28366E
```

In the previous data file, you can see that the Boston Celtics have two registered players, and if you follow the reference objects, you find that the two players are Ray Allen and Kevin Garnett. You also find LeBron James as part of his new team, the Miami Heat.

What About XML Persistent Stores?

Core Data offers another persistent store type, XML, on Mac OS X that you specify by passing NSXMLStoreType to your persistent store coordinator's addPersistentStoreWithType: method. Passing NSXMLStoreType when compiling for iOS, however, gives you a compiler error: 'NSXMLStoreType' undeclared. If you look in the Core Data header files for iOS, you'll find the following in NSPersistentStoreCoordinator.h:

```
// Persistent store types supported by Core Data:
COREDATA_EXTERN NSString * const NSSQLiteStoreType __OSX_AVAILABLE_STARTING(__MAC_10_4,
__IPHONE_3_0);
COREDATA_EXTERN NSString * const NSBinaryStoreType __OSX_AVAILABLE_STARTING(__MAC_10_4,
__IPHONE_3_0);
COREDATA_EXTERN NSString * const NSInMemoryStoreType
__OSX_AVAILABLE_STARTING(__MAC_10_4, __IPHONE_3_0);
```

Indeed, NSXMLStoreType remains undeclared, though it's emphatically available for Mac OS X. To understand why, turn to Apple's developer documentation on Core Data Persistent Store Features, found at http://developer.apple.com/mac/library/ documentation/Cocoa/Conceptual/CoreData/Articles/cdPersistentStores.html, to read the explanation for XML's exclusion on iOS:

> *iOS: The XML store is not available on iOS.*

That's all you get, keeping Apple's reputation for secrecy intact. You're left, then, to speculate. Apple probably left XML off iOS's version of Core Data for a few reasons:

- Parsing XML can consume a lot of processor cycles, making an iDevice, with its slower processor relative to an iMac, Mac Pro, and so on, slower.

- Because parsing XML uses more processing power, it can consume more battery life.

- XML, with its characters, brackets, and metadata, generally consumes more storage space than binary file types.

- Apple likes to steer its developers toward solutions it deems better, rather than providing as many options as possible. XML is superfluous for Core Data persistence.

If you miss XML and want it available for your applications, you can write your own XML custom store. If you imagine a nice, nested XML document issuing from your complex data models, however, you will probably become frustrated in your attempts to create a custom XML persistent store type. Core Data relationships have their inverses, meaning that you really can't arbitrate parenthood among entities. In the League Manager data model, for example, should Team entity tags contain Player entity tags, because the team "owns" its players, or should it be the reverse? Do players own the teams they play for (as many superstar professional athletes have demonstrated)? If you pursue an XML custom data store, you'll find that you don't produce readable XML documents that make relationships clear, but rather XML documents with lots of peers that are fit only for Core Data's consumption. For example, if you port the same League Manager data model to a Mac OS X Core Data application and enter the same data for teams and players, Core Data produces the following XML document:

```
<?xml version="1.0"?>
<!DOCTYPE database SYSTEM "file:///System/Library/DTDs/CoreData.dtd">

<database>
    <databaseInfo>
        <version>134481920</version>
        <UUID>45AD66DE-CC52-4B2B-931C-6ACA69BB5507</UUID>
        <nextObjectID>108</nextObjectID>
        <metadata>
            <plist version="1.0">
                <dict>
                    <key>NSPersistenceFrameworkVersion</key>
                    <integer>251</integer>
                    <key>NSStoreModelVersionHashes</key>
                    <dict>
                        <key>Player</key>
                        <data>
                            QRI+8jf5OXSA5dkydbK2OisvHVrWhCAttsY9Yh4oUSQ=
                        </data>
                         <key>Team</key>
                        <data>
                            V/pOfHFixiAQ1Nb7Xlg2Xu4laNYWtrsg5Br1qtI9JMY=
                        </data>
                    </dict>
                    <key>NSStoreModelVersionHashesVersion</key>
```

```xml
                    <integer>3</integer>
                    <key>NSStoreModelVersionIdentifiers</key>
                    <array></array>
                </dict>
            </plist>
        </metadata>
    </databaseInfo>
    <object type="TEAM" id="z102">
        <attribute name="uniformcolor" type="string">Red</attribute>
        <attribute name="name" type="string">Fire</attribute>
        <relationship name="players" type="0/0" destination="PLAYER"
idrefs="z103"></relationship>
    </object>
    <object type="PLAYER" id="z103">
        <attribute name="lastname" type="string">Gary</attribute>
        <attribute name="firstname" type="string">Terry</attribute>
        <attribute name="email" type="string">tgary@example.com</attribute>
        <relationship name="team" type="1/1" destination="TEAM"
idrefs="z102"></relationship>
    </object>
    <object type="PLAYER" id="z104">
        <attribute name="lastname" type="string">Sprat</attribute>
        <attribute name="firstname" type="string">Pat</attribute>
        <attribute name="email" type="string">psprat@example.com</attribute>
        <relationship name="team" type="1/1" destination="TEAM"
idrefs="z105"></relationship>
    </object>
    <object type="TEAM" id="z105">
        <attribute name="uniformcolor" type="string">Blue</attribute>
        <attribute name="name" type="string">Crew</attribute>
        <relationship name="players" type="0/0" destination="PLAYER" idrefs="z107 z104
z106"></relationship>
    </object>
    <object type="PLAYER" id="z106">
        <attribute name="lastname" type="string">Staley</attribute>
        <attribute name="firstname" type="string">Bailey</attribute>
        <attribute name="email" type="string">bstaley@example.com</attribute>
        <relationship name="team" type="1/1" destination="TEAM"
idrefs="z105"></relationship>
    </object>
    <object type="PLAYER" id="z107">
        <attribute name="lastname" type="string">Gordon</attribute>
        <attribute name="firstname" type="string">Jordan</attribute>
        <attribute name="email" type="string">jgordon@example.com</attribute>
        <relationship name="team" type="1/1" destination="TEAM"
idrefs="z105"></relationship>
    </object>
    <object type="TEAM" id="z108">
        <attribute name="uniformcolor" type="string">Green</attribute>
        <attribute name="name" type="string">Revolution</attribute>
        <relationship name="players" type="0/0" destination="PLAYER"></relationship>
    </object>
</database>
```

Core Data makes no attempt to determine parentage between teams and players, nor does it create tags for the different entity types. It relies instead on tags called `object` with entity names specified as `type` attributes, and makes players and teams peers, which sounds like a recipe for lockouts and season cancellations.

Summary

SQLite claims on its home page, `www.sqlite.org`, that it "is the most widely deployed SQL database engine in the world." It enjoys the backing of technology titans like Oracle, Mozilla, and Adobe. If you've spent much time in your career in typical corporate development roles, you probably feel like data belongs in a database. SQLite stores your data efficiently and compactly. It doesn't require atomically rewriting the persistent store every time you change it. It requires no custom coding to use it. Xcode generates all you need to get started with a SQLite-backed persistent store. Why wouldn't you use a SQLite database for all your Core Data persistent stores?

Well, you might. SQLite is probably the right choice for data storage for most, if not all, of your applications' data storage needs. You've learned in this chapter, however, that other options exist and that you can create your own store types optimized for your particular applications and data needs. Whether you're working with remote data that you should store only in memory, wanting to persist data into text files, or imagining some other scenario best served by some other custom data store type, understand that your data can live in places other than a SQLite database. Remember that you're free to store your data however you want, and Core Data will manage it for you appropriately.

Chapter 4

Creating a Data Model

You can create applications with the most intuitive user interfaces that perform tasks users can't live without, but if you don't model your data correctly, your applications will become difficult to maintain, will underperform, and might even become unusable. This chapter explains how to model your data to support, not undermine, your applications.

Designing Your Database

The American philosopher Ralph Waldo Emerson once said, "A foolish consistency is the hobgoblin of little minds." People often wield that quote to defend carelessness or inattention to detail. We hope we're not falling into that trap as we flip-flop inconsistently between claiming Core Data is not a database and treating it as if it were. This section discusses how to design your data structures, and likening this process to modeling a relational database greatly helps not only the discussion but also the resulting design. The analogy breaks down in spots, however, as all analogies do, and we point out those spots through this discussion.

Core Data entity descriptions look, act, smell, and taste an awful lot like tables in a relational database. Attributes seem like columns in the tables, relationships feel like joins on primary and foreign keys, and entities appear like rows. If your model sits on a SQLite persistent store, Core Data actually realizes the entity descriptions, attributes, relationships, and entities as the database structures you'd expect, as Chapters 2 and 3 demonstrate. Remember, though, that your data can live in memory only or in some flat-file atomic store that has no tables or rows or columns or primary and foreign keys. Core Data abstracts the data structure from a relational database structure, simplifying both how you model and interact with your data. Allow for that abstraction in your mental model of how Core Data modeling works, or you will fill your Core Data model with cruft, work against Core Data, and produce suboptimal data structures.

Newcomers to Core Data who have data modeling experience decry the lack of an autoincrement field type, believing that they have the responsibility, as they do in traditional data modeling, to define a primary key for each table. Core Data has no autoincrement type because you don't define any primary keys. Core Data assumes the responsibility to establish and maintain the uniqueness of each managed object, or row. No primary keys means no foreign keys, either; Core Data manages the relationships between entities, or tables, and performs any necessary joins for you. Get over the discomfort of not defining primary and foreign keys quickly, because agonizing over this implementation detail isn't worth your effort or angst.

Another place where too much database modeling knowledge can run you against Core Data's grain involves many-to-many relationships. Consider, for example, if players in the League Manager application could belong to more than one team. If this were true, each team could have many players, and each player could play for many teams. If you were creating a traditional relational data model, you'd create three tables: one for teams, one for players, and one to track each team-player relationship. In Core Data, you'd still have just two entities, Team and Player, and you'd change the relationship from Player to Team to a to-many relationship. Core Data would still implement this in a SQLite database as three tables, ZTEAM, ZPLAYER, and Z1TEAMS, but that's an implementation detail. You wouldn't need to know about the third table, because Core Data takes care of it for you.

> **Tip:** Here's a rule of thumb to remember as you create your Core Data models: worry about data, not data storage mechanisms.

Relational Database Normalization

Relational database theory espouses a process for designing a data model called *normalization*, which aims to reduce or eliminate redundancy and provide efficient access the data inside the database. The normalization process divides into five levels, or *forms*, and work continues on a sixth form. The five normal forms carry definitions only a logician can love, or perhaps even understand; they read something like this:

> *"A relation R is in fourth normal form (4NF) if and only if, wherever there exists an MVD in R, say A -> -> B, then all attributes of R are also functionally dependent on A. In other words, the only dependencies (FDs or MVDs) in R are of the form K -> X (i.e. a functional dependency from a candidate key K to some other attribute X). Equivalently: R is in 4NF if it is in BCNF and all MVD's in R are in fact FDs."* (www.databasedesign-resource.com/normal-forms.html)

We have neither sufficient pages in this book nor the inclination to walk through formal definitions for each of the normal forms and then explain what they mean. Instead, this section describes each of the normal forms in relation to Core Data and provides data modeling advice. Note that adherence to a given normal form requires adherence to all the normal forms that precede it.

A database that conforms to first normal form (1NF) is considered normalized. To conform to this level of normalization, each row in the database must have the same number of fields. For a Core Data model, this means that each managed object should have the same number of attributes. Since Core Data doesn't allow you to create variable numbers of attributes in your entities, your Core Data models are automatically normalized.

Second normal form (2NF) and third normal form (3NF) deal with the relationship between nonkey fields and key fields, dictating that nonkey fields should be facts about the entire key field to which they belong. Since your Core Data model has no key fields, you shouldn't run afoul of these concerns. You should, however, make sure that all the attributes for a given entity describe that entity, and not something else. For example, the Player entity should not have a uniformColor field since the uniform color describes the team rather than an independent player.

The next two normal forms, fourth normal form (4NF) and fifth normal form (5NF), can be considered the same form in the Core Data world. They deal with reducing or eliminating data redundancy, pushing you to move multiple-value attributes into separate entities and create to-many relationships between the entities. In Core Data terms, 4NF says that entities shouldn't have attributes that can have multiple values. Instead, you should move these attributes to a separate entity and create a to-many relationship between the entities. Consider, for example, the teams and players in the model in the League Manager application from the previous chapter. A model that would violate 4NF and 5NF would have a single entity, Team, with an additional attribute: player. We would then create a new Team managed object for each player, so that we'd have several redundant Team objects. Instead, the League Manager data model moves players to a Player entity and creates a to-many relationship, players, between each team and its players.

As you create your models in Core Data applications, keep database modeling in mind and consider removing redundancy by moving multiple-value attributes to separate entities. For example, in the League Manager data model, the uniformColor attribute of Team presents a normalization opportunity. Named colors represent a finite set, despite what Crayola may claim, so you could create an entity called Color that has an attribute, name, that relates to teams in a to-many relationship.

Using the Xcode Data Modeler

Some developers simply accept the tools given to them. Others build tools only when they believe the existing tools are inferior. A few, however, stubbornly insist on building all their own tools. We tend to fall into this last category of developers, and our colleagues know us as programmers who use only tools we build ourselves. We take pride in building tools and even hold celebrations after broadcasting the amount of time the tools save. We never tally the time it takes to build the tools, filing that time under "play time" because of our enjoyment for building tools. Surprisingly, however, writing a data modeler tool for Core Data never crossed our minds, probably because Xcode does a reasonable job of allowing you to model data. It's by no means flawless, but it does work, and it's perfectly integrated with the development environment, an attribute that even we would never be able to surpass with a tool we built. In fact, Xcode ships with a built-in data modeling tool that makes it easy to create data models visually rather than programming the NSManagedObjectModel by hand. We've gotten glimpses at this tool several times in the prior chapters. In this section, we spend less time dealing with how Core Data works and a little bit more time looking at the tool and how to use it.

In this section, we're not going to produce any runnable code. Instead, we will focus on the data modeler's user interface. To add a data model to a project in Xcode, select **File ➤ New File**… from the menu. In the iOS section on the left, select the Resource subsection. It reveals three file types: Data Model, Mapping Model, and Settings Bundle. Data Model and Mapping Model both relate to Core Data. Mapping models assist with migrating data across data model versions, which we cover in Chapter 8. Select Data Model, as shown in Figure 4-1, and click Next. Pick a name for the data model, and click Next. The next dialog allows you generate model entities in your new model from existing classes. For now, click Finish.

Figure 4-1. *New data model file*

Opening your new data model file in Xcode opens it in the data modeler interface. Rich in buttons and options, the Xcode data modeler interface can be confusing. Refer to Figure 4-2, which annotates the user interface to summarize the buttons relevant to data modeling, to understand how to work with the modeler to model your data.

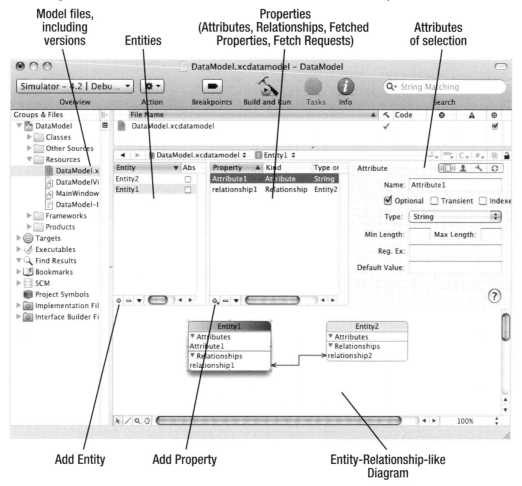

Figure 4-2. *The data modeler interface*

The main view of the modeler, the table view, allows you to navigate through the entities, fetch requests, and configurations of the data model. You get more details about the chosen artifacts as you select them. To make the model more interesting to talk about, open the League Manager data model built in Chapter 2. The Xcode interface should look as illustrated in Figure 4-3.

Figure 4-3. *The League Manager model in the Xcode data modeler*

You can see that Xcode displays the entities and properties in table form, above, and also the same information in a graph form, below. The graph view resembles a traditional entity-relationship diagram, familiar to data modelers. In the graph view, you can easily see how the entities relate to each other. You may notice that the relationship from Team to Player is double-headed. That is because it is a one-to-many relationship. A team may have several players. The inverse relationship from Player to Team is single-headed because it is a one-to-one relationship. A player has only one team at most.

You can get more information about any entity or property by selecting it. Figure 4-3, for example, shows the Player entity selected. In the upper right, you can see details about the Player entity: that it's named Player, that it's of class NSManagedObject, that it has no parent entity, and that it isn't abstract. If you select a property, that panel changes to display details for that property, appropriate to its type. If you select, for example, the email attribute for the Player entity, the panel changes to look like Figure 4-4. You see the following:

- It's named email.
- It's optional.
- It's not transient or indexed.
- It's of type String.
- It has no minimum or maximum length.

- It has no attached regular expression.
- It has no default value.

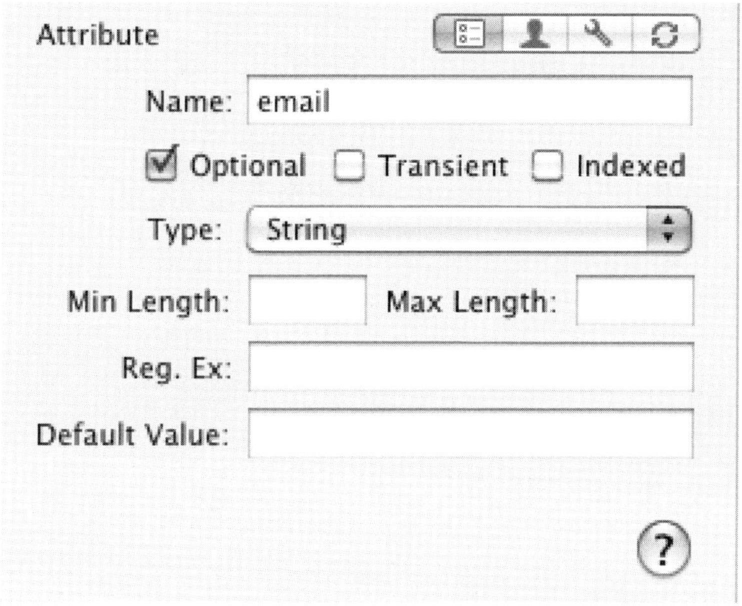

Figure 4-4. *Details for the email attribute*

Switching the selection to the team relationship of Player changes the panel to show relationship-oriented detail, as shown in Figure 4-5. From this view, we learn the following about the relationship:

- Is named team
- Is optional but not transient
- Has a destination of Team
- Has the inverse relationship "players"
- Isn't a to-many relationship
- Has a minimum count of 1 and a maximum count of 1
- Uses the delete rule called Nullify

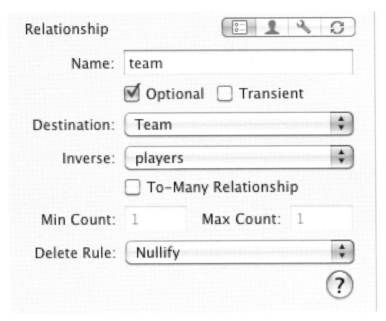

Figure 4-5. *Details for the team relationship*

Let's look back for a moment at the details for the Player entity, shown in Figure 4-6. Entities are defined by their names. Core Data also allows you to subclass NSManagedObject to provide an alternate implementation class for your managed objects. If you create a subclass of NSManagedObject and want an entity mapped to that class, then you can specify the class name in the entity details pane.

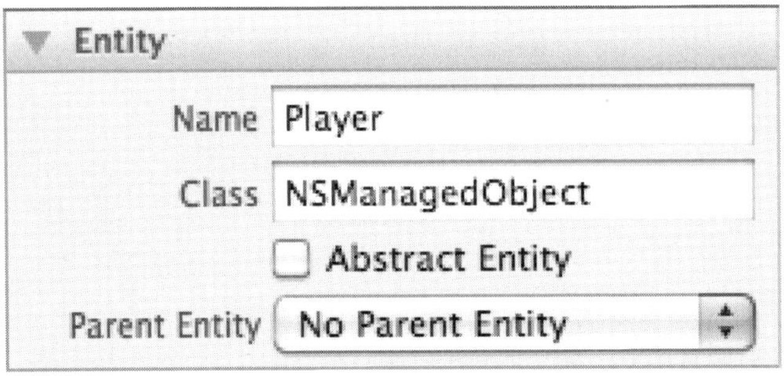

Figure 4-6. *Entity details pane*

Viewing and Editing Attribute Details

Select an attribute under the Property header in the middle column of Xcode's data modeling tool in order to switch the detail pane to display attribute details.

Table 4-1 explains the fields in the Attribute pane. The first column, Name, refers to the name of the field, while the Description column explains what this field means and how it's used.

Table 4-1. *Shows What the Different Properties Mean*

Name	Description
Name	The name of the attribute.
Transient	Tells Core Data to not persist this attribute. This is useful in conjunction with a second attribute to support nonstandard or custom types. We discuss custom types later in this chapter.
Optional	An optional attribute may have a `nil` value. Nonoptional attributes must have a non-`nil` value.
Indexed	Indexed attributes are faster to search but take up more space in the persistent store.
Type	The type of the attribute. The value you select in this column can change which validation fields display.
Min Length	For an attribute of type `String`, the minimum valid length, in characters, for the attribute.
Max Length	For an attribute of type `String`, the maximum valid length, in characters, for the attribute.
Min Value	For an attribute of a numerical type, the minimum valid value for the attribute.
Max Value	For an attribute of a numerical type, the maximum valid value for the attribute.
Default Value	A default value for this attribute when you provide no value for it.
Reg. Ex.	Regular expression used for validating data.

Viewing and Editing Relationship Details

In a similar manner, you can click a relationship to view its details.

Relationships have several properties. First, they have a name and a destination entity. The destination describes the type of objects the relationship points to. For a `Player` entity, the "team" relationship points, as expected, to a `Team` entity. The Core Data architects strongly recommend that every relationship have an *inverse relationship*—a relationship that goes in the opposite direction. For example, `Player` has a relationship to `Team`, so it is recommended, as we have implemented, that `Team` have a relationship to `Player` as well. In fact, if you don't specify an inverse relationship, the compiler will generate a warning message.

Two additional properties are available for attributes: `Transient` and `Optional`. A transient relationship does not get stored to the persistent store during the `save:` operation. If the team relationship were transient, then the information of which team a player belongs to would not be saved and would be lost when the application exits. The `Player` object itself would still be persisted, but the relationship with a team would not. Transient relationships can be useful if you want to set values at runtime, for example derived with code from other information, but don't want to store the relationship fact using Core Data. When a relationship is optional, it simply means that you may give it a `nil` value. For example, a player may not have a team.

The plurality of a relationship defines how many destination objects this source object can relate to: one or many. By default, a relationship is to-one, which means that the source object can relate to at most one destination object. This is the case for the "team" relationship of the Player entity: a player can have at most only one team. But a team can have multiple players; therefore, the "player" relationship of the Team entity is a to-many relationship. Its value is represented by a set of entities. The plurality of a relationship can also be further specified using a minimum and maximum value, which represents the cardinality of the destination entities for that relationship.

Finally, Core Data uses the delete rule to understand what to do with destination objects when a source object is deleted. Core Data can do different things to the players of a team if the team is deleted. The options are No Action, Nullify, Cascade, and Deny. The "Setting Rules" section in this chapter discusses the delete rules and what they mean.

Using Fetched Properties

So far in this book, we have mentioned attributes and relationships on several occasions. A third property can be attached to an entity: a fetched property. Fetched properties are comparable to relationships in that they allow an object to have references to other objects. While relationships directly refer to destination objects, however, fetched properties identify the destination objects by using a predicate. Fetched properties behave like the smart playlists in iTunes in which the user specifies a source list (usually the music library) and then specifies some criteria to filter the results. Fetched properties behave differently from smart playlists, however, in that they're evaluated the first time they are called, and their results are cached until you tell them to reevaluate themselves using the refreshObject:mergeChanges: method.

In the League Manager application, we could, for example, create a fetched property in the Team entity to return all the players whose last name begins with the letter *G*. Select the Team entity, click the + button below the Property section, and select Add Fetched Property button from the menu. Call it **gPlayers**. Select the destination entity (that is, the Entity type the fetched property will retrieve). Select Player for the Destination type.

You can then specify the criteria for filtering the players. Click the Edit Predicate button to display the dialog for editing predicates. In the first column, select lastName. In the second column, select starts with. Finally, in the last column, type the letter **G**. Your dialog should resemble Figure 4-7.

Figure 4-7. *Editing a predicate in the Xcode data modeler*

When you click OK, Xcode creates the predicate in the standard NSPredicate format (see Chapter 6 for more details on NSPredicate). In our example, the predicate would be as follows:

```
lastName BEGINSWITH "G"
```

Figure 4-8 illustrates the resulting fetched property configuration.

Figure 4-8. *Fetched property configuration*

The last important aspect of configuring a data model with Xcode is creating fetch requests. You use fetch requests to retrieve managed objects from the data model, just like you would using NSFetchRequest in code, except you can predefine them here. To create a fetch request that will retrieve all the teams with a blue uniform, for example, select Team in the Entity section, click the + button below the Property section in Xcode, and select Add Fetch Request from the menu. Call the fetch request **BlueTeams**. Click the Edit Predicate button to open the predicate editing dialog. In the first column, select uniformColor. In the second column, select =. Finally, in the third column, type **Blue**. Your dialog should look like Figure 4-9.

Figure 4-9. *Setting up the predicate for a fetch request*

If you click OK, you see that your predicate, in standard predicate form, is as follows:

uniformColor == "Blue"

Creating Entities

We have been talking extensively about entities up to now. Entities describe the attributes and relationships of a managed object. To add an entity in Xcode, you simply click the + button below the Entity section in Xcode, and give your entity a name.

By default, each entity is represented by objects of type NSManagedObject at runtime, but as your project evolves and matures, you typically opt for creating your own classes to represent your managed objects. Your custom managed object must extend NSManagedObject, and you must specify the custom object class name in the Class field of the Entity details pane, as shown in Figure 4-10.

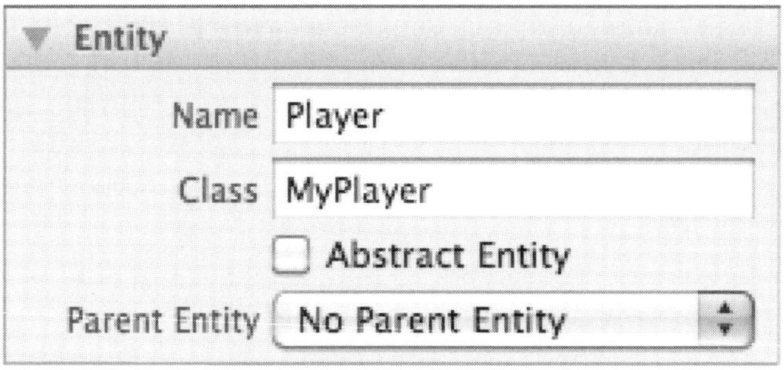

Figure 4-10. *A custom managed object class*

One topic we have not yet addressed is entity inheritance. Very similar to class inheritance in the object-oriented programming paradigm, entity inheritance allows you to create entities that inherit their properties from another entity and can add some of their own. For example, a Person entity could be created, and the Player entity could inherit from it. If we had other representations of people—Coach, for example—we could inherit from the Person entity. If we wanted to prevent the parent entity from being instantiated directly, preventing the user from creating a Person object as a stand-alone object, we could make the Person entity abstract. For example, we could create a Person entity that has a dateOfBirth attribute. Figure 4-11 shows how a Person entity could be configured. Note how it is made abstract to prevent direct instantiation.

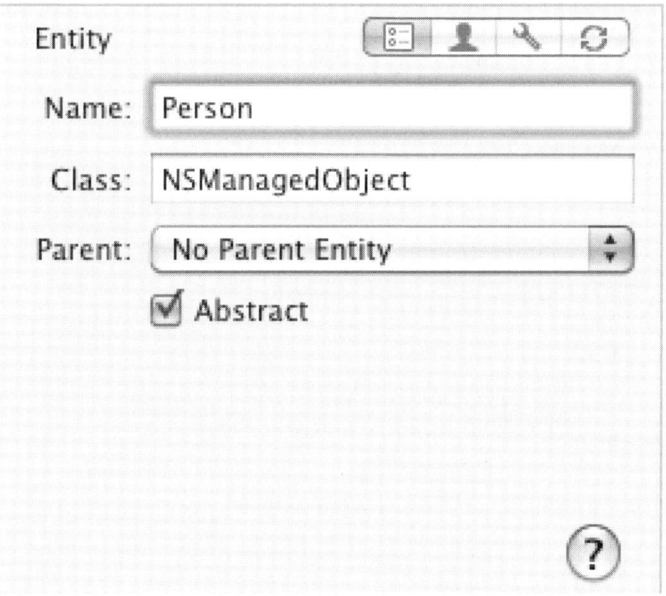

Figure 4-11. *The* Person *entity as an abstract entity*

The next step is to change the Player entity configuration and set its parent entity to Person. Select the Player entity, and change the parent field to Person, as in Figure 4-12. The Player entity now inherits from the Person entity, as illustrated in the graph view in Figure 4-13. This means that a player managed object also has a `dateOfBirth` attribute that can be set and read.

Figure 4-12. *The Player entity configured to inherit from the Person entity*

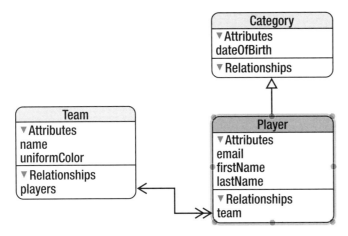

Figure 4-13. *Graph view of the Player entity configured to inherit from the Person entity*

Creating Attributes

Attributes describe an entity. Similar to the attributes of an object in object-oriented programming, entity attributes define the current state of an entity and may be represented by various data types. Select an entity, click the + button under the Property heading, and select Add Attribute from the menu to create a new attribute for the selected entity. Figure 4-14 shows the different options for configuring an attribute.

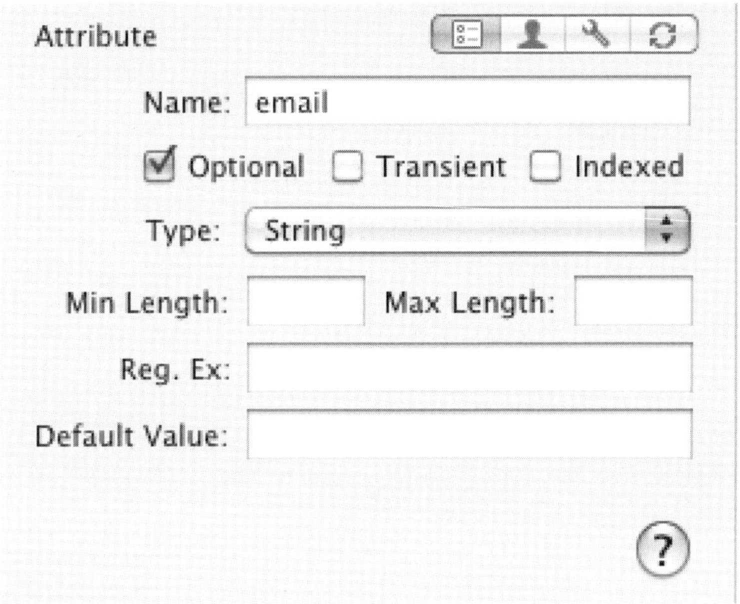

Figure 4-14. *Attribute details pane*

Earlier in this chapter, we talked about the meaning of the different properties of attributes. See Table 4-1 to review the properties. Arguably the most critical property of an attribute is its type. Several types are available by default in Core Data, as shown in Table 4-2.

Table 4-2. *Available Attribute Types*

Xcode Attribute Type	Objective-C Attribute Type	Objective-C Data Type	Description
Int16	NSInteger16AttributeType	NSNumber	A 16-bit integer
Int32	NSInteger32AttributeType	NSNumber	A 32-bit integer
Int64	NSInteger64AttributeType	NSNumber	A 64-bit integer
Decimal	NSDecimalAttributeType	NSDecimalNumber	A base-10 subclass of NSNumber
Double	NSDoubleAttributeType	NSNumber	An object wrapper for double

(Continued)

Table 4-2. *(Continued)*

Float	NSFloatAttributeType	NSNumber	An object wrapper for float
String	NSStringAttributeType	NSString	A character string
Bool	NSBooleanAttributeType	NSNumber	An object wrapper for a boolean value
Date	NSDateAttributeType	NSDate	A date object
Binary	NSBinaryDataAttributeType	NSData	Unstructured binary data
Transformable	NSTransformableAttributeType	Any nonstandard type	Any type transformed into a supported type

Most of these types are straightforward because they map directly to an Objective-C data type. Using them is just a matter of leveraging the key/value accessors of the NSManagedObject instances. The Transformable type is the only type that doesn't have an Objective-C counterpart. The Transformable type is used for custom types, which are types that aren't supported by Core Data. Use Transformable as the type when the attribute you're trying to persist doesn't fit neatly into one of the supported data types. For example, if your managed object needs to represent a color and needs to persist it, it would make sense to use the CGColorRef type. In this case, you need to set the Core Data type to Transient and Transformable and provide Core Data with the mechanism for transforming the attribute into supported data types. Custom attributes make sense to use when you create your own managed objects that extend from NSManagedObject, so we talk about them in more detail in the next chapter.

Creating Relationships

As you normalize your data model, you'll likely create several entities, depending on the complexity of the data you're modeling. Relationships allow you to tie entities together, as the League Manager application does with teams and players. Core Data allows you to tune the relationships you create to accurately reflect how your data relate to each other.

In Xcode, when you create a Core Data relationship or select an existing one, you see a set of options that you can modify to change the nature of the relationship. For example, if you select the "team" relationship from the Player entity in the League Manager data model, you see something that looks like Figure 4-15. The options in that panel allow you to configure fields of the relationship. These fields are as follows:

- Name

- Optional

- Transient

- Destination

- Inverse

- To-Many Relationship

- Min Count

- Max Count

- Delete Rule

This next sections walk through all these fields, explaining what they mean and how they impact the relationship so that you can set up your relationships correctly in your data models.

Relationship			
Name:	team		
	☑ Optional ☐ Transient		
Destination:	Team		
Inverse:	players		
	☐ To–Many Relationship		
Min Count:	1	Max Count:	1
Delete Rule:	Nullify		

Figure 4-15. *Relationship panel*

Name

The first field, Name, becomes the name of the key NSManagedObject uses to reference the relationship. By convention, it's the name of the referenced entity in lowercase. In the case of a to-many relationship, the Name field conventially is pluralized. Note that these guidelines are conventions only, but you will make your data models more understandable, maintainable, and easier to work with if you follow them. You can see that the League Manager data model follows these conventions—in the Player entity, the relationship to the Team entity is called "team." In the Team entity, the relationship to the Player entity, a to-many relationship, is called "players."

Optional

The next field, Optional, is a check box that specifies whether this relationship requires a non-nil value. Think of this like a nullable versus non-nullable column in a database. If you select the Optional check box, a managed object of this entity type can be saved to the persistent store without having anything specified for this relationship. If not selected, however, saving the context will fail. If the Player entity in the data model for League Manager, for example, left this check box unchecked, every player entity would have to belong to a team. Setting the "team" value for a player to nil (or never setting it at all) would cause all calls to save: to fail with the error description "team is a required value."

Transient

Next to the Optional check box, the Transient check box allows you to specify that a relationship should not be saved to the persistent store. A transient relationship still has support for undo and redo operations but disappears when the application exits, giving the relationship the life span of a Hollywood marriage. Here are some possible uses for transient relationships:

- Relationships between entities that are temporal and shouldn't survive beyond the current run of the application

- Relationship information that can be derived from some external source of data, whether another Core Data persistent store or some other source of information

In most cases, you'll want your relationships to be persistent, and you'll leave the Transient check box unchecked.

Destination and Inverse

The next field, Destination, specifies the entity at the other end of the relationship. The Inverse field allows you to select the same relationship, but from the destination entity's perspective. To set this properly, create the relationship in both related entities, set the names and destinations in each entity, and then select the proper inverse relationship in one entity. Core Data figures out the inverse relationship for the other entity and sets it for you.

Leaving the Inverse field with the value No Inverse Relationship gives you two compiler warnings: consistency error and misconfigured property.

You can ignore these warnings and run your application without specifying an inverse relationship—after all, these are compiler warnings, not compiler errors—but you could face unexpected consequences. Core Data uses bidirectional relationship information to maintain the consistency of the object graph (hence the Consistency Error) and manage undo and redo information. If you leave a relationship without an inverse, you imply that you will take care of the object graph consistency and undo/redo management. The Apple documentation strongly discourages this, however, especially in the case of a to-many relationship. When you don't specify an inverse relationship, the managed object at the other end of the relationship isn't marked as changed when the managed object at this end of the relationship changes. Consider the example of a `Player` object being deleted and having no inverse relationship back to its team. Any optionality rules or delete rules aren't enforced when the object graph is saved.

To-Many Relationship

To-Many Relationship is another check box. Leaving this check box unchecked makes this relationship to-one, which means this relationship has exactly one managed object (or zero, depending on optionality settings) on each end of the relationship. For the League Manager application, unchecking the To-Many Relationship check box for the "players" relationship on the `Team` entity would mean that only one player could belong on a team, which might work for golf but not soccer. Selecting this check box means the destination entity can have many managed objects that relate to each managed object instance of this entity type.

Min Count and Max Count

The next fields, Min Count and Max Count, set limits on the number of managed objects of the destination entity type that can relate to each managed object of this entity type and take effect only if the To-Many Relationship check box is selected. Unchecking that box to make the relationship to-one resets both the Min and Max values to 1.

In a to-many relationship, you can use the Min Count and Max Count fields to set limits on the number of managed objects to which this managed object can relate. Exceeding the limits causes the `save:` operation to fail with a "Too many items" or a "Too few items" error message. Note that the Optional setting overrides the Min Count setting; if Optional is checked and Min Count is 1, saving the context when the relationship count is zero succeeds. Note also that Core Data doesn't require that you set these values intelligently. You can, for example, set Min Count higher than Max Count. If you do this, calls to `save:` will always fail, because you can never meet the Count criteria set. You've probably been in relationships yourself that seem this way.

Delete Rule

The Delete Rule setting allows you to specify what happens if you try to delete a managed object of this entity type. Table 4-3 lists the four possibilities and what they mean.

Table 4-3. *Delete Rule Options*

Rule	Description
Cascade	The source object is deleted, and any related destination objects are also deleted.
Deny	If the source object is related to any destination objects, the deletion request fails, and nothing is deleted.
Nullify	The source object is deleted, and any related destination objects have their inverse relationships set to nil.
No Action	The source object is deleted, and nothing changes in any related destination objects.

The League Manager application, for example, set the Delete Rule for the "players" relationship in the Team entity to Cascade so that deleting a team would delete all the players related to it. If you set that rule to Deny and a team had any players, trying to delete the team would result in an error on any attempts to save the context with the message "team is not valid." Setting the Delete Rule to Nullify would preserve the players in the persistent store, though they would no longer belong to any team.

The No Action option represents another way, such as not specifying an inverse relationship, that Core Data allows you to accept responsibility for managing object graph consistency. If you specify this value for the Delete Rule, Core Data allows you to delete the source object but pretends to the destination objects that the source object still exists. For the League Manager application, this would mean disbanding a team but still telling the players to show up for practices and games. You won't find many compelling reasons to use the No Action setting, except perhaps for performance reasons when you have many destination objects. Chapter 7 discusses performance tuning with Core Data.

Summary

For applications that depend on data, which means most applications, the importance of designing your data model correctly cannot be overstated. The Xcode data modeler provides a solid interface for designing and defining your data models, and in this chapter, you learned to navigate the many options available as you create entities, attributes, and relationships. Make sure to understand the implications of how you've configured your data model so that your applications can run efficiently and correctly.

In most cases, you should avoid options in your model that wrest control from Core Data and make you manage the consistency of the object graph yourself. Core Data will almost always do a better job of managing object graph consistency than you will. When you must take control, make sure to debug your solutions well to prevent application crashes or data corruption.

One feature of Xcode that you may find helpful is the ability to print your data model for review. You'll find that Xcode can print your data model to any printer that Mac OS X supports.

In the next chapter, you'll learn how to use the data models you create by actually creating, retrieving, updating, and deleting data in them.

Chapter 5

Working with Data Objects

The ability to easily interact with data in a database ranks high among the features that drive the success of most new programming languages and frameworks. This chapter talks about working with the data objects you create and store in your Core Data models. You'll find Core Data provides an abstraction from the complexities of Structured Query Language (SQL) and database programming that allows you to quickly and efficiently read and write data to your persistent stores.

Understanding CRUD

Whether you claim the *R* stands for Read or Retrieve and whether you side with Destroy over Delete for the *D*, we all agree that the acronym CRUD describes the four operations you perform on a persistent data store:

- Create
- Retrieve
- Update
- Delete

These four operations apply to all persistent store interaction, whether you're working with Core Data in an iOS application, an Oracle database in a Java Enterprise Web application, a Virtual Storage Access Method (VSAM) file in a COBOL program, or any other situation in which you have a program that works with data. In fact, the CRUD concept has been extended to describe other situations in which you create, retrieve, update, and delete data. For example, the latest approach to providing services over the Web, Representation State Transfer (REST), has been called CRUD for the Web—the HTTP verbs map to the CRUD operations like this:

- POST = Create
- GET = Retrieve
- PUT = Update
- DELETE = Delete

In this chapter, you'll build one application twice: once working directly with NSManagedObject instances and the second time with custom classes that extend NSManagedObject. This section builds the raw NSManagedObject version. With a nod to Scott Hanselman's Baby Smash! (www.hanselman.com/babysmash/), this application, called Shapes, has the following requirements and characteristics:

- Each time someone taps the screen, a random shape appears where the screen was tapped.
- The shape is randomly a circle or a polygon.
- If a polygon, the shape has a random number of sides and can be concave, convex, or mixed.
- If a circle, the shape has a random radius.
- Shapes appear in random colors.
- Shaking the device deletes all the shapes.
- Rotating the device updates all the shapes to random colors.
- The screen splits down the middle, and each shape appears twice, once on each screen half.
- One of the screen halves is zoomed at 2x magnification (meaning some shapes won't appear, because they'll fall outside the screen's boundaries).
- Shapes is built for the iPad to take advantage of the extra screen space.

From a Core Data perspective, Shapes illustrates the following:

- *Create:* Each time you tap the screen, Shapes creates a shape object in the persistent store.
- *Retrieve:* Each time the screen draws the shapes, Shapes retrieves the shapes from the persistent store.
- *Update:* Each time you rotate the device, Shapes updates all the shapes in the persistent store with different random colors.
- *Delete:* Each time you shake the device, Shapes deletes all the shapes from the persistent store.
- *Inheritance:* The Polygon and Circle entities inherit from a common parent, Shape.

- *One-to-many:* One Polygon instance relates to many Vertex instances.

- *Many-to-many:* Many Shape instances relate to many Canvas instances.

- *One-to-one:* One Canvas instance relates to one Transform instance, which controls scaling.

Shapes probably can't compete with the fun of BabySmash!, but we don't want to encourage smashing iPads anyway. Shapes illustrates a wide range of Core Data fundamentals. You'll notice, however, that Shapes doesn't filter or sort results, which Chapter 6 covers.

In Xcode, create a new project, select a View-based Application under iOS, set Device Family to iPad (as Figure 5-1 shows), and click Choose…. Save the project as **Shapes**. Xcode opens with your Shapes project.

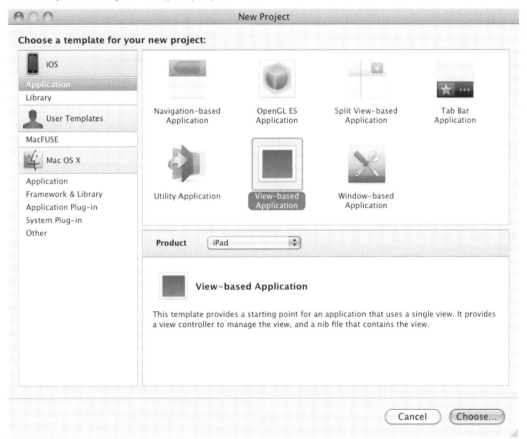

Figure 5-1. *New iPad project using the View-based Application template*

Notice that you had no opportunity in the View-based Application template to add Core Data to your application, so add Core Data now. You learned how to do that in Chapter 1, but to recap, Ctrl+click the Frameworks folder, select **Add ➤ Existing Frameworks…**, and select CoreData.framework.

Creating the Shape Application Data Model

Before writing the code for the application, create your data model. Select **File ➤ New File…**, select Resource under iOS on the left and Data Model on the right, and click Next. Call the model file **Shapes.xcdatamodel**, and add it to the Resources group. Select it to edit it, and follow these steps to finalize the model:

1. Add an entity called **Shape**, and give it a nonoptional attribute called **color** of type `String`.

2. Add an entity called **Circle**, and give it three nonoptional attributes, all of type `Float`: radius, x, and y. Set its Parent Entity to Shape.

3. Add an entity called **Polygon** with no attributes, and set its Parent Entity to `Shape`.

4. Add an entity called **Vertex** with a nonoptional attribute called `index` of type `Integer 16`. Give it two nonoptional `Float` attributes called x and y. Add a relationship called **polygon**, and set Destination to Polygon. Make it optional, and set the Delete Rule option to Nullify.

5. Add a relationship to the `Polygon` entity called **vertices**, and set its Destination to Vertex and Inverse to polygon. Uncheck the Optional check box, check the To-Many Relationship check box, set Min Count to 3, and set Delete Rule to Cascade.

6. Add an entity called **Transform**, and give a nonoptional attribute called **scale** of type `Float`.

7. Add an entity called **Canvas**, and give it a relationship called **transform**. Set Destination to Transform, uncheck the Optional check box, and set Delete Rule to Cascade. Add another relationship called **shapes**. Set Destination to Shape, leave Optional checked, and check the To-Many Relationship check box. Set Delete Rule to Nullify.

8. Select the `Shape` entity, and add a relationship called **canvases**. Set Destination to Canvas and Inverse to shapes. Check Optional and To-Many Relationship, and set Delete Rule to Nullify.

9. Select the `Transform` entity, and add a relationship called **canvas**. Set Destination to Canvas and Inverse to transform. Uncheck Optional, and set Delete Rule to Deny.

When you finish, your data model layout should look like Figure 5-2.

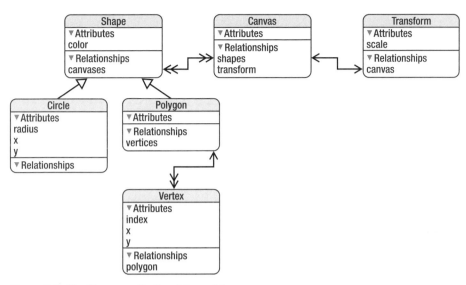

Figure 5-2. *The Shapes application data model*

With your data model in place, you're ready to add Core Data support to your application delegate. Open ShapesAppDelegate.h, import the Core Data headers, and add properties for your managed object context, managed object model, and persistent store coordinator. When you're done, your file should look like Listing 5-1, with the added lines in bold.

Listing 5-1. *ShapesAppDelegate.h*

```
#import <UIKit/UIKit.h>
#import <CoreData/CoreData.h>

@class ShapesViewController;

@interface ShapesAppDelegate : NSObject <UIApplicationDelegate> {
  UIWindow *window;
  ShapesViewController *viewController;

@private
NSManagedObjectContext *managedObjectContext_;
NSManagedObjectModel *managedObjectModel_;
NSPersistentStoreCoordinator *persistentStoreCoordinator_;
}

@property (nonatomic, retain) IBOutlet UIWindow *window;
@property (nonatomic, retain) IBOutlet ShapesViewController *viewController;

@property (nonatomic, retain, readonly) NSManagedObjectContext *managedObjectContext;
@property (nonatomic, retain, readonly) NSManagedObjectModel *managedObjectModel;
@property (nonatomic, retain, readonly) NSPersistentStoreCoordinator➥
*persistentStoreCoordinator;


@end
```

Next, open ShapesAppDelegate.m, and add the accessors for the three Core Data–
related properties you just added. You should be familiar with these by now; they should
look like this:

```
#pragma mark -
#pragma mark Core Data stack

- (NSManagedObjectModel *)managedObjectModel {
  if (managedObjectModel_ != nil) {
    return managedObjectModel_;
  }
  managedObjectModel_ = [[NSManagedObjectModel mergedModelFromBundles:nil] retain];
  return managedObjectModel_;
}

- (NSPersistentStoreCoordinator *)persistentStoreCoordinator {
  if (persistentStoreCoordinator_ != nil) {
    return persistentStoreCoordinator_;
  }
  NSString *dir = [NSSearchPathForDirectoriesInDomains(NSDocumentDirectory,➥
NSUserDomainMask, YES) lastObject];

  NSURL *storeURL = [NSURL fileURLWithPath:[dir➥
stringByAppendingPathComponent:@"Shapes.sqlite"]];

  NSError *error = nil;
  persistentStoreCoordinator_ = [[NSPersistentStoreCoordinator alloc]➥
initWithManagedObjectModel:[self managedObjectModel]];

  if (![persistentStoreCoordinator_ addPersistentStoreWithType:NSSQLiteStoreType➥
configuration:nil URL:storeURL options:nil error:&error]) {

    NSLog(@"Unresolved error %@, %@", error, [error userInfo]);
    abort();
  }
  return persistentStoreCoordinator_;
}

- (NSManagedObjectContext *)managedObjectContext {
  if (managedObjectContext_ != nil) {
    return managedObjectContext_;
  }
  NSPersistentStoreCoordinator *coordinator = [self persistentStoreCoordinator];
  if (coordinator != nil) {
    managedObjectContext_ = [[NSManagedObjectContext alloc] init];
    [managedObjectContext_ setPersistentStoreCoordinator:coordinator];
  }
  return managedObjectContext_;
}
```

According to the requirements, the Shapes application divides the screen in half and shows the same shapes on both halves, with the shapes doubled in size on one half. The Canvas entity represents these screen halves in the Core Data data model, but you need corresponding user interface elements to actually draw the shapes on the screen. To accomplish this, you'll create a class derived from UIView and then add two of these views to your existing XIB file. Start by creating the class: select **File ➤ New File…**, select Cocoa Touch Class on the left and Objective-C class on the right, and click Next. Call the class **BasicCanvasUIView**, put it in the Classes folder, and click Finish. You should see the two files for the class, BasicCanvasUIView.h and BasicCanvasUIView.m, listed in the files for your project. Open the BasicCanvasUIView.h file.

The generated class derives from NSObject, but instead you want it to derive from UIView. You also want a reference to the corresponding Canvas entity that this view will display, as well as a way to scale the view (one instance will have a 1x scale, while the other will have a 2x). Change BasicCanvasUIView.h to look like the version in Listing 5-2.

Listing 5-2. *BasicCanvasUIView.h*

```
#import <UIKit/UIKit.h>
#import <CoreData/CoreData.h>

@interface BasicCanvasUIView : UIView {
  NSManagedObject *canvas;
}
@property (nonatomic, retain) NSManagedObject *canvas;

-(float)scale;

@end
```

In the implementation file for your class, BasicCanvasUIView.m, you need an accessor and a mutator for the canvas property, so add this line:

```
@synthesize canvas;
```

The scale: method returns the value stored for the scale attribute in the Transform entity that relates to the Canvas entity that this view represents. Remember that Canvas has a one-to-one relationship with Transform ; each Canvas instance has a corresponding Transform instance. To get the value for scale, you use the Retrieve action of CRUD. You first retrieve the Transform managed object from the Canvas managed object that this BasicCanvasUIView class points to using this code:

```
NSManagedObject *transform = [canvas valueForKey:@"transform"];
```

Notice the absence of any Structured Query Language (SQL) code. Notice, also, that you retrieve the value for a relationship using the same syntax you'd use to retrieve the value of an attribute. Core Data doesn't differentiate among the types of properties in an entity.

Once you have a reference to the `Transform` managed object, you can retrieve its value for `scale` using code like this:

```
[transform valueForKey:@"scale"]
```

The `valueForKey:` method returns an object, so use the `floatValue` method to get the stored value as a `float` type. The `scale:` method, in its entirety, looks like this:

```
- (float)scale {
  NSManagedObject *transform = [canvas valueForKey:@"transform"];
  return [[transform valueForKey:@"scale"] floatValue];
}
```

The method that does the actual drawing of shapes looks a little more complex, and drawing and graphics lie outside the scope of this book. Read through the code carefully, however, and you'll find it's not as bad as it looks. Since this book covers Core Data, though, you can just type this in without understanding it. The parts relevant to Core Data are the Retrieve operations: the method retrieves all the shapes to draw using the relationship between the `Canvas` entity and the `Shape` entity and then retrieves the relevant properties for the shape to draw. In the case of `Circle` instances, the code retrieves the x, y, and `radius` attributes to construct the circle on the screen. In the case of `Polygon` instances, the code retrieves all the related `Vertex` instances using `Polygon`'s `vertices` relationship, sorts them, and draws a polygon that matches the vertices.

Here is the entire `drawRect:` method:

```
- (void)drawRect:(CGRect)rect {
  // Check to make sure we have data
  if (canvas == nil) {
    return;
  }

  // Get the current graphics context for drawing
  CGContextRef context = UIGraphicsGetCurrentContext();

  // Store the scale in a local variable so we don't hit the data store twice
  float scale = self.scale;

  // Scale the context according to the stored value
  CGContextScaleCTM(context, scale, scale);

  // Retrieve all the shapes that relate to this canvas and iterate through them
  NSSet* shapes = [canvas valueForKey:@"shapes"];
  for (NSManagedObject *shape in shapes) {
    // Get the entity name to determine whether this is a Circle or a Polygon
    NSString *entityName = [[shape entity] name];

    // Get the color, stored as RGB values in a comma-separated string, and set it into
the context
    NSString *colorCode = [shape valueForKey:@"color"];
    NSArray *colorCodes = [colorCode componentsSeparatedByString:@","];
    CGContextSetRGBFillColor(context, [[colorCodes objectAtIndex:0] floatValue] / 255,
                        [[colorCodes objectAtIndex:1] floatValue] / 255,
                        [[colorCodes objectAtIndex:2] floatValue] / 255, 1.0);
```

```
    // If this shape is a circle . . .
    if ([entityName compare:@"Circle"] == NSOrderedSame) {
        // Get the x, y, and radius from the data store and draw the circle
        float x = [[shape valueForKey:@"x"] floatValue];
        float y = [[shape valueForKey:@"y"] floatValue];
        float radius = [[shape valueForKey:@"radius"] floatValue];
        CGContextFillEllipseInRect(context, CGRectMake(x-radius, y-radius, 2*radius,➥
2*radius));

    } else if ([entityName compare:@"Polygon"] == NSOrderedSame) {
        // This is a polygon
        // Use a sort descriptor to order the vertices using the index value
        NSSortDescriptor *sortDescriptor = [[NSSortDescriptor alloc] initWithKey:➥
@"index" ascending:YES];
        NSArray *sortDescriptors = [[NSArray alloc] initWithObjects:sortDescriptor, nil];
        NSArray* vertices = [[[shape mutableSetValueForKey:@"vertices"] allObjects]➥
sortedArrayUsingDescriptors:sortDescriptors];


        // Begin drawing the polygon
        CGContextBeginPath(context);

        // Place the current graphic context point on the last vertex
        NSManagedObject *lastVertex = [vertices lastObject];
        CGContextMoveToPoint(context, [[lastVertex valueForKey:@"x"] floatValue],➥
[[lastVertex valueForKey:@"y"] floatValue]);


        // Iterate through the vertices and link them together
        for (NSManagedObject *vertex in vertices) {
            CGContextAddLineToPoint(context, [[vertex valueForKey:@"x"] floatValue],➥
[[vertex valueForKey:@"y"] floatValue]);

        }
        // Fill the polygon
        CGContextFillPath(context);

        // Clean up
        [sortDescriptors release];
        [sortDescriptor release];
    }
  }
}
```

That completes the BasicCanvasUIView class. You still must add two instances of this
class to the main view in your application, however, which is controlled by the
ShapesViewController class. Open ShapesViewController.h, add an import for
BasicCanvasUIView.h, and add two BasicCanvasUIView instances to the interface—one
to represent the top half of the screen and the other to represent the bottom half. See
Listing 5-3.

Listing 5-3. *ShapesViewController.h*

```
#import <UIKit/UIKit.h>
#import "BasicCanvasUIView.h"

@interface ShapesViewController : UIViewController {
  IBOutlet BasicCanvasUIView *topView;
  IBOutlet BasicCanvasUIView *bottomView;
}
@property (nonatomic, retain) BasicCanvasUIView *topView;
@property (nonatomic, retain) BasicCanvasUIView *bottomView;

@end
```

Add two @synthesize directives to ShapesViewController.m, like this:

```
@synthesize topView;
@synthesize bottomView;
```

Building the Shape Application User Interface

Now you are going to create the top and bottom views inside your shapes view. Double-click ShapesViewController.xib to open it in Interface Builder, which should also open the view associated with the ShapesViewController class. Drag a View object onto the view, and go to the Size tab to place and size it. Set X to 0, Y to 0, W (width) to 768, and H (height) to 502. In the Autosizing section, select all but the bottom band. See Figure 5-3 for a guide on what you're trying to accomplish.

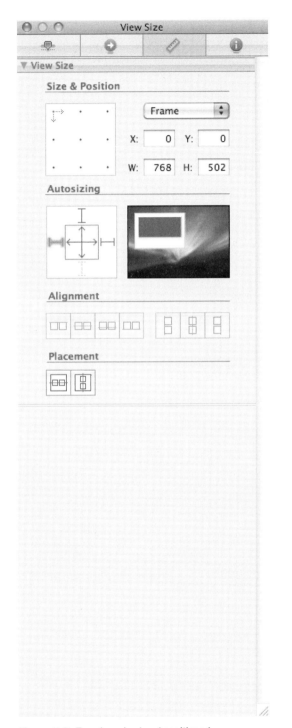

Figure 5-3. *Top view sized and positioned*

Select the view you just created and resized to the top half of the screen, and select the Identity tab. Here, you can change the class from `UIView` to `BasicCanvasUIView` by selecting it from the Class dropdown in the Class Identity section, as Figure 5-4 shows.

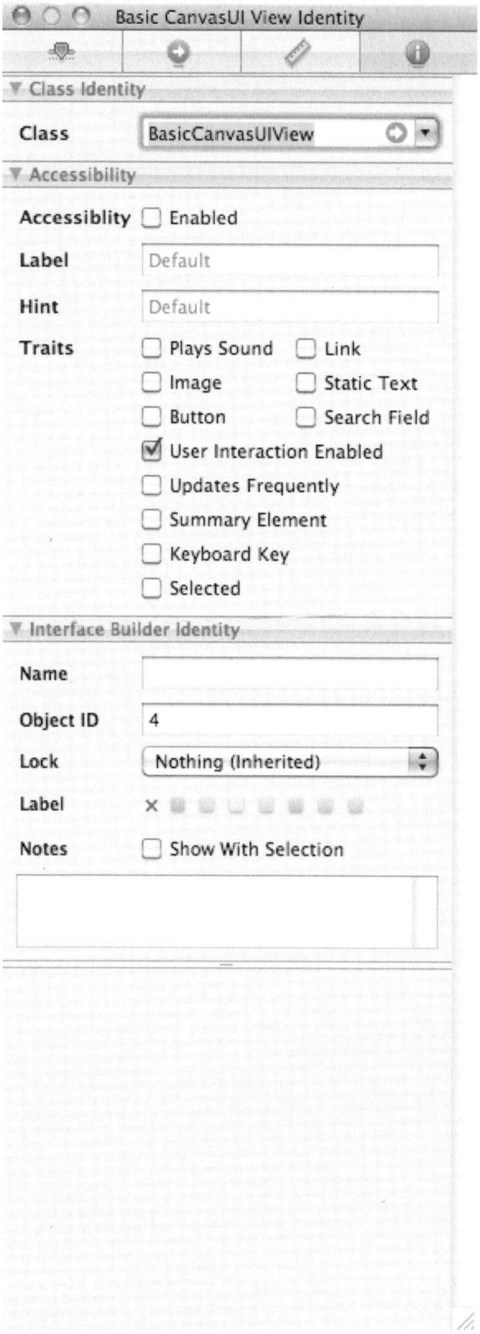

Figure 5-4. *Top view changed to BasicCanvasUIView*

Now you can Ctrl+click the File's Owner icon and drag your pointer into the view you created. When you release the mouse button, you should see a pop-up displaying the available outlets you can bind to. Select topView. Go to the Object Attributes tab, and click the background to select a different color for the background for this view. Feel free to choose your own; we chose Blueberry.

Now create the bottom view by dragging another View object onto the screen and resizing it using these values: X = 0, Y = 502, W = 768, and H = 502. In the Autosizing section, select all but the top band. Go to the Identity tab, and change Class to BasicCanvasUIView. Ctrl+click and drag from the File's Owner icon to this new view and bind it to the bottomView outlet. Change the color; we selected Tangerine.

Even though the application doesn't draw any shapes yet because you've as yet provided no mechanism to create them in the persistent store, now is a good time to build and run the application to verify that it compiles and runs. You should be able to run the application and see the views on the screen as in Figure 5-5. Rotating the device should cause the views to resize and remain on the top and bottom halves of the screen, as in Figure 5-6. If the application compiles and runs but the views don't properly display when the screen rotates, check the Autosizing settings for the views.

Figure 5-5. *Shapes without shapes in portrait mode*

Carrier 🛜   4:28 AM   100% 🔋

Figure 5-6. *Shapes without shapes in landscape mode*

The next step is to make the ShapesViewController class Core Data–aware and then add the user interfaces to Create, Update, and Delete shapes. Go back to the ShapesViewController.h file and add a property to point to the managed object context. Listing 5-4 shows what ShapesViewController.h should look like, with the added lines in bold.

Listing 5-4. *ShapesViewController.h*

```objectivec
#import <UIKit/UIKit.h>
#import <CoreData/CoreData.h>
#import "BasicCanvasUIView.h"

@interface ShapesViewController : UIViewController {
  NSManagedObjectContext *managedObjectContext;
  IBOutlet BasicCanvasUIView *topView;
  IBOutlet BasicCanvasUIView *bottomView;
}
@property (nonatomic, retain) NSManagedObjectContext *managedObjectContext;
@property (nonatomic, retain) BasicCanvasUIView *topView;
@property (nonatomic, retain) BasicCanvasUIView *bottomView;

@end
```

Now open ShapesViewController.m, where you have several tasks remaining to finish the Shapes application. Start with adding a synthesize line for the managed object context:

```
@synthesize managedObjectContext;
```

Next, create methods to create a shape, update all shapes, and delete all shapes. These methods are part of ShapeViewController's private interface, which you declare in ShapeViewController.m. The other method to add to the private interface is a helper method that returns a random color. The lines to add to ShapeViewController.m above where the implementation begins look like this:

```
@interface ShapesViewController (private)
- (void)createShapeAt:(CGPoint)point;
- (void)updateAllShapes;
- (void)deleteAllShapes;
- (NSString *)makeRandomColor;
@end

@implementation ShapesViewController
```

The implementation for the method that creates a shape receives a parameter that describes where on the screen to create the shape. The method creates an NSManagedObject of entity type Shape and then randomly creates either a Circle type or a Polygon type. If a circle, it generates a random value for the radius attribute and uses the x and y values from the passed CGPoint instance. If a polygon, it creates a random number of vertices arranged around the passed CGPoint and and stores them as Vertex types, creating relationships back to the Polygon instance just created. The implementation looks like this:

```
- (void)createShapeAt:(CGPoint)point {
  // Create a managed object to store the shape
  NSManagedObject *shape = nil;

  // Randomly choose a Circle or a Polygon
  int type = arc4random() % 2;
  if (type == 0) { // Circle
    // Create the Circle managed object
    NSEntityDescription *entity = [NSEntityDescription entityForName:@"Circle"➥
inManagedObjectContext:self.managedObjectContext];

    NSManagedObject *circle = [NSEntityDescription➥
insertNewObjectForEntityForName:[entity name]➥
inManagedObjectContext:self.managedObjectContext];

    shape = circle;

    // Randomly create a radius and set the attributes of the circle
    float radius = 10 + (arc4random() % 90);
    [circle setValue:[NSNumber numberWithFloat:point.x] forKey:@"x"];
    [circle setValue:[NSNumber numberWithFloat:point.y] forKey:@"y"];
    [circle setValue:[NSNumber numberWithFloat:radius] forKey:@"radius"];

    NSLog(@"Made a new circle at (%f,%f) with radius %f", point.x, point.y, radius);
  } else {   // Polygon
```

```objc
    // Create the Polygon managed object
    NSEntityDescription *entity = [NSEntityDescription entityForName:@"Polygon"➡
inManagedObjectContext:self.managedObjectContext];
    NSManagedObject *polygon = [NSEntityDescription➡
insertNewObjectForEntityForName:[entity name]➡
inManagedObjectContext:self.managedObjectContext];

    shape = polygon;

    // Get the vertices. At this point, no Vertex objects for this Shape exist.
    // Anything you add to the set, however, will be added to the Vertex entity.
    NSMutableSet *vertices = [polygon mutableSetValueForKey:@"vertices"];

    // Create a random number of vertices
    int nVertices = 3 + (arc4random() % 20);
    float angleIncrement = (2 * M_PI) / nVertices;
    int index = 0;
    for (float i = 0; i < nVertices; i++) {
      // Generate random values for each vertex
      float a = i * angleIncrement;
      float radius = 10 + (arc4random() % 90);
      float x = point.x + (radius * cos(a));
      float y = point.y + (radius * sin(a));

      // Create the Vertex managed object
      NSEntityDescription *vertexEntity = [NSEntityDescription entityForName:@"Vertex"➡
inManagedObjectContext:self.managedObjectContext];

      NSManagedObject *vertex = [NSEntityDescription➡
insertNewObjectForEntityForName:[vertexEntity name]➡
inManagedObjectContext:self.managedObjectContext];


      // Set the values for the vertex
      [vertex setValue:[NSNumber numberWithFloat:x] forKey:@"x"];
      [vertex setValue:[NSNumber numberWithFloat:y] forKey:@"y"];
      [vertex setValue:[NSNumber numberWithInt:index++] forKey:@"index"];

      // Add the Vertex object to the relationship
      [vertices addObject:vertex];
    }
    NSLog(@"Made a new polygon with %d vertices", nVertices);
  }
  // Set the shape's color
  [shape setValue:[self makeRandomColor] forKey:@"color"];

  // Add the same shape to both canvases
  [[topView.canvas mutableSetValueForKey:@"shapes"] addObject:shape];
  [[bottomView.canvas mutableSetValueForKey:@"shapes"] addObject:shape];

  // Save the context
  NSError *error = nil;
  if (![self.managedObjectContext save:&error]) {
    NSLog(@"Unresolved error %@, %@", error, [error userInfo]);
    abort();
  }
```

```
    // Tell the views to repaint themselves
    [topView setNeedsDisplay];
    [bottomView setNeedsDisplay];
}
```

Though the method is long, read through it, and between the codes and the comments, you should be able to see what it's doing. It uses some methods from the C standard library, so include the required headers:

```
#include <stdlib.h>
```

It also calls the makeRandomColor: method to create a random color for this shape, whether circle or polygon, so implement that method. It creates three random color values, one each for red, green, and blue, and formats them as a comma-separated string, like this:

```
- (NSString *)makeRandomColor {
    // Generate three color values
    int red = arc4random() % 256;
    int green = arc4random() % 256;
    int blue = arc4random() % 256;

    // Put them in a comma-separated string
    return [NSString stringWithFormat:@"%d,%d,%d", red, green, blue];
}
```

The method that updates all the shapes to new random colors uses this method as well. It retrieves all the shapes from the persistent store and updates them with new random colors. The method looks like this:

```
- (void)updateAllShapes {
    // Retrieve all the shapes
    NSFetchRequest *fetchRequest = [[NSFetchRequest alloc] init];
    NSEntityDescription *entity = [NSEntityDescription entityForName:@"Shape"➥
inManagedObjectContext:self.managedObjectContext];

    [fetchRequest setEntity:entity];
    NSArray *shapes = [managedObjectContext executeFetchRequest:fetchRequest error:nil];
    [fetchRequest release];

    // Go through all the shapes and update their colors randomly
    for (NSManagedObject *shape in shapes) {
        [shape setValue:[self makeRandomColor] forKey:@"color"];
    }

    // Save the context
    NSError *error = nil;
    if (![self.managedObjectContext save:&error]) {
        NSLog(@"Unresolved error %@, %@", error, [error userInfo]);
        abort();
    }

    // Tell the views to repaint themselves
    [topView setNeedsDisplay];
    [bottomView setNeedsDisplay];
```

```
}
```

The method that deletes all the shapes looks eerily similar. In fact, this would be a good opportunity to use the new block support in Objective-C and iOS 4, but for simplicity's sake, it again retrieves all the shapes from the persistent store, but this time, instead of updating them with new colors, it deletes them. Note that the Delete Rules set in the model handles what to do with any related entities. Here is the deleteAllShapes: method:

```
- (void)deleteAllShapes {
    // Retrieve all the shapes
    NSFetchRequest *fetchRequest = [[NSFetchRequest alloc] init];
    NSEntityDescription *entity = [NSEntityDescription entityForName:@"Shape"➥
inManagedObjectContext:self.managedObjectContext];

    [fetchRequest setEntity:entity];
    NSArray *shapes = [managedObjectContext executeFetchRequest:fetchRequest error:nil];
    [fetchRequest release];

    // Delete each shape.
    for (NSManagedObject *shape in shapes) {
        [managedObjectContext deleteObject:shape];
    }

    // Save the context
    NSError *error = nil;
    if (![self.managedObjectContext save:&error]) {
        NSLog(@"Unresolved error %@, %@", error, [error userInfo]);
        abort();
    }

    // Tell the views to repaint themselves
    [topView setNeedsDisplay];
    [bottomView setNeedsDisplay];
}
```

You might notice that the ShapesViewController class has a member for the managed object context, but you haven't yet set any value into that member. Open ShapesAppDelegate.m and add code to set that value. The method definition, with the added line in bold, looks like this:

```
- (BOOL)application:(UIApplication *)application➥
didFinishLaunchingWithOptions:(NSDictionary *)launchOptions {
    viewController.managedObjectContext = self.managedObjectContext;
    [window addSubview:viewController.view];
    [window makeKeyAndVisible];
    return YES;
}
```

One final Core Data–related piece remains to build into the Shapes application: the code to create the Canvas instances and tie them to the views and to create the Transform instances, one for each Canvas. This code should go into the viewDidLoad: method of ShapesViewController.m.

```objc
- (void)viewDidLoad {
  // Create the Canvas entities
  NSManagedObject *canvas1 = nil;
  NSManagedObject *canvas2 = nil;

  // Load the canvases
  NSFetchRequest *fetchRequest = [[NSFetchRequest alloc] init];
  NSEntityDescription *entity = [NSEntityDescription entityForName:@"Canvas"➥
inManagedObjectContext:self.managedObjectContext];

  [fetchRequest setEntity:entity];
  NSArray *canvases = [managedObjectContext executeFetchRequest:fetchRequest error:nil];
  [fetchRequest release];

  // If the canvases already exist in the persistent store, load them
  if([canvases count] >=2) {
    NSLog(@"Loading existing canvases");
    canvas1 = [canvases objectAtIndex:0];
    canvas2 = [canvases objectAtIndex:1];
  } else { // No canvases exist in the persistent store, so create them
    NSLog(@"Making new canvases");
    canvas1 = [NSEntityDescription insertNewObjectForEntityForName:[entity name]➥
inManagedObjectContext:self.managedObjectContext];

    canvas2 = [NSEntityDescription insertNewObjectForEntityForName:[entity name]➥
inManagedObjectContext:self.managedObjectContext];

    // Create the Transform instance for each canvas. The first has a scale of 1
    NSManagedObject *transform1 = [NSEntityDescription➥
insertNewObjectForEntityForName:@"Transform"➥
inManagedObjectContext:self.managedObjectContext];

    [transform1 setValue:[NSNumber numberWithFloat:1] forKey:@"scale"];
    [canvas1 setValue:transform1 forKey:@"transform"];

    // The second Transform for the second Canvas has a scale of 0.5
    NSManagedObject *transform2 = [NSEntityDescription➥
insertNewObjectForEntityForName:@"Transform"➥
inManagedObjectContext:self.managedObjectContext];

    [transform2 setValue:[NSNumber numberWithFloat:0.5] forKey:@"scale"];
    [canvas2 setValue:transform2 forKey:@"transform"];

    // Save the context
    NSError *error = nil;
    if (![self.managedObjectContext save:&error]) {
      NSLog(@"Unresolved error %@, %@", error, [error userInfo]);
      abort();
    }
  }
  // Set the Canvas instances into the views
  topView.canvas = canvas1;
  bottomView.canvas = canvas2;

}
```

Enabling User Interactions with the Shapes Application

That completes the Core Data parts of the application. You could build and run it, but nothing visible has changed. You need to add user interface elements to create, update, and delete shapes. Start with creation. The user interface for creating a shape is to tap the screen, so add a method to capture any screen taps, determine the location of the tap, scale the location appropriately according to the canvas, and call the `createShapeAt:` method, passing in the tapped point:

```
#pragma mark -
#pragma mark Touch events handling

- (void)touchesBegan:(NSSet *)touches withEvent:(UIEvent *)event {
    UITouch *touch = [touches anyObject];

    // Where did the view get touched?
    CGPoint location = [touch locationInView: touch.view];

    // Scale according to the canvas' transform
    float scale = [(BasicCanvasUIView *)touch.view scale];
    location = CGPointMake(location.x / scale, location.y / scale);

    // Create the shape
    [self createShapeAt:location];
}
```

Now the application merits building and running. You haven't finished yet—you can't update or delete shapes—but you deserve some gratification for having worked this long. Build and run the application, and tap the screen a few times. Notice that you can tap either screen half, and the shapes appear on both, with the shapes twice as big on the top half. Rotate the screen, and see that the shapes still display. See Figure 5-7 for an example of what your screen should look like.

Figure 5-7. *Some shapes*

Stop the running application, and add the user interface elements to update and delete the shapes. The user interface for updating the shapes is rotating the device, so add a method to detect any device rotation, and call the updateAllShapes method from within that:

```
- (void) willRotateToInterfaceOrientation:(UIInterfaceOrientation)toInterfaceOrientation
duration:(NSTimeInterval)duration {
  [self updateAllShapes];
}
```

Adding support for detecting whether the device is shaken, so the application can delete all the shapes, is slightly more complicated. ShapeViewController must become the first responder when its view displays, so add the method that makes it eligible to be a first responder, and then make it become the first responder in the viewDidAppear method:

```
- (BOOL)canBecomeFirstResponder {
  return YES;
}

- (void)viewDidAppear:(BOOL)animated {
  [super viewDidAppear:animated];
  [self becomeFirstResponder];
}
```

Now, add the method to detect any shakes, and call the `deleteAllObjects` method from within it.

```
#pragma mark -
#pragma mark Shake events handling

- (void)motionEnded:(UIEventSubtype)motion withEvent:(UIEvent *)event {
  if (event.subtype == UIEventSubtypeMotionShake) {
    [self deleteAllShapes];
  }
}
```

This completes the Shapes application. Build it, run it, tap it, rotate it, shake it. You should see shapes appear, change colors, and disappear. Through the easy Core Data interface, you can create, retrieve, update, and delete data from your persistent store.

If you have any problems building or running the Shapes application, check the accuracy of your data model and also of your code. The complete source code of the Shapes application is available online at `http://apress.com/book/sourcecode`.

The next section enhances the Shapes application by adding custom data objects instead of using `NSManagedObject` instances. In the typical life cycle of a Core Data–enabled application, you will likely start by using `NSManagedObject`. As your application evolves, you will eventually feel the need to introduce custom data objects for code clarity and maintainability.

Generating Classes

This is the first time in this book that we are on the verge of enhancing our managed objects to a level that makes them truly blend with the rest of your code. Core Data gives you so much flexibility to implement your own managed objects that you can almost completely hide the fact that they are backed by the framework. In this section, we rework the Shapes application in order to use custom managed objects.

The first step is to create the data object classes themselves. You can create them manually or let Xcode generate them for you. Getting Xcode to generate them for you involves a bit of trickery: open your data model (`Shapes.xcdatamodel`) and click somewhere on the background, outside any of the entities. Now select File ►New File…, select Cocoa Touch Class under iOS on the left, and you should see a new option on the right: Managed Object Class, as shown in Figure 5-8. Select it and click Next. In the ensuing dialog, set the Location field to save the classes into your project's Classes directory and click Next. You then have the opportunity to select any or all of your model's entities and generate classes for them, as shown in Figure 5-9. Once you've selected what you want, which for our purposes is all of them, click Finish, and the classes are generated.

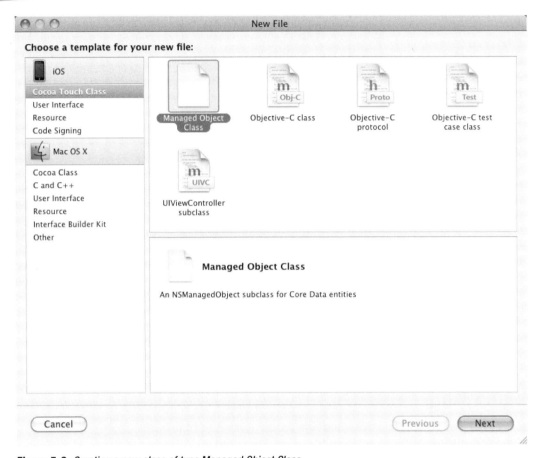

Figure 5-8. *Creating a new class of type Managed Object Class*

Figure 5-9. *Selecting which entities to generate classes for*

To keep the code organized, a good practice is to create a group of classes where you will store your data objects. In Xcode, right-click the Classes group, and select New Group. Rename the new group to **Managed Objects** and drag all the newly generated classes to it. Figure 5-10 shows what your source tree should look like.

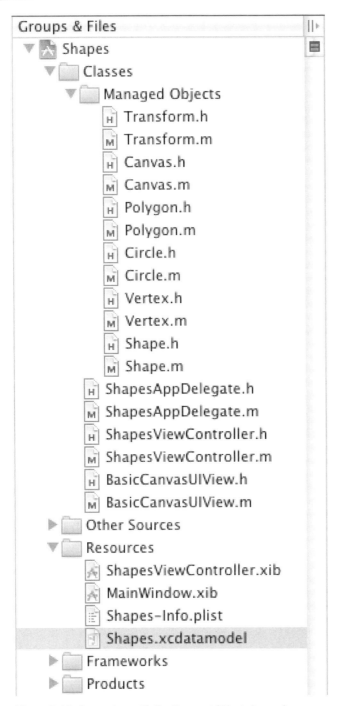

Figure 5-10. *Source tree with the Managed Object classes in a group*

Besides generating the classes, Xcode also updates the class for the entities in your data model from `NSManagedObject` to the newly generated class.

To perform the same task manually, without having Xcode generate your classes, you would do two things:

1. Create the code for the class (open any of the new files to see examples)

2. Update the Class field for the entity in your data model to point to the new class

That's good information to know, in case you ever have to create those classes manually, but it's nice to have Xcode do the work for you.

Now, let's look at some of these classes. Open Vertex.h, shown in Listing 5-5. You can see that it imports the Core Data framework header file, that it derives from NSManagedObject, and that it exposes the properties (both attributes and relationships) of the Vertex entity as Objective-C properties.

Listing 5-5. *Vertex.h*

```
#import <CoreData/CoreData.h>

@class Polygon;

@interface Vertex :  NSManagedObject
{
}

@property (nonatomic, retain) NSNumber * y;
@property (nonatomic, retain) NSNumber * x;
@property (nonatomic, retain) NSNumber * index;
@property (nonatomic, retain) Polygon * polygon;

@end
```

Listing 5-6 shows the implementation file, Vertex.m. You probably can't help but notice how light this implementation is. The magic happens when using the @dynamic directive in the code. You already know the more common @synthesize directive, which tells the compiler to generate basic stubs for property accessors in order to fulfill the API contract with @property directives in the header file. The @dynamic directive is used to tell the compiler that even though it can't find the methods that fulfill the contract, they will be there by the time the runtime needs to invoke them. In essence, you are telling the compiler to trust you. Of course, if you lied to the compiler, break your promise, and do not provide the accessors at runtime, you will be punished with an application crash. Because your class extends NSManagedObject, the accessors are generated for you so you don't have to worry about any punishment. It is safe to use the @dynamic directive for entity properties.

Listing 5-6. *Vertex.m*

```
#import "Vertex.h"

#import "Polygon.h"
```

```
@implementation Vertex

@dynamic y;
@dynamic x;
@dynamic index;
@dynamic polygon;

@end
```

Finally, verify that Xcode updated your data model for the Vertex entity and changed the associated class from NSManagedObject to Vertex. Open the data model, select the Vertex entity, and look at its properties. The value in the Class field should say Vertex, as shown in Figure 5-11.

Figure 5-11. *The* Vertex *entity set to the* Vertex *class*

Again, you could have written this code yourself and updated the model manually, but it's nice to have Xcode do that work for you.

You can start the application, and it still runs even though the rest of the code doesn't use the newly generated classes. It still, for example, accesses the properties of any vertices using the valueForKey: method. Since Vertex is an instance of NSManagedObject, accessing its properties through valueForKey: is still valid.

Let's look next at the header file for Circle, shown in Listing 5-7. Notice that it doesn't extend NSManagedObject but instead extends Shape. Because we made the Circle entity a subentity of Shape in the data model, the Circle class must extend Shape. Circle is still an NSManagedObject by inheritance since Shape extends NSManagedObject.

Listing 5-7. *Circle.h*

```
#import <CoreData/CoreData.h>
#import "Shape.h"


@interface Circle :  Shape
{
}

@property (nonatomic, retain) NSNumber * x;
@property (nonatomic, retain) NSNumber * y;
@property (nonatomic, retain) NSNumber * radius;

@end
```

Next in line to review is Polygon. Polygons are slightly different from the other objects created so far because they have a to-many relationship to another class.

Because a Polygon is a subclass of NSManagedObject, it benefits from its Key-Value Coding (KVC) compliance. Core Data provides accessor methods for attributes and relationships you modeled in your data model. For attributes, we have seen that it provides simple get/set methods. For to-many relationships, it automatically creates KVC mutable proxy methods for the NSSet. The methods are named after the key:

```
- (void)add<Key>Object:(id)value;
- (void)remove<Key>Object:(id)value;
- (void)add<Key>:(NSSet *)value;
- (void)remove<Key>:(NSSet *)value;
```

This feature means that it is possible to call addVerticesObject:(Vertex*) where before we called [[managedObject mutableSetValueForKey:key] addObject:value]. To silence compiler warnings, however, it is necessary to create a category and list the methods for the relationships, as shown in Listing 5-8.

Listing 5-8. *Polygon.h*
```
#import <CoreData/CoreData.h>
#import "Shape.h"


@interface Polygon :  Shape
{
}

@property (nonatomic, retain) NSSet* vertices;

@end


@interface Polygon (CoreDataGeneratedAccessors)
- (void)addVerticesObject:(NSManagedObject *)value;
- (void)removeVerticesObject:(NSManagedObject *)value;
- (void)addVertices:(NSSet *)value;
- (void)removeVertices:(NSSet *)value;
```

```
@end
```

You won't see implementations for these methods in `Polygon.m`, however, because they're automatically provided by the KVC mechanism.

Feel free to peruse the rest of the code for the generated classes. Armed with your knowledge of Core Data and the previous information, you should understand what's happening with this code.

Now that we have our custom objects, we can go back to the application code to use their properties directly, rather than going through `valueForKey:`. Open `ShapesViewController.m`, and add import statements for all the new objects you've created, as shown here:

```
#include <stdlib.h>
#import "ShapesViewController.h"

#import "Polygon.h"
#import "Circle.h"
#import "Shape.h"
#import "Canvas.h"
#import "Vertex.h"
#import "Transform.h"

@interface ShapesViewController (private)
- (void)createShapeAt:(CGPoint)point;
- (void)updateAllShapes;
- (void)deleteAllShapes;
-(UIColor*)makeRandomColor;
@end

@implementation ShapesViewController
...
```

Next, update the `createShapeAt:` method to use your new classes. The revised implementation of `createShapeAt:` is slightly cleaner. In this first wave of cleanup, we've removed all references to `NSManagedObject` and put the actual type instead. This allows us to then set the properties directly instead of calling `setValue:forKey:`. Later in this chapter, we run a second wave of cleanup that illustrates how to get rid of all references to Core Data in the code to make the framework even more seamless.

```
- (void)createShapeAt:(CGPoint)point {
  Shape *shape = nil;
  int type = arc4random() % 2;

  if(type == 0) { // Circle
    Circle *circle = [NSEntityDescription insertNewObjectForEntityForName:@"Circle"
inManagedObjectContext:self.managedObjectContext];

    float radius = 10 + (arc4random() % 90);
    circle.x = [NSNumber numberWithFloat:point.x];
    circle.y = [NSNumber numberWithFloat:point.y];
    circle.radius = [NSNumber numberWithFloat:radius];
```

```
    NSLog(@"Made a new circle at %f,%f with radius %f", point.x, point.y, radius);

    shape = circle;
  }
  else {  // Polygon
    Polygon *polygon = [NSEntityDescription insertNewObjectForEntityForName:@"Polygon"
inManagedObjectContext:self.managedObjectContext];

    // Set the vertices
    int nVertices = 3 + (arc4random() % 20);
    float angleIncrement = (2 * M_PI) / nVertices;
    int index = 0;
    for (float i = 0; i < nVertices; i++) {
      float a = i * angleIncrement;

      float radius = 10 + (arc4random() % 90);
      float x = point.x + (radius * cos(a));
      float y = point.y + (radius * sin(a));

      Vertex *vertex= [NSEntityDescription insertNewObjectForEntityForName:@"Vertex"
inManagedObjectContext:self.managedObjectContext];

      vertex.x = [NSNumber numberWithFloat:x];
      vertex.y = [NSNumber numberWithFloat:y];
      vertex.index = [NSNumber numberWithFloat:index++];

      [polygon addVerticesObject:vertex];
    }

    NSLog(@"Made a new polygon with %d vertices", nVertices);
    shape = polygon;
  }
  // Set the shape's color
  shape.color = [self makeRandomColor];

  // Add the same shape to both canvases
  [[topView.canvas mutableSetValueForKey:@"shapes"] addObject:shape];
  [[bottomView.canvas mutableSetValueForKey:@"shapes"] addObject:shape];

  // Save the context
  NSError *error = nil;
  if (![self.managedObjectContext save:&error]) {
    NSLog(@"Unresolved error %@, %@", error, [error userInfo]);
    abort();
  }

  // Tell the views to repaint themselves
  [topView setNeedsDisplay];
  [bottomView setNeedsDisplay];
}
```

Note how each vertex is added to the polygon by calling addVerticesObject:.

There still isn't anything groundbreaking at this point because we have simply removed references to NSManagedObject and calls to the key/value store. The resulting code is still slightly better because it enforces stronger typing with the managed objects and their properties. The real value of custom managed objects comes from enhancing them with more specialized methods. The next section explains how to do that.

Modifying Generated Classes

Now that the application is outfitted with custom objects, it's time to exhibit the real power of custom managed objects. Having to constantly refer to the Core Data framework or key/value store for everything that relates to managed objects gets distracting very quickly when building an application. The framework should assist, not hinder, the developers in building data store–driven applications. With custom objects, we've gone halfway to a better place and have created an anemic object model and a set of objects that have a state but no behavior. Martin Fowler, chief scientist at ThoughtWorks and self-labeled general loudmouth on software development, first identified the anemic domain model antipattern as well as the antidote. The injection of business logic into objects has been proven to rapidly cure anemia. The next step in refactoring the Core Data managed objects is to add the business logic that will make our objects useful and easier to use.

Adding a static managed object initializer method is a usual way to further detach Core Data from the rest of the code. In ShapesViewController, we created a canvas and its transform by doing the following:

```
canvas1 = [NSEntityDescription insertNewObjectForEntityForName:@"Canvas"
inManagedObjectContext:self.managedObjectContext];
Transform *transform1 = [NSEntityDescription
insertNewObjectForEntityForName:@"Transform"
inManagedObjectContext:self.managedObjectContext];
transform1.scale = [NSNumber numberWithFloat:1];
canvas1.transform = transform1;
```

Our application code still reeks of Core Data. A better way to create a Canvas and its Transform is to define a method for creating transforms and canvases. We first declare the initializer in Transform.h, shown in bold in Listing 5-9.

Listing 5-9. *Transform.h*

```
#import <CoreData/CoreData.h>


@interface Transform :  NSManagedObject
{
}

@property (nonatomic, retain) NSNumber * scale;
@property (nonatomic, retain) NSManagedObject * canvas;

+ (Transform *)initWithScale:(float)scale inContext:(NSManagedObjectContext *)context;
```

@end

The implementation for the new initializer goes in Transform.m, shown in bold in Listing 5-10.

Listing 5-10. *Transform.m*

```objc
#import "Transform.h"


@implementation Transform

@dynamic scale;
@dynamic canvas;

+ (Transform *)initWithScale:(float)scale inContext:(NSManagedObjectContext *)context {
  Transform *transform = [NSEntityDescription➥
insertNewObjectForEntityForName:@"Transform" inManagedObjectContext:context];
  transform.scale = [NSNumber numberWithFloat:scale];
  return transform;
}


@end
```

We do the same for Canvas, which can be initialized with its Transform instead of setting it later. This is a better design since the transform attribute of the Canvas entity is required. Canvas.h can be modified to look like Listing 5-11.

Listing 5-11. *Canvas.h*

```objc
#import <CoreData/CoreData.h>

@class Transform;

@interface Canvas :  NSManagedObject
{
}

@property (nonatomic, retain) NSSet* shapes;
@property (nonatomic, retain) Transform * transform;

+ (Canvas *)initWithTransform:(Transform *)transform inContext:(NSManagedObjectContext➥
*)context;


@end


@interface Canvas (CoreDataGeneratedAccessors)
- (void)addShapesObject:(NSManagedObject *)value;
- (void)removeShapesObject:(NSManagedObject *)value;
- (void)addShapes:(NSSet *)value;
- (void)removeShapes:(NSSet *)value;

@end
```

And we can then add the code in the implementation file, `Canvas.m`, shown in Listing 5-12.

Listing 5-12. *Canvas.m*

```
#import "Canvas.h"
#import "Transform.h"

@implementation Canvas

@dynamic shapes;
@dynamic transform;

+ (Canvas *)initWithTransform:(Transform *)transform inContext:(NSManagedObjectContext➥
*)context {

  Canvas *canvas = [NSEntityDescription insertNewObjectForEntityForName:@"Canvas"➥
inManagedObjectContext:context];

  canvas.transform = transform;
  return canvas;
}

@end
```

Finally, we are ready to alter the `viewDidLoad:` method in the `ShapesViewController` implementation:

```
- (void)viewDidLoad {
  Canvas *canvas1 = nil;
  Canvas *canvas2 = nil;

  // Load the canvases
  NSFetchRequest *fetchRequest = [[NSFetchRequest alloc] init];
  NSEntityDescription *entity = [NSEntityDescription entityForName:@"Canvas"➥
inManagedObjectContext:self.managedObjectContext];

  [fetchRequest setEntity:entity];

  NSArray *canvases = [managedObjectContext executeFetchRequest:fetchRequest error:nil];
  [fetchRequest release];

  if ([canvases count] >= 2) {
    NSLog(@"Loading existing canvases");
    canvas1 = [canvases objectAtIndex:0];
    canvas2 = [canvases objectAtIndex:1];
  } else {
    NSLog(@"Making new canvases");
    // If there aren't any canvases, then we create them
    Transform *transform1 = [Transform initWithScale:1➥
inContext:self.managedObjectContext];

    canvas1 = [Canvas initWithTransform:transform1 inContext:self.managedObjectContext];

    Transform *transform2 = [Transform initWithScale:0.5➥
inContext:self.managedObjectContext];
```

```
  canvas2 = [Canvas initWithTransform:transform2 inContext:self.managedObjectContext];

    NSError *error = nil;
    if (![self.managedObjectContext save:&error]) {
      NSLog(@"Unresolved error %@, %@", error, [error uscrInfo]);
      abort();
    }
  }
  topView.canvas = canvas1;
  bottomView.canvas = canvas2;
}
```

The code is getting a lot cleaner, and using the managed objects is becoming more and more like using regular objects because the ties to Core Data get encapsulated in the classes themselves.

Turn your attention now to the creation of the shapes. The shapes view controller has code that will create a random circle. In the context of our application, this is business logic that could be encapsulated in the `Circle` class. Instead of building a circle ourselves, we could ask the `Circle` class to give us a random instance of itself based on a given origin. We could then create a circle by calling [Circle randomInstance:origin inContext:managedObjectContext].

To do this, we add a static initializer method in the `Circle` class:

```
+ (Circle *)randomInstance:(CGPoint)origin inContext:(NSManagedObjectContext *)context;
```

And provide an implementation in `Circle.m`:

```
+ (Circle *)randomInstance:(CGPoint)origin inContext:(NSManagedObjectContext *)context {
  Circle *circle = [NSEntityDescription insertNewObjectForEntityForName:@"Circle"➠
inManagedObjectContext:context];

  float radius = 10 + (arc4random() % 90);
  circle.x = [NSNumber numberWithFloat:origin.x];
  circle.y = [NSNumber numberWithFloat:origin.y];
  circle.radius = [NSNumber numberWithFloat:radius];

  return circle;
}
```

Do the same for `Polygon` by adding a similar method to `Polygon.h`:

```
+ (Polygon *)randomInstance:(CGPoint)origin inContext:(NSManagedObjectContext *)context;
```

And provide an implementation in `Polygon.m`:

```
+ (Polygon *)randomInstance:(CGPoint)origin inContext:(NSManagedObjectContext *)context
{
  Polygon *polygon = [NSEntityDescription insertNewObjectForEntityForName:@"Polygon"➠
inManagedObjectContext:context];

  // Set the vertices
  int nVertices = 3 + (arc4random() % 20);
  float angleIncrement = (2 * M_PI) / nVertices;
```

```
  int index = 0;
  for (float i = 0; i < nVertices; i++) {
    float a = i * angleIncrement;
    float radius = 10 + (arc4random() % 90);
    float x = origin.x + (radius * cos(a));
    float y = origin.y + (radius * sin(a));

    Vertex *vertex = [NSEntityDescription insertNewObjectForEntityForName:@"Vertex"➥
inManagedObjectContext:context];

    vertex.x = [NSNumber numberWithFloat:x];
    vertex.y = [NSNumber numberWithFloat:y];
    vertex.index = [NSNumber numberWithFloat:index++];

    [polygon addVerticesObject:vertex];
  }
  return polygon;
}
```

You also must add an import for Vertex at the top of Polygon.m:

```
#import "Vertex.h"
```

You can now modify the implementation of createShapeAt: as follows:

```
- (void)createShapeAt:(CGPoint)point {
  Shape *shape = nil;
  int type = arc4random() % 2;

  if(type == 0) { // Circle
    shape = [Circle randomInstance:point inContext:self.managedObjectContext];
  }
  else {   // Polygon
    shape = [Polygon randomInstance:point inContext:self.managedObjectContext];
  }

  // Set the shape's color
  shape.color = [self makeRandomColor];

  // Add the same shape to both canvases
  [[topView.canvas mutableSetValueForKey:@"shapes"] addObject:shape];
  [[bottomView.canvas mutableSetValueForKey:@"shapes"] addObject:shape];

  // Save the context
  NSError *error = nil;
  if (![self.managedObjectContext save:&error]) {
    NSLog(@"Unresolved error %@, %@", error, [error userInfo]);
    abort();
  }

  // Tell the views to repaint themselves
  [topView setNeedsDisplay];
  [bottomView setNeedsDisplay];
}
```

The tidiness of the application code speaks for itself at this point. Most of the logic has been encapsulated into the custom managed objects.

Using the Transformable Type

Despite all the efforts to hide Core Data, it is likely that some properties of the custom objects just feel like they are using the "wrong" type simply to satisfy Core Data. For this type of situation, the framework allows you to use the Transformable type (NSTransformableAttributeType). In our Shapes application, the color property of the Shape object gives this sensation of type misuse. In the current implementation, the color is represented by a comma-delimited string so that we could use the NSStringAttributeType in the data model. It works well, but it makes using the object more complicated because we find ourselves having to decode the value back and forth between a string and a color. The first step is to change the data model. Select the Shape entity, pick the color attribute, and change its type to Transformable. In the Transformer field, use NSKeyedUnarchiveFromDataTransformerName.

> **Note:** Value transformers are part of the Foundation framework in Cocoa. As its name indicates, it facilitates the transformation of data from one format to another. In Core Data, it is typical to use NSKeyedUnarchiveFromDataTransformerName, which converts objects into NSData. Alternatively, you may extend NSValueTransformer in order to provide a custom transformer.

In the code, we now edit Shape.h to change the property type from NSString to UIColor.

```
@property (nonatomic, retain) UIColor *color;
```

Naturally, using the Transformable type isn't all good news. Because the transformer creates an NSData representation of the color property, the data store will use a binary field. In the case of SQLite, for example, a BLOB column will be created to store your data. This means that you can no longer use the data in the query. For instance, you would no longer be able to query for all red shapes. Note that with the string encoding we used before, it wasn't trivial either, but it was at least possible.

Since you changed the attribute type, you need to go back to the application code to make it use the new type. First, alter the ShapesViewController.m to change the implementation of the makeRandomColor: method:

```
- (UIColor *)makeRandomColor {
    // Set the shape's color
    float red = (arc4random() % 256) / 255.0;
    float green = (arc4random() % 256) / 255.0;
    float blue = (arc4random() % 256) / 255.0;

    return [UIColor colorWithRed:red green:green blue:blue alpha:1.0];
}
```

Don't forget to change the return type in the method definition in the category at the top of the file. The second place to modify is the implementation of the drawRect: method in BasicCanvasUIView.m. Be sure to import Shape.h, Circle.h, Polygon.h, and Vertex.h in BasicCanvasUIView.m and then update the drawRect: method like this:

```objc
- (void)drawRect:(CGRect)rect {
  if (canvas == nil) return;

  CGContextRef context = UIGraphicsGetCurrentContext();

  float scale = self.scale;
  CGContextScaleCTM(context, scale, scale);

  NSSet* shapes = [canvas valueForKey:@"shapes"];
  for (Shape *shape in shapes) {
    NSString *entityName = [[shape entity] name];

    const CGFloat *rgb = CGColorGetComponents(shape.color.CGColor);
    CGContextSetRGBFillColor(context, rgb[0], rgb[1], rgb[2], 1.0);

    if ([entityName compare:@"Circle"] == NSOrderedSame) {
      Circle *circle = (Circle *)shape;
      float x = [circle.x floatValue];
      float y = [circle.y floatValue];
      float radius = [circle.radius floatValue];
      CGContextFillEllipseInRect(context, CGRectMake(x-radius, y-radius, 2*radius,➥
2*radius));

    } else if ([entityName compare:@"Polygon"] == NSOrderedSame) {
      Polygon *polygon = (Polygon *)shape;
      // Use a sort descriptor to order the vertices using the index value
      NSSortDescriptor *sortDescriptor = [[NSSortDescriptor alloc] initWithKey:➥
@"index" ascending:YES];
      NSArray *sortDescriptors = [[NSArray alloc] initWithObjects:sortDescriptor, nil];

      NSArray* vertices = [polygon.vertices➥
sortedArrayUsingDescriptors:sortDescriptors];

      CGContextBeginPath(UIGraphicsGetCurrentContext());

      // Place the current graphic context point on the last vertex
      Vertex *lastVertex = [vertices lastObject];
      CGContextMoveToPoint(context, [lastVertex.x floatValue], [lastVertex.y➥
floatValue]);

      // Iterate through the vertices and link them together
      for(Vertex *vertex in vertices) {
        CGContextAddLineToPoint(context, [vertex.x floatValue], [vertex.y floatValue]);
      }

      CGContextFillPath(context);

      [sortDescriptors release];
      [sortDescriptor release];
    }
  }
}
```

We've noted that it is possible to use an alternate value transformer. You must use an alternate value transformer for objects that cannot be naturally serialized to NSData, and you can use one for any of your attributes.

> **Tip:** If a class conforms to the NSCoding protocol, then NSKeyedUnarchiveFromDataTransformerName can be used.

We are now implementing a custom value transformer for our UIColor object. In Xcode, add a new class called UIColorTransformer, and edit the header file to extend NSValueTransformer:

```
#import <Foundation/Foundation.h>

@interface UIColorTransformer : NSValueTransformer {
}

@end
```

NSValueTransformer has several methods that must be implemented in UIColorTransformer.m in order to provide the functionality that Core Data requires. You first must make sure the transformer is reversible, which means it can transform a UIColor object into an NSData as well as transforming the NSData back into a UIColor. This is critical in order to be able to store and retrieve the color attribute. For this, open the UIColorTransformer.m file, and override the allowsReverseTransformation: method:

```
+ (BOOL)allowsReverseTransformation {
  return YES;
}
```

You also indicate that the transformed object will be represented as an NSData:

```
+ (Class)transformedValueClass {
  return [NSData class];
}
```

Finally, you provide the two transformation methods. One will transform from UIColor to NSData, and the reverse method does the opposite. Note that we present here a simplified implementation for color transformation that assumes that the UIColor object was created in the RGB color space, which is the case in the Shapes application. Color spaces fall outside the scope of this book, but we encourage you to read further about colors and transformers if you want to implement a more complete color value transformer.

```
- (id)transformedValue:(id)value {
  UIColor* color = (UIColor *)value;
  const CGFloat *components = CGColorGetComponents(color.CGColor);

  NSString* result = [NSString stringWithFormat:@"%f,%f,%f", components[0],➡
components[1], components[2]];

  return [result dataUsingEncoding:[NSString defaultCStringEncoding]];
}
```

```
- (id)reverseTransformedValue:(id)value {
  NSString *string = [[NSString alloc] initWithData:value➥
encoding:[NSString defaultCStringEncoding]];

  NSArray *components = [string componentsSeparatedByString:@","];
  CGFloat red = [[components objectAtIndex:0] floatValue];
  CGFloat green = [[components objectAtIndex:1] floatValue];
  CGFloat blue = [[components objectAtIndex:2] floatValue];
  [string release];

  return [UIColor colorWithRed:red green:green blue:blue alpha:1.0];
}
```

The last step for using your custom attribute transformer is to register the transformer in
ShapesAppDelegate.m. This can be done simply by importing UIColorTransformer.h and
adding the following two lines at the beginning of the
application:didFinishLaunchingWithOptions: method so that they are called before
the Core Data stack is initialized:

```
UIColorTransformer* transformer = [[[UIColorTransformer alloc] init] autorelease];
[UIColorTransformer setValueTransformer:transformer forName:(NSString
*)@"UIColorTransformerName"];
```

In this section, we have seen how to take advantage of our custom objects to hide Core
Data from our application code as much as possible in order to make the persistence
layer as transparent as possible.

Validating Data

Core Data won't allow you to stuff data that doesn't fit into any of the attributes in your
model. Try, for example, to put a string like "Books for Professionals by Professionals,"
the Apress tag line, into an attribute of type Integer 16, and you'll raise an
NSInvalidArgumentException that looks something like this:

```
'NSInvalidArgumentException', reason: 'Unacceptable type of value for attribute:
property = "x"; desired type = NSNumber; given type = NSCFString; value = Books for
Professionals by Professionals.'
```

Core Data enforces data integrity, but sometimes you want more than that. Sometimes
you want to enforce what corporate-speak terms *business rules*, though they might or
might not have anything to do with business. Take, for example, the Polygon instances
in the Shapes application and their relationships with Vertex instances. A real-world
polygon with no vertices doesn't exist, so you set the "vertices" relationship to
nonoptional. A polygon with one vertex isn't a polygon, either. It's a point. And a two-
vertex polygon is a line. A polygon must have at least three vertices to make the club.
For that reason, you set the value for Min Count in the "vertices" relationship to three.
Relating a Polygon instance to only one or two Vertex instances prevents the managed
object context from saving successfully. Instead, you get an error that looks like this:
"Operation could not be completed. (Cocoa error 1580.)." The error codes come from
the header file CoreDataErrors.h and are listed, along with descriptions, in Table 5-1.

Note that the descriptions are lifted directly from the header file. Checking this table reveals that error code 1580 means "to-many relationship with too few destination objects," which describes exactly what you tried to do.

Table 5-1. *Core Data Validation Errors*

Constant	Code	Description
NSManagedObjectValidationError	1550	Generic validation error
NSValidationMultipleErrorsError	1560	Generic message for error containing multiple validation errors
NSValidationMissingMandatoryPropertyError	1570	Nonoptional property with a nil value
NSValidationRelationshipLacksMinimumCountError	1580	To-many relationship with too few destination objects
NSValidationRelationshipExceedsMaximumCountError	1590	Bounded, to-many relationship with too many destination objects
NSValidationRelationshipDeniedDeleteError	1600	Some relationship with NSDeleteRuleDeny is nonempty
NSValidationNumberTooLargeError	1610	Some numerical value is too large
NSValidationNumberTooSmallError	1620	Some numerical value is too small
NSValidationDateTooLateError	1630	Some date value is too late
NSValidationDateTooSoonError	1640	Some date value is too soon
NSValidationInvalidDateError	1650	Some date value fails to match date pattern
NSValidationStringTooLongError	1660	Some string value is too long
NSValidationStringTooShortError	1670	Some string value is too short
NSValidationStringPatternMatchingError	1680	Some string value fails to match some pattern

The table of error codes gives us some clues about what Core Data will validate for us. The Core Data modeling tool for defining attributes and relationships gives us the same clues. For relationships, you can validate that to-many relationships have a valid number of destination objects—not too many and not too few. For attributes, however, you have a larger number of parameters we can validate, depending on the attribute type. For all the number types, you can specify a Min value and a Max value:

- Integer 16

- Integer 32

- Integer 64

- Decimal

- Double

- Float

Violating the acceptable range gives you an `NSValidationNumberTooSmallError` or an `NSValidationNumberTooLargeError`, depending on which is appropriate. If, for example, you set the Min value to 7.0 and the Max value to 10.0 for the `radius` attribute of the `Circle` entity, random circles that don't fall within that radius range would not save to the persistent store.

For the `String` type, you can specify values for the Min Length and Max Length of the string, as well as provide a regular expression to which the value must conform. The `Date` attribute is a little more tricky, however, because the Core Data modeling tool provides only text entry fields to enter Min and Max values, with no hint for how to format the values or whether any "magic" values like Today, Yesterday, 3 Days Ago, or 1 Year From Now are available. Scouring Apple's documentation yields nothing, but a little Google work uncovers blog posts by Shane Crawford (http://shanecrawford.org/2008/57/coredatas-default-date-value/) and Jeff LaMarche (http://iphonedevelopment.blogspot.com/2009/07/core-data-default-dates-in-data-model.html) that make Date Min and Max values (and Default values; see the "Default Values" section) sound really cool: you can specify natural-language strings like "now," "today," or "last Saturday." Just as the thrill factor hits, you read in the posts that the natural-language strings are interpreted at compile time, not runtime, so they're not updated to reflect the current date, ever. This renders them useless.

You can put specific dates in these fields, however, like 1/1/1900, but it's difficult to find much use for that. Read on in the next section, "Custom Validation," to understand how to validate relative dates.

Custom Validation

If you've generated your own `NSManagedObject`-derived classes for your data model, you can easily create your own validation routines that Core Data automatically invokes when customizing your objects. One option is to edit your `NSManagedObject` implementation (*.m) file and override the `validateValue:forKey:error` method, which has this signature:

```
- (BOOL)validateValue:(id *)ioValue forKey:(NSString *)key error:(NSError **)outError
```

It returns `YES` for valid and `NO` for not valid. This method gets called for each of the properties of your object, with the `key` value holding the property's name for each invocation. You are responsible for validating all the properties of your object by determining which key has been passed and doing appropriate validation for the property with that key.

Core Data offers a second, cleaner option that allows you to write individual validation routines for any or all of your properties and allows the default validation to process for any properties you haven't explicitly written validation routines for. To use this validation option, you write methods in your NSManagedObject-derived class's implementation file that take this form:

```
- (BOOL)validate<AttributeName>:(id *)ioValue error:(NSError **)outError
```

Substitute the name of the attribute you're trying to validate for <AttributeName>. For example, remove any validation you have on the radius attribute of the Circle entity in the Core Data modeler, and create a method in Circle.m that looks like this:

```
- (BOOL)validateRadius:(id *)ioValue error:(NSError **)outError {
  NSLog(@"Validating radius using custom method");

  if ([*ioValue floatValue] < 7.0 || [*ioValue floatValue] > 10.0) {
    // Fill out the error object
    if (outError != NULL) {
      NSString *msg = @"Radius must be between 7.0 and 10.0";
      NSDictionary *dict = [NSDictionary dictionaryWithObject:msg➥
forKey:NSLocalizedDescriptionKey];

      NSError *error = [[[NSError alloc] initWithDomain:@"Shapes" code:10 userInfo:➥
dict] autorelease];
      *outError = error;
    }
    return NO;
  }
  return YES;
}
```

This code retrieves the value passed in the ioValue parameter as a float and then compares it to the acceptable boundaries: 7.0 and 10.0. If the comparison fails, the code fills out an NSError object, if one was passed, with an arbitrary error code of 10. The code then returns NO to fail the validation. If the comparison passes, the code returns YES.

If you run this code and create a few shapes that include some circles, eventually the application will crash. You'll see messages in the log that look something like this:

```
2010-09-12 10:49:16.696 Shapes[9888:207] Validating radius using custom method
```

If any shapes fail validation, you'll see log messages that look like this:

```
Error Domain=Shapes Code=10 UserInfo=0x4e2c980 "Radius must be between 7.0 and 10.0"
```

Use this same mechanism to create date validations that validate date ranges relative to the current date. The following example validates that a date called myDate in the Core Data model falls between a week ago and a week from now:

```
- (BOOL)validateMyDate:(id *)ioValue error:(NSError **)outError {
  // 1 week = 60 sec/min * 60 min/hr * 24 hr/day * 7 day/week
  static int SECONDS_IN_A_WEEK = 60 * 60 * 24 * 7;
```

```
NSLog(@"Validating myDate using custom method");

// Get the passed date and calculate the valid dates
NSDate *myDate = (NSDate *)(*ioValue);
NSDate *minDate = [NSDate dateWithTimeIntervalSinceNow:-SECONDS_IN_A_WEEK];
NSDate *maxDate = [NSDate dateWithTimeIntervalSinceNow:SECONDS_IN_A_WEEK];

// Check if it's valid
if ([myDate earlierDate:minDate] == myDate || [myDate laterDate:maxDate] == myDate) {
    // The date isn't valid, so construct an NSError if one was passed and return NO
    if (outError != NULL) {
        NSString *msg = @"myDate must fall between a week ago and a week from now";
        NSDictionary *dict = [NSDictionary dictionaryWithObject:msg➥
forKey:NSLocalizedDescriptionKey];

        NSError *error = [[[NSError alloc] initWithDomain:@"Shapes" code:20 userInfo:➥
dict] autorelease];
        *outError = error;
    }
    return NO;
}
return YES;
}
```

Although ioValue is a pointer to an object reference, which would allow you to change the input value in the object graph, Apple's documentation strongly discourages you from doing this, because it could create memory management issues.

The first method of validation, validateValue:forKey:error, trumps the validate<AttributeName> way. If you've provided a validateValue implementation, none of your validate<AttributeName> methods get called, and Core Data uses the answer that validateValue returns to determine the validity of an object.

You can also override the three other validation methods offered by NSManagedObject:

- ■ validateForInsert
- ■ validateForUpdate
- ■ validateForDelete

Core Data calls these methods to invoke validation before inserting, updating, or deleting an object, respectively. These are the methods that call the validateValue methods, whether yours or the default NSManagedObject implementation. You can override these to do your own custom validation, but be sure to call the superclass implementation first so that you get all the appropriate validation. One tricky piece to doing this is that if your code detects an error, it shouldn't override any existing errors from the validation in the superclass. Instead, it should combine any errors. Apple's documentation offers a method, errorFromOriginalError, that combines errors. You can use this method, listed here, or you can write your own. Either way, be sure to combine errors and not overwrite them.

```
- (NSError *)errorFromOriginalError:(NSError *)originalError error:(NSError
*)secondError
```

```
{
  NSMutableDictionary *userInfo = [NSMutableDictionary dictionary];
  NSMutableArray *errors = [NSMutableArray arrayWithObject:secondError];

  if ([originalError code] == NSValidationMultipleErrorsError) {
    [userInfo addEntriesFromDictionary:[originalError userInfo]];
    [errors addObjectsFromArray:[userInfo objectForKey:NSDetailedErrorsKey]];
  } else {
    [errors addObject:originalError];
  }

  [userInfo setObject:errors forKey:NSDetailedErrorsKey];

  return [NSError errorWithDomain:NSCocoaErrorDomain
                             code:NSValidationMultipleErrorsError
                         userInfo:userInfo];
}
```

You typically override one of the validateFor... methods to perform validation that depends on multiple properties. Each property might be valid on its own, but some combinations may not be valid. Consider, for instance, that you want to make a circle invalid for insertion if the x value is more than twice the y value. You create a method in Circle.m that first calls the superclass implementation of validateForInsert and then does its validation to make sure x isn't more than twice y. It could look like this:

```
- (BOOL)validateForInsert:(NSError **)outError {
  BOOL valid = [super validateForInsert:outError];

  // x can't be more than twice as much as y
  float fx = [self.x floatValue], fy = [self.y floatValue];
  if (fx >= (2 * fy)) {
    // Create the error if one was passed
    if (outError != NULL) {
      NSString *msg = @"x can't be more than twice as much as y";
      NSDictionary *dict = [NSDictionary dictionaryWithObject:msg➥
forKey:NSLocalizedDescriptionKey];

      NSError *error = [[[NSError alloc] initWithDomain:@"Shapes" code:30 userInfo:➥
dict] autorelease];

      // Check to see if [super validateForInsert] returned errors
      if (*outError == nil) {
        *outError = error;
      } else {
        // Combine this error with any existing ones
        *outError = [self errorFromOriginalError:*outError error:error];
      }
    }
    valid = NO;
  }
  return valid;
}
```

Note that it calls the errorFromOriginalError method listed earlier to combine any existing errors.

Invoking Validation

Core Data allows you to create objects with invalid attributes and invokes the validation routines when you save the managed object context. Objects with invalid values in their attributes or incorrect numbers of relationships can live comfortably in the managed object context. The validation doesn't occur until you try to save the managed object, at which time the save fails with the appropriate error codes.

If you don't want to wait for the save method to be invoked, however, you can invoke validation manually. To do so, simply call any of the validation methods that you just learned about.

Default Values

Core Data allows you to set default values for each of your attributes. You might have noticed that setting validation rules in your attributes without setting default values that pass those rules nets you compiler warnings that look something like this:

```
Misconfigured Property. Circle.radius has default value smaller than minimum value.
```

The compiler tries to protect you from creating attributes that violate your validation rules. You can safely ignore them and make sure to set valid values yourself, or you can take advantage of Core Data's offer to help.

Setting default values works exactly as you'd suppose: you type a valid default value into the Default field, and any new instance of that entity type will begin life with that value for that attribute. Try setting the default value for radius to 8.0, for example, and comment out the code that sets a random radius. You'll find that all created circles have a radius of 8.0.

The one oddity for default values is an attribute of type Date, as noted earlier. You can use an explicit date or a natural-language string like "today," but that string evaluates at compile time, not runtime, so doesn't do what you probably want (unless you want your dates to all commemorate your application's ship day by default). To create a default date that's based on the runtime date, add a method to your NSManagedObject-derived class that overrides NSManagedObject's awakeFromInsert: method. In this method, called when the object is inserted into the managed object context, you can provide your own default value for any default fields. The following implementation inserts today's date into the attribute myDate so that any new instances of this object automatically have today's date.

```
- (void)awakeFromInsert {
  [super awakeFromInsert];
  [self setValue:[NSDate date] forKey:@"myDate"];
}
```

Undoing and Redoing

Golfers call it a mulligan. School-yard children call it a do-over. Computer users call it
Edit ➤ Undo. Whatever you call it, you've realized that you've blundered and want to
take back your last action. Not all scenarios afford you that opportunity, to which many
broken-hearted lovers will attest, but Core Data forgives and allows you to undo what
you've done using the standard Cocoa NSUndoManager mechanism. This section instructs
you how to use it to allow your users to undo their Core Data changes.

The Core Data undo manager, an object of type NSUndoManager, lives in your managed
object context, and NSManagedObjectContext provides a getter and a setter for the undo
manager. Unlike Core Data on Mac OS X, however, the managed object context in iOS's
Core Data doesn't provide an undo manager by default for performance reasons. If you
want undo capabilities for your Core Data objects, you must set the undo manager in
your managed object context yourself.

> **Note:** Core Data on iOS doesn't provide an undo manager by default. You must set it yourself.

If you want to support undoing actions in your iOS application, you typically create the
undo manager when you set up your managed object context, which usually happens in
the getter for the managed object context. The Shapes application, for example, sets up
the managed object context in the application delegate, as shown here. Note the code
in bold, which adds an undo manager to the managed object context.

```
- (NSManagedObjectContext *)managedObjectContext {
  if (managedObjectContext_ != nil) {
    return managedObjectContext_;
  }
  NSPersistentStoreCoordinator *coordinator = [self persistentStoreCoordinator];
  if (coordinator != nil) {
    managedObjectContext_ = [[NSManagedObjectContext alloc] init];
    [managedObjectContext_ setPersistentStoreCoordinator:coordinator];

    NSUndoManager *undoManager = [[NSUndoManager alloc] init];
    [managedObjectContext_ setUndoManager:undoManager];
    [undoManager release];
  }
  return managedObjectContext_;
}
```

As you can see, the code allocates and initializes the undo manager, sets it into the
managed object context (passing the responsibility for its life-cycle management to the
context), and releases it to decrement the reference count.

Once the undo manager is set into the managed object context, it tracks any changes in
the managed object context and adds them to the undo stack. You can undo those
changes by calling the undo method of NSUndoManager, and each change (actually, each
undo group, as explained in the section "Undo Groups") is rolled back from the

managed object context. You can also replay changes that have been undone by calling NSUndoManager's redo method.

The undo and redo methods perform their magic only if the managed object context has any change to undo or redo, so calling them when no changes can be undone or redone does nothing. You can check, however, if the undo manager can undo or redo any changes by calling the canUndo: and canRedo: methods, respectively.

Undo Groups

By default, the undo manager groups all changes that happen during a single pass through the application's run loop into a single change that can be undone or redone as a unit. This means, for example, that in the Shapes application, each shape creation can be undone or redone individually, because each shape is created in response to a touch event. When you shake the device, however, a single shake event occurs, and all the shapes are deleted in the method you call in response to that event. You can undo the deletion of all the shapes or call redo to undo the deletion of all the shapes, but by default you can't undo the deletion or redo the creation of single shapes.

You alter this behavior by turning off automatic grouping completely and managing the undo groups yourself. To accomplish this, pass NO to setGroupsByEvent. You become responsible, then, for creating all undo groups, because the undo manager will no longer create them for you. You create the undo group by calling beginUndoGrouping to start creating the group and endUndoGrouping to complete the undo group. These calls must be matched, or an exception of type NSInternalInconsistencyException is raised. You could, for example, create an undo group for each shape deletion in Shapes so that you can undo the deletion one shape at a time. You can also span undo groups across events, so you could, for example, group three shape creations and undo the three shapes with a single call to undo.

Limiting the Undo Stack

By default, the undo manager tracks an unlimited number of changes for you to undo and redo. This can cause memory issues, especially on iOS devices. You can limit the size of the undo stack by calling NSUndoManager's setLevelsOfUndo: method, passing an unsigned integer that represents the number of undo groups to retain on the undo stack. You can inspect the current undo stack size, measured in the number of undo groups, by calling levelsOfUndo, which returns an unsigned integer. A value of 0 represents no limit. If you've imposed a limit on the size of the undo stack, the oldest undo groups roll off the stack to accommodate the newer groups.

Disabling Undo Tracking

Once you create an undo manager and set it into the managed object context, any changes you make to the managed object context are tracked and can be undone. You can disable undo tracking, however, by calling NSUndoManager's disableUndoRegistration method. To reenable undo tracking, call NSUndoManager's enableUndoRegistration method. Disabling and enabling undo tracking uses a reference counting mechanism, so multiple calls to disableUndoRegistration require an equal number of calls to enableUndoRegistration before undo tracking becomes enabled again.

Calling enableUndoRegistration when undo tracking is already enabled raises an exception of type NSInternalInconsistencyException, which will likely crash your application. To avoid this embarrassment, you can call NSUndoManager's isUndoRegistrationEnabled, which returns a BOOL, before calling enableUndoRegistration. For example, the following code checks whether undo tracking is enabled before enabling it:

```
if (![undoManager isUndoRegistrationEnabled]) {
  [undoManager enableUndoRegistration];
}
```

You can clear the undo stack entirely by calling the removeAllActions method. This method has the side effect of reenabling undo tracking.

Adding Undo to Shapes

The rest of this section puts into practice the concepts explained about undo managers by adding undo and redo support to the Shapes application. To begin, change the accessor for the managed object context in the application delegate to create an undo manager for the context. Set the undo stack to an arbitrary size of 10, as this code shows:

```
- (NSManagedObjectContext *)managedObjectContext {
    if (managedObjectContext_ != nil) {
        return managedObjectContext_;
    }

    NSPersistentStoreCoordinator *coordinator = [self persistentStoreCoordinator];
    if (coordinator != nil) {
        managedObjectContext_ = [[NSManagedObjectContext alloc] init];
        [managedObjectContext_ setPersistentStoreCoordinator:coordinator];

        // Set up the undo manager
        NSUndoManager *undoManager = [[NSUndoManager alloc] init];
        [undoManager setLevelsOfUndo:10];
        [managedObjectContext_ setUndoManager:undoManager];
        [undoManager release];
    }
    return managedObjectContext_;
}
```

The default interface for undoing actions on an iOS device is to shake the device, but Shapes already uses that to delete all the shapes from the persistent store. Instead, Shapes will provide two buttons, one to undo the last change and one to redo it. Open the ShapesViewController.h file, and add members for the two buttons, methods to invoke when the buttons are pressed, and a method that hides the buttons when the

managed object context has no changes to undo or redo. The code should look like
Listing 5-13 with the added lines in bold.

Listing 5-13. ShapesViewController.h

```
#import <UIKit/UIKit.h>
#import <CoreData/CoreData.h>

#import "BasicCanvasUIView.h"

@interface ShapesViewController : UIViewController {
    NSManagedObjectContext *managedObjectContext;

    IBOutlet BasicCanvasUIView *topView;
    IBOutlet BasicCanvasUIView *bottomView;
    IBOutlet UIButton *undoButton;
    IBOutlet UIButton *redoButton;
}

@property (nonatomic, retain) NSManagedObjectContext *managedObjectContext;
@property (nonatomic, retain) BasicCanvasUIView *topView;
@property (nonatomic, retain) BasicCanvasUIView *bottomView;
@property (nonatomic, retain) UIButton *undoButton;
@property (nonatomic, retain) UIButton *redoButton;

- (void)deleteAllShapes;
- (void)updateAllShapes;
- (IBAction)undo:(id)sender;
- (IBAction)redo:(id)sender;
- (void)updateUndoAndRedoButtons:(NSNotification *)notification;

@end
```

Add @synthesize directives to ShapesViewController.m for undoButton and redoButton.
Open ShapesViewController.xib, and drag two Round Rect Button instances to the top
corners of the screen—one on the left and one on the right. Change the label on the one
on the left to Undo and the one on the right to Redo. Set the Autosizing appropriately for
each button. The Undo button should have the bands on the top and left only, and the
Redo button should have the bands on the top and right only. Ctrl+drag from the File's
Owner icon to the Undo button, and wire it to undoButton; repeat the process to wire the
Redo button to redoButton. Wire the Touch Up Inside events for each button to the
methods you created—the Undo button to the undo: method and the Redo button to
the redo: method.

The undo method should get the undo manager from the managed object context and
call the undo: method and then tell the views to repaint themselves, like this:

```
- (IBAction)undo:(id)sender {
    [[self.managedObjectContext undoManager] undo];
    [topView setNeedsDisplay];
    [bottomView setNeedsDisplay];
}
```

The redo: method should do the same thing but call the undo manager's redo: method instead of its undo: method:

```
- (IBAction)redo:(id)sender {
    [[self.managedObjectContext undoManager] redo];
    [topView setNeedsDisplay];
    [bottomView setNeedsDisplay];
}
```

To show the Undo button only when the user can undo a change and the Redo button only when the user can redo a change, you could insert code everywhere you make data changes to update the buttons. Take advantage of Cocoa Touch's notification mechanism, however, and have the managed object context notify you whenever its managed data changes. In the viewDidLoad: method, add code to call your updateUndoAndRedoButtons: method any time the data changes. You also want to call the updateUndoAndRedoButtons: method when the view first loads, so tack on a call to that method. This is the code you should add to viewDidLoad:

```
    // Register for changes to the managed object context
    NSNotificationCenter *notificationCenter = [NSNotificationCenter defaultCenter];
    [notificationCenter addObserver:self selector:@selector(updateUndoAndRedoButtons:)
name:NSManagedObjectContextObjectsDidChangeNotification object:nil];
    [self updateUndoAndRedoButtons:nil];
```

In the viewDidUnload: method, undo the notifications:

```
- (void)viewDidUnload {
    [[NSNotificationCenter defaultCenter] removeObserver:self];
}
```

The updateUndoAndRedoButtons: method hides the buttons appropriately when the application has nothing to undo or redo. It looks like this:

```
- (void)updateUndoAndRedoButtons:(NSNotification *)notification {
    NSUndoManager *undoManager = [self.managedObjectContext undoManager];
    undoButton.hidden = ![undoManager canUndo];
    redoButton.hidden = ![undoManager canRedo];
}
```

After making these changes, build and run the Shapes application. As you add shapes and undo changes, you should see the Undo and Redo buttons as in Figure 5-12. Add shapes, change the colors of shapes by rotating the device, and delete the shapes. Click Undo and Redo and see the data changes undo and redo themselves.

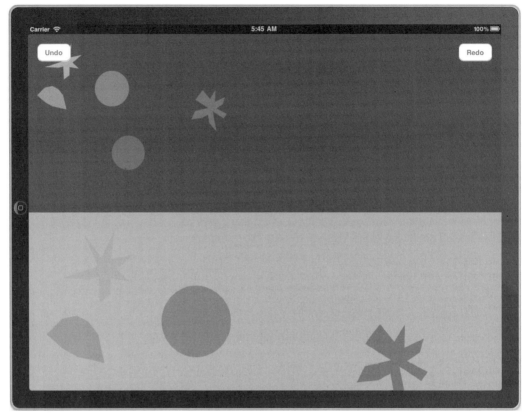

Figure 5-12. *The Undo and Redo buttons*

For a small amount of work, you can support undoing and redoing actions in your Core Data applications. Users expect mulligans, so make the small effort to give them to your users.

Summary

This chapter covered the heart of the purpose of Core Data: to create, retrieve, update, and delete data in a persistent store. Like Ruby on Rails, Core Data provides simple yet powerful mechanisms to carry out these CRUD operations. Whether talking directly to your NSManagedObject instances or generating classes to represent your data objects, you can perform CRUD operations through the interfaces Core Data provides you without getting into the messy details of SQL or other data storage details.

One area where Core Data trumps Ruby on Rails is its native support for undoing data operations. Although efforts continue to add Undo/Redo support for Rails, no solution built into Rails provides easy ways to undo data-related operation like Core Data does.

Although now you know almost all you need for writing usable Core Data applications, don't stop here. The next chapter talks about how to refine result sets so that you can filter, sort, and aggregate the data you retrieve from your persistent store.

Chapter 6

Refining Result Sets

Billing itself as "the ultimate automotive marketplace," AutoTrader.com allows consumers in the United States to buy and sell cars. According to census data, the United States has around 250 million registered motor vehicles, so you can imagine that finding the perfect car to buy can daunt even the most intrepid prospective car buyer. To help car buyers cut through the lots of cars they don't want to find the one they do, AutoTrader.com provides tools on its web site to filter available cars by criteria such as body style, make, model, year, price, and location. Its television commercials tout these filtering tools by such means as showing cars zooming past car shoppers or automotive armadas driving to their homes until only the perfect car appears.

When dealing with large sets of data, refining result sets becomes essential for analysts to extract any meaning from the data. Computers, including iDevices, excel at narrowing data sets to make it easier for computer users to understand the data they're working with. Imagine, for example, how much more difficult calling someone from your iPhone would be if the Contacts application didn't sort your contacts alphabetically or allow you to search for a contact.

This chapter demonstrates how to sort, filter, and aggregate data using Core Data's mechanisms so you can help your application's users find the data they're looking for.

Building the Test Application

You can get data out of a Core Data persistent store in two ways. If you already have handles to existing managed objects, then you can follow the object graph and relationships to pull more objects out. If you don't have any objects yet, such as when the application first starts, then you must go get them directly out of the persistent store. In this case, you typically use an instance of NSFetchRequest to go get objects. You initialize an NSFetchRequest with an NSEntityDescription, which helps narrow the result set by constraining the type of managed objects to retrieve. This chapter shows you how to narrow your fetch requests in various ways using the NSFetchRequest class.

To support the examples in this chapter, we'll reuse the OrgChart application from Chapter 2. We suggest you make a copy of the application because you will make some changes to Chapter 2's data model in this chapter. Since Chapter 2, you've learned that Core Data can better deal with managing the object graph if all the relationships have an inverse, so go back to the OrgChart application and add reverse relationships for "leader" and "employees." To accomplish this, open the OrgChart.xcdatamodel data model, and select the Person entity. Since Organization already has the "leader" relationship to the Person entity, add a relationship called "organization" in Person, set the destination to Organization, and select "leader" as the inverse relationship. Person also has a self-referencing relationship called "employees," so create a relationship from Person to Person, call it **manager**, and select "employees" as the inverse relationship. Also, rename the id attribute of Person to age. Your Person entity should look like Figure 6-1.

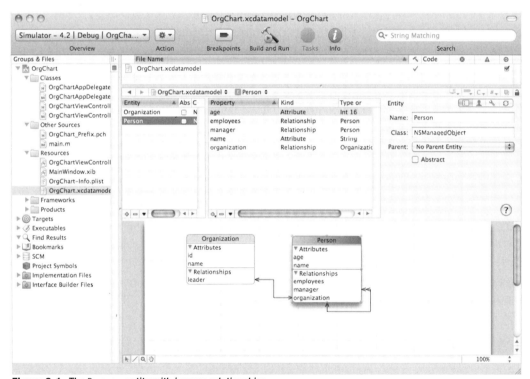

Figure 6-1. *The* Person *entity with inverse relationships*

> **Note:** If you did not make a copy of the OrgChart application and simply modified the code from Chapter 2, you will need to delete the OrgChart.sqlite SQLite database before the application can start.

Creating the Org Chart Data

The OrgChart application is a very simple application with no fancy user interface—just a blank, gray window. What interests us about the OrgChart application, for the purposes of this chapter, is how to retrieve the data from the persistent store. In the OrgChartAppDelegate.m file, the createData method populates the data store. The data it uses to populate the data store represents the org chart shown in Figure 6-2.

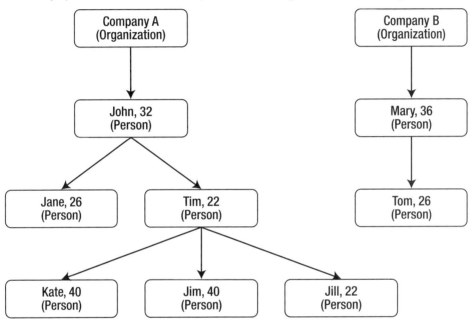

Figure 6-2. *The sample org chart data set*

Listing 6-1 shows the createData method that populates the data according to Figure 6-2. Open OrgChartAppDelegate.m, and replace the createData method from Chapter 2 with Listing 6-1's code.

Listing 6-1. *The createData Method That Populates the Org Chart*

```
-(void)createData {
  NSManagedObjectContext *context = [self managedObjectContext];

  NSEntityDescription *orgEntity = [NSEntityDescription entityForName:@"Organization"➧
inManagedObjectContext:context];

  NSEntityDescription *personEntity = [NSEntityDescription entityForName:@"Person"➧
inManagedObjectContext:context];

  { // Company A
```

```objc
    NSManagedObject *organization = [NSEntityDescription➡
insertNewObjectForEntityForName:[orgEntity name] inManagedObjectContext:context];


    [organization setValue:@"Company A" forKey:@"name"];
    int orgId = [organization hash];
    [organization setValue:[NSNumber numberWithInt:orgId] forKey:@"id"];

    NSManagedObject *john = [NSEntityDescription➡
insertNewObjectForEntityForName:[personEntity name] inManagedObjectContext:context];

    [john setValue:@"John" forKey:@"name"];
    [john setValue:[NSNumber numberWithInt:32] forKey:@"age"];

    NSManagedObject *jane = [NSEntityDescription➡
insertNewObjectForEntityForName:[personEntity name] inManagedObjectContext:context];

    [jane setValue:@"Jane" forKey:@"name"];
    [jane setValue:[NSNumber numberWithInt:26] forKey:@"age"];

    NSManagedObject *tim = [NSEntityDescription➡
insertNewObjectForEntityForName:[personEntity name] inManagedObjectContext:context];

    [tim setValue:@"Tim" forKey:@"name"];
    [tim setValue:[NSNumber numberWithInt:22] forKey:@"age"];

    NSManagedObject *jim = [NSEntityDescription➡
insertNewObjectForEntityForName:[personEntity name] inManagedObjectContext:context];

    [jim setValue:@"Jim" forKey:@"name"];
    [jim setValue:[NSNumber numberWithInt:40] forKey:@"age"];

    NSManagedObject *kate = [NSEntityDescription➡
insertNewObjectForEntityForName:[personEntity name] inManagedObjectContext:context];

    [kate setValue:@"Kate" forKey:@"name"];
    [kate setValue:[NSNumber numberWithInt:40] forKey:@"age"];

    NSManagedObject *jill = [NSEntityDescription➡
insertNewObjectForEntityForName:[personEntity name] inManagedObjectContext:context];

    [jill setValue:@"Jill" forKey:@"name"];
    [jill setValue:[NSNumber numberWithInt:22] forKey:@"age"];

    NSMutableSet *johnsEmployees = [john mutableSetValueForKey:@"employees"];
    [johnsEmployees addObject:jane];
    [johnsEmployees addObject:tim];

    NSMutableSet *timsEmployees = [tim mutableSetValueForKey:@"employees"];

    [timsEmployees addObject:jim];
    [timsEmployees addObject:kate];
    [timsEmployees addObject:jill];

    [organization setValue:john forKey:@"leader"];
}
```

```
  { // Company B
    NSManagedObject *organization = [NSEntityDescription➡
insertNewObjectForEntityForName:[orgEntity name] inManagedObjectContext:context];

    [organization setValue:@"Company B" forKey:@"name"];
    int orgId = [organization hash];
    [organization setValue:[NSNumber numberWithInt:orgId] forKey:@"id"];

    NSManagedObject *mary = [NSEntityDescription➡
insertNewObjectForEntityForName:[personEntity name] inManagedObjectContext:context];

    [mary setValue:@"Mary" forKey:@"name"];
    [mary setValue:[NSNumber numberWithInt:36] forKey:@"age"];

    NSManagedObject *tom = [NSEntityDescription➡
insertNewObjectForEntityForName:[personEntity name] inManagedObjectContext:context];

    [tom setValue:@"Tom" forKey:@"name"];
    [tom setValue:[NSNumber numberWithInt:26] forKey:@"age"];

    [[mary mutableSetValueForKey:@"employees"] addObject:tom];

    [organization setValue:mary forKey:@"leader"];
  }

  NSError *error = nil;
  if (![context save:&error]) {
    NSLog(@"Unresolved error %@, %@", error, [error userInfo]);
    abort();
  }
}
```

The next step is to edit the `application:didFinishLaunchingWithOptions:` method to call `createData`.

```
- (BOOL)application:(UIApplication *)application➡
didFinishLaunchingWithOptions:(NSDictionary *)launchOptions {
  [self createData];

  [window addSubview:viewController.view];
  [window makeKeyAndVisible];
  return YES;
}
```

Launch the application. It should start, display the gray screen, and have no output. The application has created the persistent store and populated it with the org chart data that we use throughout the rest of the chapter for sorting, filtering, and aggregating result sets. You can verify that the application created the persistent store using the techniques outlined in earlier chapters to find the SQLite data store and run queries against it using the `sqlite3` command-line tool. See Chapter 2 for more information.

Reading and Outputting the Data

Now that you've created your persistent store and inserted all the org chart test data, you don't need to call the `createData:` method anymore. Stop the application and comment out the `createData:` call in the `application:didFinishLaunchingWithOptions:` method. Right below it, add a call to the `readData:` method so that the application reads the data and outputs it to the Debugger Console when the application launches. Through this chapter, you'll replace the `readData:` method multiple times to read and output different data from your org chart data model. The `application:didFinishLaunchingWithOptions:` method should now look like this:

```
- (BOOL)application:(UIApplication *)application➡
didFinishLaunchingWithOptions:(NSDictionary *)launchOptions {
//[self createData];
  [self readData];

  [window addSubview:viewController.view];
  [window makeKeyAndVisible];
  return YES;
}
```

Next, edit the `displayPerson:withIndentation:` method to display the person's age since you just added this new field:

```
-(void)displayPerson:(NSManagedObject*)person withIndentation:(NSString*)indentation {
  NSLog(@"%@Name: %@ (%@)", indentation, [person valueForKey:@"name"], [person➡
valueForKey:@"age"]);

  // Increase the indentation for sub-levels
  indentation = [NSString stringWithFormat:@"%@  ", indentation];

  NSSet *employees = [person valueForKey:@"employees"];
  id employee;
  NSEnumerator *it = [employees objectEnumerator];
  while((employee = [it nextObject]) != NULL) {
    [self displayPerson:employee withIndentation:indentation];
  }
}
```

Launch the application again, and the log output will look similar to the following example, showing that your two organizations are there with the proper org charts. The ordering in your output may differ—for example, Company B could come before Company A—but that's not important.

> **Tip:** To view the application log, go to the Xcode menu and select **Run ➤ Console**, or use the ⇧+⌘+R keyboard shortcut.

```
2010-12-16 07:16:51.427 OrgChart[37749:207] Organization: Company B
2010-12-16 07:16:51.430 OrgChart[37749:207]   Name: Mary (36)
2010-12-16 07:16:51.431 OrgChart[37749:207]     Name: Tom (26)
```

```
2010-12-16 07:16:51.432 OrgChart[37749:207] Organization: Company A
2010-12-16 07:16:51.432 OrgChart[37749:207]   Name: John (32)
2010-12-16 07:16:51.433 OrgChart[37749:207]   Name: Jane (26)
2010-12-16 07:16:51.434 OrgChart[37749:207]   Name: Tim (22)
2010-12-16 07:16:51.434 OrgChart[37749:207]    Name: Kate (40)
2010-12-16 07:16:51.435 OrgChart[37749:207]    Name: Jim (40)
2010-12-16 07:16:51.436 OrgChart[37749:207]    Name: Jill (22)
```

Your data set is now ready and verified. The remainder of this chapter deals with extracting only certain objects and rearranging them based on constraints you specify.

Filtering

Core Data uses the NSPredicate class from the Foundation framework to specify how to select the objects that should be part of the result set when executing a fetch request. Predicates can be built in two ways: either you can build the object and its graph manually or you can use the query language NSPredicate implements. You will find that most of the time, you will prefer the convenience and readability of the latter method.

In this section, we look at both ways of building predicates for each example in order to help draw a parallel between the query language and the NSPredicate object graph. Understanding both ways will help you determine your preferred approach. You can also mix and match the approaches depending on your applications and data scenarios.

The predicate query language builds an NSPredicate object graph from a string representation that has similarities with a SQL WHERE clause. The method that builds a predicate from the language is +predicateWithFormat:(NSString*). For instance, if you want to get the managed object that represents Jane, you build the predicate by calling [NSPredicate predicateWithFormat:@"name = 'Jane'"].

To test this, modify the readData: method as follows:

```
-(void)readData {
  NSManagedObjectContext *context = [self managedObjectContext];
  NSEntityDescription *entity = [NSEntityDescription entityForName:@"Person"➥
inManagedObjectContext:context];

  NSFetchRequest *fetchRequest = [[NSFetchRequest alloc] init];➥
  [fetchRequest setEntity:entity];

  NSPredicate *predicate = [NSPredicate predicateWithFormat:@"name='Jane'"];
  [fetchRequest setPredicate:predicate];

  NSArray *persons = [context executeFetchRequest:fetchRequest error:nil];

  for(NSManagedObject *person in persons) {
    NSLog(@"name=%@ age=%@", [person valueForKey:@"name"], [person valueForKey:@"age"]);
  }
  [fetchRequest release];
}
```

Running the application again yields the expected output:

```
name=Jane age=26
```

In its simplest form, a predicate executes a test on an object. If the test succeeds, then the object is part of the result set. If the test is negative, then the object isn't included in the result set. In the previous example, name='Jane' is an example of a simple predicate. The key path name and the constant string value 'Jane' are called *expressions*. The operator = is called a *comparator*.

Expressions for a Single Value

Expressions, represented by the NSExpression class, are the basic building blocks of a predicate. They represent values that can be compared with each other or simply evaluated by themselves. The simplest and most common type of expression is the expression that represents a single value (as opposed to representing a collection of values). NSPredicate supports four types of single-value expressions, as shown in Table 6-1.

Table 6-1. *The Four Types of Single-Value Expressions*

Type	Static Initializer Method	Description
Constant value	+expressionForConstantValue:	Creates an expression to represent the given objec
Evaluated object	+expressionForEvaluatedObject	When the predicate is run in order to decide whether an object should be part of the result, the evaluated object is the object in question. This method creates an expression that represents the object being evaluated for inclusion in the result set.
Key path	+expressionForKeyPath:	Managed objects are Key-Value Coding (KVO) compliant. This method creates an expression tha represents the value for the given key in the evaluated object.
Variable	+expressionForVariable:	A value from the variable bindings dictionary associated with the evaluated object.

Our previous example using the query language had two expressions: name and Jane. The name expression is a key path into the managed object, while the Jane expression is a constant value. Creating the same expressions in code looks like this:

```
NSExpression *exprName = [NSExpression expressionForKeyPath:@"name"];
NSExpression *exprJane = [NSExpression expressionForConstantValue:@"Jane"];
```

Expressions for a Collection

Some comparisons require more than one right-side expression. This is the case, for example, when you want to compare a value against a range of values. In this situation, you need to provide a lower bound value and an upper bound value. Predicates use arrays of expressions to represent multiple values. The following example shows how a range of values is built. First, the expressions representing the single values are created; they are then put into an expression representing the array using the `expressionForAggregate:` method.

```
NSExpression *lower = [NSExpression expressionForConstantValue:[NSNumber➡
numberWithInt:20]];
NSExpression *upper = [NSExpression expressionForConstantValue:[NSNumber➡
numberWithInt:35]];

NSExpression *exprRange = [NSExpression expressionForAggregate:[NSArray➡
arrayWithObjects:lower, upper, nil]];
```

> **Note:** Although the `NSExpression` class provides a way to build an expression from a selector using the `expressionForFunction:arguments:` method, this mechanism is not supported by Core Data.

Comparison Predicates

Expressions aren't predicates by themselves. The other element required is a comparator to evaluate the predicate. Two expressions are compared with each other using the `NSComparisonPredicate` class, which is a subclass of `NSPredicate`. The comparator is a binary operator between a left expression and a right expression. Table 6-2 lists them and describes how `NSComparisonPredicate` uses the left (L) and the right (R) expressions to determine the outcome of the comparison based on the selected type.

Table 6-2. *The Predefined Comparators*

Type	Query Language	Logical Description
NSLessThanPredicateOperatorType	L < R	L less than R.
NSLessThanOrEqualToPredicateOperatorType	L <= R	L less than or equal to R.
NSGreaterThanPredicateOperatorType	L > R	L greater than R.
NSGreaterThanOrEqualToPredicateOperatorType	L >= R	L greater than or equal to R.

(Continued)

Table 6-2. *(Continued)*

Type	Query Language	Logical Description
NSEqualToPredicateOperatorType	L = R	L equals R.
NSNotEqualToPredicateOperatorType	L != R	L different from R.
NSMatchesPredicateOperatorType	L MATCHES R	L matches the R regular expression
NSLikePredicateOperatorType	L LIKE R	L = R where R can contain * wildcards.
NSBeginsWithPredicateOperatorType	L BEGINSWITH R	L starts with R.
NSEndsWithPredicateOperatorType	L ENDSWITH R	L ends with R.
NSInPredicateOperatorType	L IN R	L belongs to the collection R.
NSContainsPredicateOperatorType	L CONTAINS R	L is a collection that contains item R.
NSBetweenPredicateOperatorType	L BETWEEN R	L is a value between the two values of the array R.

> **Note:** NSLikePredicateOperatorType is a simplified version of NSMatchesPredicateOperatorType. While NSMatchesPredicateOperatorType can use complex regular expressions, the NSLikePredicateOperatorType type uses simple wildcard replacement (*) characters. So, name like 'J*n*' would match Jane and John but not Jim.

The name='Jane' predicate could be written in code, without going through the query language, using NSExpression and NSComparisonPredicate:

```
NSExpression *exprName = [NSExpression expressionForKeyPath:@"name"];
NSExpression *exprJane = [NSExpression expressionForConstantValue:@"Jane"];
NSPredicate *predicate = [NSComparisonPredicate predicateWithLeftExpression:exprName➥
rightExpression:exprJane modifier:NSDirectPredicateModifier➥
type:NSEqualToPredicateOperatorType options:0];
```

We could rewrite the readData: method using the predicate object graph rather than the query language, and the output would still be the same. Obviously, most programmers prefer using the query language, but it is a good exercise to see how the query language translates into predicate objects behind the scenes.

```
-(void)readData {
```

```
    NSManagedObjectContext *context = [self managedObjectContext];
    NSEntityDescription *entity = [NSEntityDescription entityForName:@"Person"➥
inManagedObjectContext:context];


    NSFetchRequest *fetchRequest = [[NSFetchRequest alloc] init];
    [fetchRequest setEntity:entity];

    NSExpression *exprName = [NSExpression expressionForKeyPath:@"name"];
    NSExpression *exprJane = [NSExpression expressionForConstantValue:@"Jane"];
    NSPredicate *predicate = [NSComparisonPredicate predicateWithLeftExpression:exprName➥
rightExpression:exprJane modifier:NSDirectPredicateModifier➥
type:NSEqualToPredicateOperatorType options:0];


    [fetchRequest setPredicate:predicate];

    NSArray *persons = [context executeFetchRequest:fetchRequest error:nil];

    for(NSManagedObject *person in persons) {
        NSLog(@"name=%@ age=%@", [person valueForKey:@"name"], [person valueForKey:@"age"]);
    }
    [fetchRequest release];
}
```

Running the application with this version of readData: reveals the same output as before:

```
name=Jane age=26
```

You might have noticed that the fifth argument of the static init method you just used is options. Options are used to modify the behavior of the comparator. Options are not always applicable but are used with the string comparison comparators only. They can also be specified in the query language by appending the option code between square brackets right after the operator. Table 6-3 lists the available options as well as how to use them in the query language.

Table 6-3. *The String Comparison Options*

Option	Code	Description	Query Language Example
NSCaseInsensitivePredicateOption	c	The comparison should not be case sensitive.	"X" =[c] "x"
NSDiacriticInsensitivePredicateOption	d	The comparison should overlook accents.	"é" =[d] "e"

(Continued)

Table 6-3. *(Continued)*

Option	Code	Description	Query Language Example
NSNormalizedPredicateOption	n	Indicates that the operands have been preprocessed (that is, made all the same case, accents removed, and so on), so NSCaseInsensitivePredicateOption and NSDiacriticInsensitivePredicateOption options can be overlooked if specified.	"abc" =[n] "abc"
NSLocaleSensitivePredicateOption	l	Indicates that the comparison should take the current locale into consideration.	"straße" =[l] "strasse"

To specify multiple options, you simply use the binary or (|) operator between them. In the query language, you append the codes together, as shown in the following example:

```
NSPredicate *predicate = [NSPredicate predicateWithFormat:@"name =[cd] 'jàne'"];
```

predicateWithFormat: accepts string formats. So, the previous example could also be written as [NSPredicate predicateWithFormat:@"name =[cd] %@", @"jàne"];

In the event where the right expression is a collection rather than a single object, the modifier can be used to indicate what the right expression is referring to. The modifiers are explained in Table 6-4.

Table 6-4. *The Comparison Predicate Modifiers*

Modifier	Query Language Example	Description
NSDirectPredicateModifier	X	The right expression refers to the given expression itself.
NSAllPredicateModifier	ALL X	The comparator returns true only if the comparison returns TRUE for every object in the collection.
NSAnyPredicateModifier	ANY X	The comparator returns true only if there is at least one object in the collection for which the comparison returns TRUE.

Compound Predicates

We've just looked at a simple example for a predicate that used only one criterion (name = 'Jane'). Predicates are often formed by a logical combination of multiple subpredicates. If we wanted to find all the people where the first name starts with the letter *J* and with an age between 20 and 35, the system should find John, Jane, and Jill, who are 32, 26, and 22 years old, respectively, but not Jim, who is 40 years old. Core Data allows you to build compound predicates using the NSCompoundPredicate class. The compounding operator is one of the three main logic operators: OR, AND, and NOT. Compound predicates can be built from one the three following methods, as shown in Table 6-5.

Table 6-5. *Methods for Creating Compound Predicates*

Method Name	Query Language Example	Description
andPredicateWithSubpredicates:	P1 AND P2 AND P3	Returns TRUE only if all the predicates in the given collection of predicates are TRUE as well
orPredicateWithSubpredicates:	P1 OR P2 OR P3	Returns TRUE only if at least one of the predicates in the given collection of predicates is TRUE
notPredicateWithSubpredicate:	NOT P	Returns TRUE only if the given predicate is FALSE

For this example, you build the predicate manually as follows:

```
NSExpression *exprName = [NSExpression expressionForKeyPath:@"name"];
NSExpression *exprJ = [NSExpression expressionForConstantValue:@"J"];

NSPredicate *p1 = [NSComparisonPredicate predicateWithLeftExpression:exprName➡
rightExpression:exprJ modifier:NSDirectPredicateModifier➡
type:NSBeginsWithPredicateOperatorType options:0];

NSExpression *exprAge = [NSExpression expressionForKeyPath:@"age"];

NSExpression *lower = [NSExpression expressionForConstantValue:[NSNumber➡
numberWithInt:20]];

NSExpression *upper = [NSExpression expressionForConstantValue:[NSNumber➡
numberWithInt:35]];

NSExpression *exprRange = [NSExpression expressionForAggregate:[NSArray➡
arrayWithObjects:lower, upper, nil]];

NSPredicate *p2 = [NSComparisonPredicate predicateWithLeftExpression:exprAge➡
rightExpression:exprRange modifier:NSDirectPredicateModifier➡
type:NSBetweenPredicateOperatorType options:0];

NSPredicate *predicate = [NSCompoundPredicate andPredicateWithSubpredicates:[NSArray➡
arrayWithObjects:p1, p2, nil]];
```

After updating the readData: method with this predicate, running the application yields the following expected output:

```
name=John age=32
name=Jane age=26
name=Jill age=22
```

As shown in Table 6-5, the query language also supports compound predicates using the OR, AND, and NOT operators. The same example could be rewritten more simply using the query language:

```
NSPredicate *predicate = [NSPredicate predicateWithFormat:@"name BEGINSWITH %@ AND age
BETWEEN {%d, %d}", @"J", 20, 35];
```

> **Note:** If you can't figure out the syntax of the query language. You can always build the predicate object graph and then print it to the console using NSLog(@"%@", myPredicate). It will give you the exact syntax to use.

The result of rewriting the readData method with the string-based predicated is shown here. Running it yields the same result, as expected.

```
-(void)readData {
  NSManagedObjectContext *context = [self managedObjectContext];
  NSEntityDescription *entity = [NSEntityDescription entityForName:@"Person"➡
inManagedObjectContext:context];

  NSFetchRequest *fetchRequest = [[NSFetchRequest alloc] init];
  [fetchRequest setEntity:entity];

  NSPredicate *predicate = [NSPredicate predicateWithFormat:@"name BEGINSWITH %@ AND➡
age BETWEEN {%d, %d}", @"J", 20, 35];

  [fetchRequest setPredicate:predicate];

  NSArray *persons = [context executeFetchRequest:fetchRequest error:nil];

  for(NSManagedObject *person in persons) {
    NSLog(@"name=%@ age=%@", [person valueForKey:@"name"], [person valueForKey:@"age"]);
  }
  [fetchRequest release];
}
```

Subqueries

In some cases, you want to find objects based on criteria that pertain to other related objects. For example, you might want to find all the managers who have at least one direct report whose age is 26. According to our test data set, this should return Mary and John since both have 26-year-old direct reports. Without subqueries, you can't fetch this result set directly. Instead, you could do this using two steps where you first fetch all the persons of the right age and then iterate through each of them to find their managers. This solution is shown here:

```objc
-(void)readData {
  NSManagedObjectContext *context = [self managedObjectContext];
  NSEntityDescription *entity = [NSEntityDescription entityForName:@"Person"➦
inManagedObjectContext:context];

  NSFetchRequest *fetchRequest = [[NSFetchRequest alloc] init];
  [fetchRequest setEntity:entity];

  NSPredicate *predicate = [NSPredicate predicateWithFormat:@"age=26"];
  [fetchRequest setPredicate:predicate];

  NSArray *matches = [context executeFetchRequest:fetchRequest error:nil];

  NSMutableArray *persons = [[NSMutableArray alloc] init];
  for(NSManagedObject *obj in matches) {
    [persons addObject:[obj valueForKey:@"manager"]];
  }

  for(NSManagedObject *person in persons) {
    NSLog(@"name=%@ age=%@", [person valueForKey:@"name"], [person valueForKey:@"age"]);
  }

  [persons release];
  [fetchRequest release];
}
```

Subquery expressions provide a way to encapsulate the solution into a single query, eliminating the need to manually post-process the data after retrieving it. Our entire predicate and logic can be replaced with "SUBQUERY(employees, $x, $x.age == 26).@count > 0", which returns true for any person with an employees relationship that has at least one employee who is 26 years old. A subquery iterates through a collection expression (employees in this case) and creates a temporary variable ($x in this example, but name it however you'd like), which takes the value of each item in the collection to evaluate the predicate. The syntax @count returns a count of the items in the collection. We talk more about aggregators later in this chapter. Using this predicate, you can clean up the readData: method:

```objc
-(void)readData {
  NSManagedObjectContext *context = [self managedObjectContext];
  NSEntityDescription *entity = [NSEntityDescription entityForName:@"Person"➦
inManagedObjectContext:context];

  NSFetchRequest *fetchRequest = [[NSFetchRequest alloc] init];
  [fetchRequest setEntity:entity];

  NSPredicate *predicate = [NSPredicate predicateWithFormat:@"(SUBQUERY(employees,➦
$x, $x.age -= %d).@count > 0)", 26];
  [fetchRequest setPredicate:predicate];

  NSArray *persons = [context executeFetchRequest:fetchRequest error:nil];
```

```
    for(NSManagedObject *person in persons) {
        NSLog(@"name=%@ age=%@", [person valueForKey:@"name"], [person valueForKey:@"age"]);
    }
    [fetchRequest release];
}
```

Another way to return the same result would be to use the expression modifier and apply the predicate to any of the evaluated object's employees. The predicate would then look like this: [NSPredicate predicateWithFormat:@"ANY employees.age == %d", 26]. Unfortunately, this kind of logic is risky because it works only with simple predicates. If you had a compound predicate, the logic would be flawed. Imagine, for example, that you wanted to return all the managers who not only have a direct report whose age is 26 years old but also have a name that starts with the letter *T*. According to your test data, this would only match Mary because she has an employee named Tom who is 26 years old. It would no longer match John because although Jane is 26 years old, her name does not start with *T*. If you tried to use the expression modifier ANY, you would write your predicate like this:

```
[NSPredicate predicateWithFormat:@"ANY employees.age == %d AND ANY employees.name BEGINS
WITH %@", 26, @"T"];
```

The resulting readData: method is as follows:

```
-(void)readData {
    NSManagedObjectContext *context = [self managedObjectContext];
    NSEntityDescription *entity = [NSEntityDescription entityForName:@"Person"➥
inManagedObjectContext:context];

    NSFetchRequest *fetchRequest = [[NSFetchRequest alloc] init];
    [fetchRequest setEntity:entity];

    NSPredicate *predicate = [NSPredicate predicateWithFormat:@"ANY employees.age == %d➥
AND ANY employees.name BEGINSWITH %@", 26, @"T"];

    [fetchRequest setPredicate:predicate];

    NSArray *persons = [context executeFetchRequest:fetchRequest error:nil];

    for(NSManagedObject *person in persons) {
        NSLog(@"name=%@ age=%@", [person valueForKey:@"name"], [person valueForKey:@"age"]);
    }
    [fetchRequest release];
}
```

Running the test yields the following output, which is wrong:

```
name=John age=32
name=Mary age=36
```

The problem you run into is that John has two employees: Jane, age 26, and Tim, age 22. Jane matches the criterion for age, and Tim matches the criterion for the first letter in the name. The problem is that we want the ANY modifier to encapsulate both conditions instead of ANY one and ANY the other. This negative example illustrates why subqueries are a more adapted tool for this problem. The following implementation of `readData:` shows how to use the subquery with the compounded predicate:

```
-(void)readData {
  NSManagedObjectContext *context = [self managedObjectContext];
  NSEntityDescription *entity = [NSEntityDescription entityForName:@"Person"➥
inManagedObjectContext:context];

  NSFetchRequest *fetchRequest = [[NSFetchRequest alloc] init];
  [fetchRequest setEntity:entity];

  NSPredicate *predicate = [NSPredicate predicateWithFormat:@"(SUBQUERY(employees,➥
$x, $x.age == %d and $x.name BEGINSWITH %@).@count > 0)", 26, @"T"];
  [fetchRequest setPredicate:predicate];

  NSArray *persons = [context executeFetchRequest:fetchRequest error:nil];

  for(NSManagedObject *person in persons) {
    NSLog(@"name=%@ age=%@", [person valueForKey:@"name"], [person valueForKey:@"age"]);
  }
  [fetchRequest release];
}
```

This time, it yields the correct output:

```
name=Mary age=36
```

Aggregating

When we think about aggregating data, we think about gathering a global statistic on a collection. This was the case in the previous example where we wanted to know how many items there were in the collection returned by the subquery. Collection operators are part of the Key-Value Coding paradigm. They can be embedded in a key path to signify that an aggregation operation should be executed. Figure 6-3 shows the general syntax for collection operators.

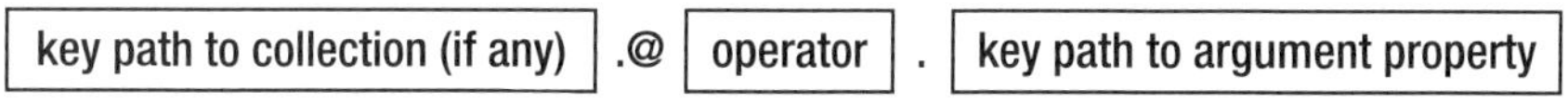

| key path to collection (if any) | .@ | operator | . | key path to argument property |

Figure 6-3. *The syntax of collection operators*

You currently cannot define your own custom operators, but the most common are already available by default, as shown in Table 6-6.

Table 6-6. *The Comparison Predicate Modifiers*

Operator	Description
avg	Computes the average of the argument property in the collection
count	Computes the number of items in the collection (does not need an argument property)
min	Computes the minimum value of the argument property in the collection
max	Computes the maximum value of the argument property in the collection
sum	Computes the sum value of the argument property in the collection

Let's play around with these operators. Go back to your test data, and this time you want to return any managers whose direct reports' average age is 24 years old. The result from your query should contain only John, since Jane is 26 and Tim is 22. Using the avg operator, the predicate is surprisingly simple:

```
"employees.@avg.age = 24"
```

Replace the readData: method with the following implementation:

```
-(void)readData {
  NSManagedObjectContext *context = [self managedObjectContext];
  NSEntityDescription *entity = [NSEntityDescription entityForName:@"Person"➡
inManagedObjectContext:context];

  NSFetchRequest *fetchRequest = [[NSFetchRequest alloc] init];
  [fetchRequest setEntity:entity];

  NSPredicate *predicate = [NSPredicate predicateWithFormat:@"employees.@avg.age = ➡
%d", 24];
  [fetchRequest setPredicate:predicate];

  NSArray *persons = [context executeFetchRequest:fetchRequest error:nil];

  for(NSManagedObject *person in persons) {
    NSLog(@"name=%@ age=%@", [person valueForKey:@"name"], [person valueForKey:@"age"]);
  }
  [fetchRequest release];
}
```

Running this code returns John, as expected.

The other operators work the same way. To pull, for example, all managers whose youngest direct report is 22 years old, use the min operator and construct a predicate like this:

```
NSPredicate *predicate = [NSPredicate predicateWithFormat:@"employees.@min.age = %d"➡
, 22];
```

This predicate returns John, who has Tim (age 22) working for him, and Tim, who has Jill (age 22) working for him:

```
name=John age=32
name=Tim age=22
```

The one operator that behaves somewhat differently is the count operator, which doesn't take an argument property. To pull all managers, for example, that have exactly one direct report, use this predicate:

```
NSPredicate *predicate = [NSPredicate predicateWithFormat:@"employees.@count = %d", 1];
```

This pulls only Mary, who has only one employee, Tom, reporting to her, as the Debugging Console shows:

```
name=Mary age=36
```

Sorting

Sorting is the operation of ordering the resulting data set based on some criteria. Let's imagine we want to find all the people whose managers' names contain the letter *M*, but we want to sort the result set by age.

Returning Unsorted Data

Using the data set you just set up in the previous section, your query should return Mary's employee (Tom) and Tim's employees (Kate, Jim, and Jill). For such an example, the readData: method would look as follows:

```
-(void)readData {
  NSManagedObjectContext *context = [self managedObjectContext];
  NSEntityDescription *entity = [NSEntityDescription entityForName:@"Person"➡
inManagedObjectContext:context];

  NSFetchRequest *fetchRequest = [[NSFetchRequest alloc] init];
  [fetchRequest setEntity:entity];

  NSPredicate *predicate = [NSPredicate predicateWithFormat:@"manager.name ➡
CONTAINS[c] %@", @"m"];
  [fetchRequest setPredicate:predicate];

  NSArray *persons = [context executeFetchRequest:fetchRequest error:nil];

  for(NSManagedObject *person in persons) {
    NSLog(@"name=%@ age=%@", [person valueForKey:@"name"], [person valueForKey:@"age"]);
  }
  [fetchRequest release];
}
```

Replace the existing readData: method with the code listed earlier, and rerun the application. In Xcode's Debugger Console, you should see this output (with each line preceded by date, time, and application information, deleted here), with the objects in no particular order:

```
name=Jill age=22
name=Jim age=40
name=Kate age=40
name=Tom age=26
```

Sorting Data on One Criterion

In many cases, especially when dealing with user interfaces, sorting the data provides value, whether to make it more visually appealing or to make data easier to find. This is where NSSortDescriptor comes into play. Using this class, you can specify sort orders in a manner similar to what you would do in SQL using the ORDER BY keyword. If you wanted your result sorted by age, alter the readData: method to include a sort descriptor:

```
-(void)readData {
  NSManagedObjectContext *context = [self managedObjectContext];
  NSEntityDescription *entity = [NSEntityDescription entityForName:@"Person"➥
inManagedObjectContext:context];

  NSFetchRequest *fetchRequest = [[NSFetchRequest alloc] init];
  [fetchRequest setEntity:entity];

  NSPredicate *predicate = [NSPredicate predicateWithFormat:@"manager.name➥
CONTAINS[c] %@", @"m"];
  [fetchRequest setPredicate:predicate];

  NSSortDescriptor *sortDescriptorByAge = [[NSSortDescriptor alloc] initWithKey:@"age"➥
ascending:YES];

  NSArray *sortDescriptors = [[NSArray alloc] initWithObjects:sortDescriptorByAge, nil];
  [fetchRequest setSortDescriptors:sortDescriptors];
  [sortDescriptorByAge release];

  NSArray *persons = [context executeFetchRequest:fetchRequest error:nil];

  for(NSManagedObject *person in persons) {
    NSLog(@"name=%@ age=%@", [person valueForKey:@"name"], [person valueForKey:@"age"]);
  }
  [sortDescriptors release];
  [fetchRequest release];
}
```

Again, replace the readData: method in OrgChartAppDelegate.m with the code listed earlier and run the application. This time, the output comes back sorted by age. Note that Jim and Kate have the same age, 40, so your output could have them reversed. Either way, your output should look similar to this:

```
name=Jill age=22
name=Tom age=26
name=Kate age=40
```

```
name=Jim age=40
```

Just like some expressions in a predicate, sort descriptors also rely on key paths to specify the property to use when sorting. The second attribute of the initWithKey:ascending method specifies whether the order should be ascending or descending. Changing this value has the effect of reversing the order.

Sorting on Multiple Criteria

You can also add additional sorting criteria to obtain a multilevel sort. For example, you might want to sort the data by age, and if multiple ages are the same, use a complementary sort order such as alphabetically arranging the names. This would remove the arbitrary return order of Jim and Kate in the previous example. You may have noticed that the setSortDescriptors: expects an array of sort descriptors. Adding a secondary sort level is simply a matter of adding another sort descriptor to the array:

```
-(void)readData {
  NSManagedObjectContext *context = [self managedObjectContext];
  NSEntityDescription *entity = [NSEntityDescription entityForName:@"Person"➥
inManagedObjectContext:context];


  NSFetchRequest *fetchRequest = [[NSFetchRequest alloc] init];
  [fetchRequest setEntity:entity];


  NSPredicate *predicate = [NSPredicate predicateWithFormat:@"manager.name ➥
CONTAINS[c] %@", @"m"];
  [fetchRequest setPredicate:predicate];


  NSSortDescriptor *sortDescriptorByAge = [[NSSortDescriptor alloc] initWithKey:@"age"➥
ascending:YES];
  NSSortDescriptor *sortDescriptorByName = [[NSSortDescriptor alloc] initWithKey:➥
@"name" ascending:YES];
  NSArray *sortDescriptors = [[NSArray alloc] initWithObjects:sortDescriptorByAge,➥
sortDescriptorByName, nil];


  [sortDescriptorByAge release];
  [sortDescriptorByName release];
  [fetchRequest setSortDescriptors:sortDescriptors];


  NSArray *persons = [context executeFetchRequest:fetchRequest error:nil];


  for(NSManagedObject *person in persons) {
    NSLog(@"name=%@ age=%@", [person valueForKey:@"name"], [person valueForKey:@"age"]);
  }
  [sortDescriptors release];
  [fetchRequest release];
}
```

Since Kate and Jim have the same age but Kate comes after Jim in alphabetical order, the output changes from an arbitrary order to a deterministic one.

```
name=Jill age=22
name=Tom age=26
name=Jim age=40
name=Kate age=40
```

You can verify that you control the order of Jim's and Kate's names by changing the `sortDescriptorByName` instance to sort descending by passing NO to the ascending parameter, like this:

```
NSSortDescriptor *sortDescriptorByName = [[NSSortDescriptor alloc] initWithKey:@"name"
ascending:NO];
```

The resulting output confirms that Kate now comes before Jim:

```
name=Jill age=22
name=Tom age=26
name=Kate age=40
name=Jim age=40
```

Summary

Dumping an entire data set on someone overwhelms them and prevents them from finding what they're looking for. AutoTrader.com recognizes this and uses its ability to filter results as a marketing ploy to attract customers. You should recognize this, too, as you build Core Data applications. Use the information presented in this chapter to sort, filter, and aggregate results so that you can narrow your data into what users seek.

Chapter 7

Tuning Performance and Memory Usage

In this computer age, people have grown to hate hourglasses, spinning beach balls, and pop-ups that say, "Please Wait." Although giving a visual clue that the computer is working beats giving no such clue and letting customers think their computers have locked up, better still would be to never have episodes of slowness that make users wait. You may not always be able to achieve that goal, but you should always try.

Fetching and storing data in a persistent store can take a long time, especially when a lot of data is involved. This chapter helps assure you that you understand how Core Data helps you, and how you must help yourself, to make sure you don't pepper your users with "Please Wait" spinners or, worse, an unresponsive application that appears locked up while it retrieves or saves large object graphs. We show you how to utilize the various tools and strategies, such as caching, faulting, and using the Instruments application that comes with Xcode.

Building the Application for Testing

You need a way to perform all this performance testing so that you can verify results. This section walks you through building an application that will allow you to run various tests and see the results. The application presents a list of tests you can run in a standard picker view. To run a test, select it in the picker, click the Run Selected Test button, and wait for the results. After the test runs, you'll see the start time, the stop time, the number of elapsed seconds for the test, and some text describing the results of the test.

Creating the Core Data Project

Start by creating a new view-based application with the Product option set to iPhone. Call it **PerformanceTuning**, and add the Core Data framework. In your application delegate (`PerformanceTuningApplicationDelegate`), add a managed object context, a managed object model, and a persistent store coordinator. See Listing 7-1 for guidance on `PerformanceTuningApplicationDelegate.h`, and see Listing 7-2 for guidance on `PerformanceTuningApplicationDelegate.m`.

Listing 7-1. *PerformanceTuningApplicationDelegate.h*

```
#import <UIKit/UIKit.h>
#import <CoreData/CoreData.h>

@class PerformanceTuningViewController;

@interface PerformanceTuningAppDelegate : NSObject <UIApplicationDelegate> {
  UIWindow *window;
  PerformanceTuningViewController *viewController;

@private
  NSManagedObjectContext *managedObjectContext_;
  NSManagedObjectModel *managedObjectModel_;
  NSPersistentStoreCoordinator *persistentStoreCoordinator_;
}
@property (nonatomic, retain) IBOutlet UIWindow *window;
@property (nonatomic, retain) IBOutlet PerformanceTuningViewController *viewController;
@property (nonatomic, retain, readonly) NSManagedObjectContext *managedObjectContext;
@property (nonatomic, retain, readonly) NSManagedObjectModel *managedObjectModel;
@property (nonatomic, retain, readonly) NSPersistentStoreCoordinator➡
*persistentStoreCoordinator;


@end
```

Listing 7-2. *PerformanceTuningApplicationDelegate.m*

```
#import "PerformanceTuningAppDelegate.h"
#import "PerformanceTuningViewController.h"

@implementation PerformanceTuningAppDelegate

@synthesize window;
@synthesize viewController;

- (BOOL)application:(UIApplication *)application➡
didFinishLaunchingWithOptions:(NSDictionary *)launchOptions {

  [window addSubview:viewController.view];
  [window makeKeyAndVisible];
  return YES;
```

```objc
}

- (void)applicationWillTerminate:(UIApplication *)application {
}

#pragma mark -
#pragma mark Core Data stack
- (NSManagedObjectModel *)managedObjectModel {
  if (managedObjectModel_ != nil) {
    return managedObjectModel_;
  }
  managedObjectModel_ = [[NSManagedObjectModel mergedModelFromBundles:nil] retain];
  return managedObjectModel_;
}

- (NSPersistentStoreCoordinator *)persistentStoreCoordinator {
  if (persistentStoreCoordinator_ != nil) {
    return persistentStoreCoordinator_;
  }

  NSString* dir = [NSSearchPathForDirectoriesInDomains(NSDocumentDirectory,➡
NSUserDomainMask, YES) lastObject];

  NSURL *storeURL = [NSURL fileURLWithPath: [dir stringByAppendingPathComponent:➡
@"PerformanceTuning.sqlite"]];

  NSError *error = nil;
  persistentStoreCoordinator_ = [[NSPersistentStoreCoordinator alloc]➡
initWithManagedObjectModel:[self managedObjectModel]];

  if (![persistentStoreCoordinator_ addPersistentStoreWithType:NSSQLiteStoreType➡
configuration:nil URL:storeURL options:nil error:&error]) {

    NSLog(@"Unresolved error %@, %@", error, [error userInfo]);
    abort();
  }

  return persistentStoreCoordinator_;
}

- (NSManagedObjectContext *)managedObjectContext {
  if (managedObjectContext_ != nil) {
    return managedObjectContext_;
  }

  NSPersistentStoreCoordinator *coordinator = [self persistentStoreCoordinator];
  if (coordinator != nil) {
    managedObjectContext_ = [[NSManagedObjectContext alloc] init];
    [managedObjectContext_ setPersistentStoreCoordinator:coordinator];
  }
  return managedObjectContext_;
}

- (void)dealloc {
  [window release];
```

```
    [viewController release];
    [super dealloc];
}

@end
```

Creating the Data Model and Data

The data model for this performance-testing application consists of three entities: Actor, Movie, and Studio. Actor and Movie have a many-to-many relationship, and Movie and Studio have a many-to-many relationship. Each entity has two attributes: name, of type String, and rating, of type Integer 16. Create your data model by selecting **File ➤ New File...** from the Xcode menu and then selecting Resource on the left and Data Model on the right. Call it PerformanceTuning.xcdatamodel, and save it in the Resources group. Create entities for Actor, Movie, and Studio; give them each attributes called name of type String and rating of type Integer 16; and create optional to-many relationships between Actor and Movie and between Movie and Studio. Your completed data model should look like Figure 7-1.

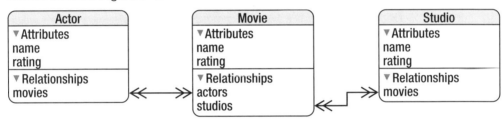

Figure 7-1. *The performance-tuning data model*

Now that you've completed your data model, it's time to stuff data into it. You want enough data to be able to do performance testing and differentiate between results, so the plan is to create 200 actors, 200 movies, and 200 studios and then to relate each actor to each movie, and vice versa, and to relate each movie to each studio, and vice versa. When you're done, you'll have three tables with 200 rows each (Actor, Movie, and Studio) and two join tables with 40,000 rows each (Actor-to-Movie and Movie-to-Studio).

To insert the data, open the PerformanceTuningAppDelegate.h file, and declare two methods: one that loads the data into the persistent data store and the other that acts as a helper method to create an entity. The helper method takes two strings: the name of the entity to create and the value for the name attribute. For the rating attribute, the helper will insert a random number between one and ten. Your two method declarations should look like this:

```
- (void)loadData;
- (NSManagedObject *)insertObjectForName:(NSString *)entityName withName:(NSString➡
*)name;
```

Now, open `PerformanceTuningAppDelegate.m`, and define those methods. The helper method creates the object within the specified entity type and then sets the value for the name attribute. It looks like this:

```
- (NSManagedObject *)insertObjectForName:(NSString *)entityName withName:(NSString
*)name {
  NSManagedObjectContext *context = [self managedObjectContext];
  NSManagedObject *object = [NSEntityDescription➡
insertNewObjectForEntityForName:entityName inManagedObjectContext:context];

  [object setValue:name forKey:@"name"];
  [object setValue:[NSNumber numberWithInteger:((arc4random() % 10) + 1)]➡
forKey:@"rating"];

  return object;
}
```

The method to load the data, `loadData:`, first checks the persistent store to determine whether the data have already been loaded so that subsequent runs of the program don't take several minutes to launch. If the data have not been created, it creates 200 actors with names like `Actor 1`, `Actor 2`, and so on; 200 movies named like `Movie 1`; and 200 studios with names like `Studio 1`. After creating all the objects, the code loops through all the movies and adds relationships to all the actors and to all the studios. Finally, `loadData:` saves the object graph to the persistent data store. See Listing 7-3 for the complete implementation of the `loadData` method.

Listing 7-3. *The loadData Method*

```
- (void)loadData {
  // Pull the movies. If we have 200, assume our db is set up.
  NSManagedObjectContext *context = [self managedObjectContext];
  NSFetchRequest *request = [[NSFetchRequest alloc] init];
  [request setEntity:[NSEntityDescription entityForName:@"Movie"➡
inManagedObjectContext:context]];

  NSArray *results = [context executeFetchRequest:request error:nil];
  if ([results count] != 200) {
    // Add 200 actors, movies, and studios
    for (int i = 1; i <= 200; i++) {
      [self insertObjectForName:@"Actor" withName:[NSString stringWithFormat:➡
@"Actor %d", i]];
      [self insertObjectForName:@"Movie" withName:[NSString stringWithFormat:➡
@"Movie %d", i]];
      [self insertObjectForName:@"Studio" withName:[NSString stringWithFormat:➡
@"Studio %d", i]];
    }

    // Relate all the actors and all the studios to all the movies
    NSManagedObjectContext *context = [self managedObjectContext];
    NSFetchRequest *request = [[NSFetchRequest alloc] init];
    [request setEntity:[NSEntityDescription entityForName:@"Movie"➡
inManagedObjectContext:context]];

    NSArray *results = [context executeFetchRequest:request error:nil];
    for (NSManagedObject *movie in results) {
```

```
        [request setEntity:[NSEntityDescription entityForName:@"Actor"➡
inManagedObjectContext:context]];

        NSArray *actors = [context executeFetchRequest:request error:nil];
        NSMutableSet *set = [movie mutableSetValueForKey:@"actors"];
        [set addObjectsFromArray:actors];

        [request setEntity:[NSEntityDescription entityForName:@"Studio"➡
inManagedObjectContext:context]];

        NSArray *studios = [context executeFetchRequest:request error:nil];
        set = [movie mutableSetValueForKey:@"studios"];
        [set addObjectsFromArray:studios];
    }
  }
  [request release];

  NSError *error = nil;
  if (![context save:&error]) {
    NSLog(@"Unresolved error %@, %@", error, [error userInfo]);
    abort();
  }
}
```

Go to the `application:didFinishLaunchingWithOptions:` method, and add a call to your `loadData:` method before it displays the window and view so it looks like this:

```
- (BOOL)application:(UIApplication *)application➡
didFinishLaunchingWithOptions:(NSDictionary *)launchOptions {
  [self loadData];
  [window addSubview:viewController.view];
  [window makeKeyAndVisible];
  return YES;
}
```

Build and run the program to create your persistent data store.

Creating the Testing View

The application you're building will present a picker with a list of tests you can run and a button to launch the selected test. It will list the start time, the stop time, and the elapsed time for the test, as well as a string describing the results of the test. Start creating this user interface by opening the `PerformanceTuningViewController.h` file, declaring that it implements the protocols for your picker view, declaring fields for your user interface elements, and declaring a method to be called when someone clicks the Run Selected Test button. Listing 7-4 contains the contents of `PerformanceTuningViewController.h`.

Listing 7-4. *PerformanceTuningViewController.h*

```
#import <UIKit/UIKit.h>

@interface PerformanceTuningViewController : UIViewController <UIPickerViewDataSource,
UIPickerViewDelegate> {
```

```
    IBOutlet UILabel *startTime;
    IBOutlet UILabel *stopTime;
    IBOutlet UILabel *elapsedTime;
    IBOutlet UITextView *results;
    IBOutlet UIPickcrView *testPicker;
}
@property (nonatomic, retain) UILabel *startTime;
@property (nonatomic, retain) UILabel *stopTime;
@property (nonatomic, retain) UILabel *elapsedTime;
@property (nonatomic, retain) UITextView *results;
@property (nonatomic, retain) UIPickerView *testPicker;

- (IBAction)runTest:(id)sender;

@end
```

In `PerformanceTuningViewController.m`, add `@synthesize` directives for your fields, stub implementations for the picker view protocols you promised to implement, and a stub implementation for `runTest:`

```
@synthesize startTime, stopTime, elapsedTime, results, testPicker;

#pragma mark -
#pragma mark UIPickerViewDataSource methods

- (NSInteger)numberOfComponentsInPickerView:(UIPickerView *)pickerView {
    return 1;
}

- (NSInteger)pickerView:(UIPickerView *)pickerView➥
numberOfRowsInComponent:(NSInteger)component {

    return 1;
}

#pragma mark -
#pragma mark UIPickerViewDelegate methods

- (NSString *)pickerView:(UIPickerView *)pickerView titleForRow:(NSInteger)row➥
forComponent:(NSInteger)component {

    return @"Test";
}

#pragma mark -
#pragma mark Run the test
- (IBAction)runTest:(id)sender {
}
```

Open the `PerformanceTuningViewController.xib` file, and start building the view. You want labels for Start Time, Stop Time, and Elapsed, as well as right-aligned labels to store the actual start time, stop time, and elapsed. You want a Text View to store the results of any test that runs. You want a button for launching a test, and finally you want a picker view to show the available tests. Drag all those items to the screen, and arrange them so they look like Figure 7-2.

Figure 7-2. *Building the view in Interface Builder*

The next step is to wire all the controls to the fields you created in the PerformanceTuningViewController class. Ctrl+drag from the File's Owner icon to each of the labels for start time, stop time, and elapsed time, and pick the appropriate outlet for each. Ctrl+drag from File's Owner to the Text View, and select results. Ctrl+drag from File's Owner to the picker view, select testPicker, and then Ctrl+drag twice from the picker view back to File's Owner: the first time select dataSource, and the second time select delegate. You'll know if you forget to do this, because the picker view won't appear when you run your application. Finally, Ctrl+drag from the Run Selected Test button to File's Owner, and select runTest: from the pop-up. Save everything, build your application, and run it. You should see something that looks like Figure 7-3.

Figure 7-3. *The first run of the performance-tuning application*

Building the Testing Framework

The approach for adding tests for the performance testing application to run is to create an Objective-C protocol called `PerformanceTest` and then create an array of tests that all implement that protocol. The application will display the names of the tests in the picker view and execute the selected test when the user taps the Run Selected Test button. The protocol, then, requires two methods:

- One to return the name of the test for display in the picker view
- One to execute the selected test in the application's managed object context

To keep the project organized, create a new group under Classes (Ctrl+click Classes and select **Add ➤ New Group** from the pop-up menu), and call it **Tests**. The tests you add throughout this chapter will go in this group. To create the protocol, select **File ➤ New File...**, select Cocoa Touch Class on the left and Objective-C protocol on the right, and click Next. Call the protocol `PerformanceTest.h`, and put it in the Tests group. Open `PerformanceTest.h`, and modify it to match Listing 7-5.

Listing 7-5. *PerformanceTest.h*

```
#import <CoreData/CoreData.h>

@protocol PerformanceTest

- (NSString *)name;
- (NSString *)runWithContext:(NSManagedObjectContext *)context;

@end
```

Before integrating the testing framework into the application, create a test—a "test" test, if you will—so that you have something to both see in the picker view and run. The first test you create will retrieve all the movies, actors, and studios from the persistent store. Create a new class called `FetchAllMoviesActorsAndStudiosTest`, and add it to the Tests group you just created. Listing 7-6 shows the header file, and Listing 7-7 shows the implementation file. Modify your files to look like these.

Listing 7-6. *FetchAllMoviesActorsAndStudiosTest.h*

```
#import <Foundation/Foundation.h>
#import "PerformanceTest.h"

@interface FetchAllMoviesActorsAndStudiosTest : NSObject <PerformanceTest> {

}

@end
```

Listing 7-7. *FetchAllMoviesActorsAndStudiosTest.m*

```
#import <CoreData/CoreData.h>
#import "FetchAllMoviesActorsAndStudiosTest.h"

@implementation FetchAllMoviesActorsAndStudiosTest

- (NSString *)name {
  return @"Fetch all test";
}

- (NSString *)runWithContext:(NSManagedObjectContext *)context {
  NSFetchRequest *request = [[NSFetchRequest alloc] init];
  [request setEntity:[NSEntityDescription entityForName:@"Movie"➥
inManagedObjectContext:context]];

  NSArray *results = [context executeFetchRequest:request error:nil];
  int actorsRead = 0, studiosRead = 0;
  for (NSManagedObject *movie in results) {
    actorsRead += [[movie valueForKey:@"actors"] count];
    studiosRead += [[movie valueForKey:@"studios"] count];
```

```
    [context refreshObject:movie mergeChanges:NO];
  }
  [request release];
  return [NSString stringWithFormat:@"Fetched %d actors and %d studios", actorsRead,➡
studiosRead];

}

@end
```

Adding the Testing Framework to the Application

Now you must modify the view controller to use the testing framework. Open
PerformanceTuningViewController.h, and add an instance of NSArray to hold the tests.
Listing 7-8 shows the updated version of the file with the lines to add in bold. Save the
file, and move on to PerformanceTuningViewController.m.

Listing 7-8. *PerformanceTuningViewController.h*

```
#import <UIKit/UIKit.h>

@interface PerformanceTuningViewController : UIViewController <UIPickerViewDataSource,
UIPickerViewDelegate> {
  IBOutlet UILabel *startTime;
  IBOutlet UILabel *stopTime;
  IBOutlet UILabel *elapsedTime;
  IBOutlet UITextView *results;
  IBOutlet UIPickerView *testPicker;
  NSArray *tests;
}
@property (nonatomic, retain) UILabel *startTime;
@property (nonatomic, retain) UILabel *stopTime;
@property (nonatomic, retain) UILabel *elapsedTime;
@property (nonatomic, retain) UITextView *results;
@property (nonatomic, retain) UIPickerView *testPicker;
@property (nonatomic, retain) NSArray *tests;

- (IBAction)runTest:(id)sender;

@end
```

In PerformanceTuningViewController.m, add the new tests member to your @synthesize
line, which now looks like this:

```
@synthesize startTime, stopTime, elapsedTime, results, testPicker, tests;
```

Add the following import statements to support the changes you're going to make to
allow your new test, and the subsequent tests you build in this chapter, to run:

```
#import "PerformanceTuningAppDelegate.h"
#import "PerformanceTest.h"
#import "FetchAllMoviesActorsAndStudiosTest.h"
```

Now, create a `viewDidLoad:` method that blanks out the fields that tests will fill in after they run and adds the new test to the `tests` array. Your implementation should match this:

```
- (void)viewDidLoad {
    [super viewDidLoad];

    startTime.text = @"";
    stopTime.text = @"";
    elapsedTime.text = @"";
    results.text = @"";

    FetchAllMoviesActorsAndStudiosTest *famaasTest =➡
[[FetchAllMoviesActorsAndStudiosTest alloc] init];

    self.tests = [[NSArray alloc] initWithObjects:famaasTest, nil];
    [famaasTest release];
}
```

Also, be sure to call `[tests release]` in your `dealloc:` method.

Since you still have only one component to show in the picker view, you can leave the `numberOfComponentsInPickerView:` method alone and continue to allow it to return 1. Your `pickerView:numberOfRowsInComponent:` method, however, should return the number of tests in your `tests` array:

```
- (NSInteger)pickerView:(UIPickerView *)pickerView➡
numberOfRowsInComponent:(NSInteger)component {
    return [self.tests count];
}
```

The `pickerView:titleForRow:forComponent:` method allows you to use your new `PerformanceTest` protocol. This method should retrieve the test for the corresponding row from the `tests` array and return the name for the test so the picker view displays this name. The method should now look like this:

```
- (NSString *)pickerView:(UIPickerView *)pickerView titleForRow:(NSInteger)row➡
forComponent:(NSInteger)component {
    id <PerformanceTest> test = [self.tests objectAtIndex:row];
    return [test name];
}
```

Finally, you must instruct the `runTest:` method to do the following:

1. Get the managed object context from the application delegate.

2. Determine which test is selected.

3. Get the start time.

4. Run the selected test.

5. Get the stop time.

6. Update the fields with the times and results.

That implementation looks like this:

```
- (IBAction)runTest:(id)sender {
  PerformanceTuningAppDelegate *delegate = (PerformanceTuningAppDelegate➥
*)[[UIApplication sharedApplication] delegate];

  NSManagedObjectContext *context = [delegate managedObjectContext];
  id <PerformanceTest> test = [self.tests objectAtIndex:[testPicker➥
selectedRowInComponent:0]];

  NSDate *start = [NSDate date];
  results.text = [test runWithContext:context];
  NSDate *stop  = [NSDate date];

  startTime.text = [start description];
  stopTime.text = [stop description];
  elapsedTime.text = [NSString stringWithFormat:@"%.03f seconds", [stop➥
timeIntervalSinceDate:start]];
}
```

You have completed the performance-tuning application—for now. As you work through this chapter, you will add tests to cover the scenarios you read about.

Running Your First Test

Build and run the application. One important thing to note is that you're loading a lot of data into the managed object context and stressing the memory handling of iOS. You will likely see some instability in the application throughout the chapter if you run a few tests in a row. When the application crashes, simply restart it and carry on.

When you run the application, you should see the iPhone Simulator with the screen shown in Figure 7-4. The only test you've created so far, "Fetch all test," stands alone in the picker view, selected and ready for you to run. Click the Run Selected Test button, and wait. Be patient. We didn't add any spinners or progress indicators or any feedback mechanisms to the user interface while it runs, so all you'll see for a few moments is that the button turns blue and stays that way, but the test will eventually complete, and you'll see something like Figure 7-5. You can see in Figure 7-5 that the test took 1.312 seconds to run on our machine.

Figure 7-4. *The performance-tuning application with a single test available*

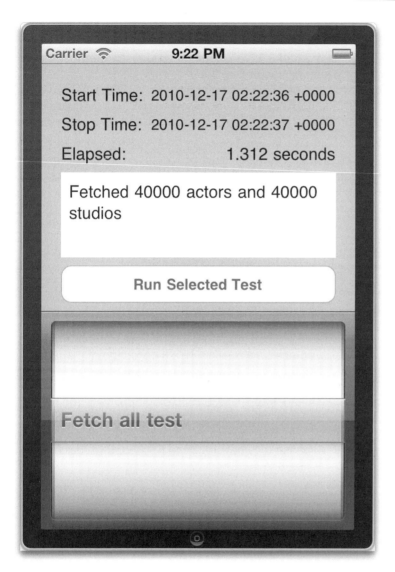

Figure 7-5. *The performance-tuning application after running a test*

The rest of this chapter explains the various performance considerations imposed by Core Data on iOS and the devices it runs on. As you learn these performance considerations, you'll add new tests to the application you built in this section. Feel free to add your own tests as well so that you always give the users of your applications the best possible experience.

Faulting

When you run SQL queries against a database, you know the depth and range of the data you're pulling. You know if you're joining tables, you know the columns you're pulling back, and, if you're careful, you can limit the number of rows you yank from the database into working memory. You may have to work harder to get data than you do with Core Data, but you have more control. You know about how much memory you're using to hold the data you fetch.

With Core Data, however, you've given up some amount of control in exchange for ease of use. With the Shapes application from Chapter 5, for example, each `Polygon` instance had a collection of vertices, which you accessed in an object-oriented, not a data-oriented, way. You didn't have to care whether Core Data pulled the vertex data from the database when the application started, when the polygon was loaded, or when you first accessed the vertices. Core Data cares, however, and attempts to delay loading data from the persistent store into the object graph until necessary, reducing both fetch time and memory usage. It does this using what's termed *faults*.

Think of a fault like a symlink on a Unix file system, which is not the actual file it points to nor does it contain the file's data. The symlink represents the file, though, and when called upon can get to the file and its data, just as if it were the file itself. Like a symlink, a fault is a placeholder that can get to the persistent store's data. A fault can represent either a managed object or, when it represents a relationship, a collection of managed objects. As a link to or a shadow of the data, a fault occupies much less memory than the actual data does. See Figure 7-6 for a depiction of a managed object and a fault. In this case, the managed object is an instance of Shape, and the fault points to the related collection of Vertex objects. The Shape is boldly depicted, representing the fact that it has been fetched from the persistent store and resides in memory. The vertices, however, are faint and grayed out, because they haven't been fetched from the persistent store and do not reside in memory.

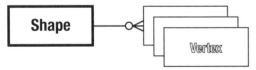

Figure 7-6. *A shape and its faulted vertices*

Firing Faults

Core Data uses the term *firing faults* when it must pull the data from the persistent store that a fault points to and then put it into memory. Core Data has "fired" off a request to fetch data from the data store, and the fault has been "fired" from its job to represent the actual data. You cause a fault to fire any time you request a managed object's persistent data, whether through `valueForKey:` or through methods of a custom class that either return or access the object's persistent data. Methods that access a managed object's metadata and not any of the data stored in the persistent store don't fire a fault. This means you can query a managed object's class, hash, description, entity, and object ID, among other things, and not cause a fault to fire. For the complete

list of which methods don't fire a fault, see Apple's documentation at
`http://developer.apple.com/library/ios/#documentation/Cocoa/Conceptual/CoreData`
`/Articles/cdPerformance.html` under the section Faulting Behavior.

Explicitly asking a managed object for its persistent data causes a fault to fire, but so
does calling any methods or constructs that access persistent data from a managed
object. You can, for example, access a collection through a managed object's
relationships without causing a fault to fire. Sorting the collection, however, will fire a
fault because any logical sorting will sort by some of the object's persistent data. The
test you build later in this section demonstrates this behavior.

Faulting and Caching

We fibbed a bit when we said that firing faults fetches data from the persistent store.
That's often true, but before Core Data treks all the way to the persistent store to
retrieve data, it first checks its cache for the data it seeks. If Core Data finds its intended
data in the cache, it pulls the data from cache and skips the longer trip to the persistent
store. The sections "Caching" and "Expiring" discuss caching in more detail.

Refaulting

One way to take control of your application's persistent data and memory use is to turn
managed objects back into faults, thereby relinquishing the memory its data was
occupying. You turn objects back into faults by calling the managed object context's
`refreshObject:mergeChanges:` method, passing the object you want to fault and NO for
the `mergeChanges:` parameter. If, for example, I had a managed object called `foo` that I
wanted to turn back into a fault, I would use code similar to this:

```
[context refreshObject:foo mergeChanges:NO];
```

After this call, `foo` is now a fault, and `[foo isFault]` returns YES. If you look at the code
for the test we wrote previously, you'll see a call within the loop that iterates over all
`movie` instances to turn each `movie` instance back into a fault:

```
[context refreshObject:movie mergeChanges:NO];
```

Understanding the `mergeChanges:` parameter is important. Passing NO, as the previous
code does, throws away any changed data that has not yet been saved to the persistent
store. Take care when doing this because you lose all data changes in this object you're
faulting, and all the objects to which the faulted object relates are released. If any of the
relationships have changed and the context is then saved, your faulted object is out of
sync with its relationships, and you have created data integrity issues in your persistent
store.

> **Note:** Because faulting an object by calling `refreshObject:mergeChanges:NO` releases relationships, you can use this to prune your object graph in memory. Faulting a movie in the PerformanccTuning application, for example, would release its 200 related actors and 200 related studios.

Passing `YES` to `mergeChanges:` doesn't fault the object. Instead, it reloads all the object's persistent data from the persistent store (or the last cached state) and then reapplies any changes that existed before the call to `refreshObject:` that have not yet been saved.

When you turn a managed object into a fault, Core Data sends two messages to the managed object:

- `willTurnIntoFault:` before the object faults
- `didTurnIntoFault:` after the object faults

If you have implemented custom classes for your managed objects, you can implement either or both of these methods in your classes to perform some action on the object. Suppose, for example, that your custom managed object performs an expensive calculation on some persistent values and caches the result, and you want to nullify that cached result if the values it depends on aren't present. You could nullify the calculation in `didTurnIntoFault:`.

Building the Faulting Test

To test what you've learned about faulting in this section, build a test that will do the following:

1. Retrieve the first movie from the persistent store.

2. Grab an actor from that movie.

3. Check whether the actor is a fault.

4. Get the name of the actor.

5. Check whether the actor is a fault.

6. Turn the actor back into a fault.

7. Check whether the actor is a fault.

To start, generate an `Actor` class from your data model that will represent the `Actor` entity. You can, if you want, create it manually. Listing 7-9 shows the header file, `Actor.h`, and Listing 7-10 shows the implementation file, `Actor.m`. In the implementation file, implement the methods `willTurnIntoFault:` and `didTurnIntoFault:`, so that you can verify that Core Data indeed does call those methods when you turn the object back into a fault. You don't do anything special in those methods but simply log that the events happened.

Listing 7-9. *Actor.h*

```
#import <CoreData/CoreData.h>


@interface Actor :  NSManagedObject
{
}

@property (nonatomic, retain) NSString * name;
@property (nonatomic, retain) NSNumber * rating;
@property (nonatomic, retain) NSSet* movies;

@end


@interface Actor (CoreDataGeneratedAccessors)
- (void)addMoviesObject:(NSManagedObject *)value;
- (void)removeMoviesObject:(NSManagedObject *)value;
- (void)addMovies:(NSSet *)value;
- (void)removeMovies:(NSSet *)value;

@end
```

Listing 7-10. *Actor.m*

```
#import "Actor.h"


@implementation Actor

@dynamic name;
@dynamic rating;
@dynamic movies;

- (void)willTurnIntoFault {
  NSLog(@"Actor named %@ will turn into fault", self.name);
}

- (void)didTurnIntoFault {
  NSLog(@"Actor named %@ did turn into fault", self.name);
}

@end
```

If you created the Actor class manually, go to your data model and change the class for the Actor entity from NSManagedObject to Actor. If you forget this step, Core Data will not use your custom class for Actor objects, and your methods will not be called.

Now, create a class called `DidTurnIntoFaultTest` that implements the `PerformanceTest` protocol. Listing 7-11 shows `DidTurnIntoFaultTest.h`, and Listing 7-12 shows `DidTurnIntoFaultTest.m`.

Listing 7-11. *DidTurnIntoFaultTest.h*

```
#import <Foundation/Foundation.h>
#import "PerformanceTest.h"

@interface DidTurnIntoFaultTest : NSObject <PerformanceTest> {

}

@end
```

Listing 7-12. *DidTurnIntoFaultTest.m*

```
#import <CoreData/CoreData.h>
#import "DidTurnIntoFaultTest.h"
#import "Actor.h"

@implementation DidTurnIntoFaultTest

- (NSString *)name {
  return @"Did Turn Into Fault Test";
}

// Pull all the movies and verify that each of their actor objects are pointing to the➡
same actors

- (NSString *)runWithContext:(NSManagedObjectContext *)context {
  NSString *result = nil;

  // Fetch the first movie
  NSFetchRequest *request = [[NSFetchRequest alloc] init];
  [request setEntity:[NSEntityDescription entityForName:@"Movie"➡
inManagedObjectContext:context]];

  NSPredicate *predicate = [NSPredicate predicateWithFormat:@"name = %@", @"Movie 1"];
  [request setPredicate:predicate];
  NSArray *results = [context executeFetchRequest:request error:nil];
  [request release];

  if ([results count] == 1) {
    NSManagedObject *movie = (NSManagedObject *)[results objectAtIndex:0];
    NSSet *actors = [movie valueForKey:@"actors"];
    if ([actors count] != 200) {
      result = @"Failed to find the 200 actors for the first movie";
    } else {
      // Get an actor
      Actor *actor = (Actor *)[actors anyObject];

      // Check if it's a fault
      result = [actor isFault] ? @"Actor is a fault.\n" : @"Actor is NOT a fault.\n";

      // Get its name and rating
```

```
        result = [result stringByAppendingFormat:@"Actor is named %@\n", actor.name];
        result = [result stringByAppendingFormat:@"Actor has rating %d\n", [actor.rating➡
    intigerValue]];


        // Check if it's a fault
        result = [result stringByAppendingString:[actor isFault] ? ➡
@"Actor is a fault.\n" : @"Actor is NOT a fault.\n"];


        // Turn actor back into a fault
        result = [result stringByAppendingString:@"Turning actor back into a fault.\n"];
        [context refreshObject:actor mergeChanges:NO];


        // Check if it's a fault
        result = [result stringByAppendingString:[actor isFault] ? ➡
@"Actor is a fault.\n" : @"Actor is NOT a fault.\n"];
    }
  } else {
    result = @"Failed to fetch the first movie";
  }
  return result;
}

@end
```

Turn your attention to the `runWithContext:` method, which fetches the first movie from the persistent store. It then grabs any one of the actors related to that movie and checks to see whether this actor is a fault. Note that, although you have done nothing to this point in the code to cause a fault to fire for the actor, the actor may not be a fault at this point, depending on what you've been doing in the application before this point. The code then accesses the actor's name and checks again whether the actor is a fault. It won't be. The access to the name fired a fault, if it hadn't already been fired elsewhere. The code then turns the actor into a fault and verifies that the actor, indeed, is a fault.

To add your new test to the application, open `PerformanceTuningViewController.m`, make sure you import `DidTurnIntoFaultTest.h`, find the line in `viewDidLoad:` that adds the tests to the `tests` array, and add the new test like this:

```
FetchAllMoviesActorsAndStudiosTest *famaasTest = [[FetchAllMoviesActorsAndStudiosTest➡
alloc] init];
DidTurnIntoFaultTest *dtifTest = [[DidTurnIntoFaultTest alloc] init];
self.tests = [[NSArray alloc] initWithObjects:famaasTest, dtifTest, nil];
[famaasTest release];
[dtifTest release];
```

Build the application, and run the test. You should see output similar to this:

```
Actor is a fault.
Actor is named Actor 42
Actor has rating 8
Actor is NOT a fault.
Turning actor back into a fault.
Actor is a fault.
```

Taking Control: Firing Faults on Purpose

This section on faulting began by explaining that you had more control over memory usage when you ran SQL queries yourself than you do by allowing Core Data to manage data fetches. Although true, you can exert some amount of control over Core Data's fault management by firing faults yourself. By firing faults yourself, you can avoid inefficient scenarios in which Core Data must fire several small faults to fetch your data, incurring several trips to the persistent store.

Core Data provides two means for optimizing the firing of faults:

- Batch faulting
- Prefetching

As a control group, create a test called `SinglyFiringFaultTest`. This test should fetch all the movies, loop through them one by one, and do the following:

- Access the `name` attribute so that a fault fires for this movie only
- Loop through all the related actors and access their `name` attributes, one at a time, so each access fires a fault
- Reset each actor so the next movie will have to fire faults for each actor
- Do the same for all the related studios

The files for this test are in Listing 7-13 and Listing 7-14. Create these files, and add an instance of `SinglyFiringFaultTest` to your `tests` array. Don't forget to import `SinglyFiringFaultTest.h`. Build the application, launch the simulator, and run the test. Running this test on our machine took about 34 seconds, so be patient. By using prefetching, we should be able to improve on those results!

Listing 7-13. *SinglyFiringFaultTest.h*

```
#import <Foundation/Foundation.h>
#import "PerformanceTest.h"

@interface SinglyFiringFaultTest : NSObject <PerformanceTest> {

}

@end
```

Listing 7-14. *SinglyFiringFaultTest.m*

```
#import <CoreData/CoreData.h>
#import "SinglyFiringFaultTest.h"

@implementation SinglyFiringFaultTest
```

```
- (NSString *)name {
  return @"Singly Firing Fault Test";
}

- (NSString *)runWithContext:(NSManagedObjectContext *)context {
  NSString *result = @"Singly Firing Fault Test Complete!";

  // Fetch all the movies
  NSFetchRequest *request = [[NSFetchRequest alloc] init];
  [request setEntity:[NSEntityDescription entityForName:@"Movie"➥
inManagedObjectContext:context]];

  NSArray *results = [context executeFetchRequest:request error:nil];
  [request release];

  // Loop through all the movies
  for (NSManagedObject *movie in results) {
    // Fire a fault just for this movie
    [movie valueForKey:@"name"];

    // Loop through all the actors for this movie
    for (NSManagedObject *actor in [movie valueForKey:@"actors"]) {
      // Fire a fault just for this actor
      [actor valueForKey:@"name"];

      // Put this actor back in fault so the next movie
      // will have to fire a fault
      [context refreshObject:actor mergeChanges:NO];
    }

    // Loop through all the studios for this movie
    for (NSManagedObject *studio in [movie valueForKey:@"studios"]) {
      // Fire a fault just for this studio
      [studio valueForKey:@"name"];

      // Put this studio back in fault so the next movie
      // will have to fire a fault
      [context refreshObject:studio mergeChanges:NO];
    }
  }
  return result;
}

@end
```

Prefetching

Similar to batch faulting, prefetching minimizes the number of times that Core Data has to fire faults and go fetch data. With prefetching, though, you tell Core Data when you perform a fetch to also fetch the related objects you specify. For example, using this chapter's data model, when you fetch the movies, you can tell Core Data to prefetch the related actors, studios, or both.

To prefetch related objects, call NSFetchRequest's
setRelationshipKeyPathsForPrefetching: method, passing an array that contains the
names of the relationships that you want Core Data to prefetch. To prefetch the related
actors and studios when you fetch the movies, for example, you use this code:

```
NSFetchRequest *request = [[NSFetchRequest alloc] init];
  [request setEntity:[NSEntityDescription entityForName:@"Movie"➥
inManagedObjectContext:context]];
```

**[request setRelationshipKeyPathsForPrefetching:[NSArray arrayWithObjects:@"actors",➥
@"studios", nil]];**

```
  NSArray *results = [context executeFetchRequest:request error:nil];
  [request release];
```

The line in bold instructs Core Data to prefetch all the related actors and studios when it
fetches the movies.

Before testing this, recognize that your baseline numbers depend on turning each actor
and studio back into a fault after triggering the fault to load the data for a given movie.
You did this because each movie relates to the same 200 actors and the same 200
studios, so the only time the actors and movies would normally be faults would be for
the first movie, not the remaining 199. Turning each actor and each studio back into a
fault for each movie allows you to measure firing faults for each actor and studio for
each movie.

Turning each actor and each studio back into a fault negates the performance gains
offered by prefetching them, however, so you're not going to refault them. To get good
comparison numbers, then, you must change the code for SinglyFiringFaultTest to
not reset the Actor and Studio objects. Open SinglyFiringFaultTest.m, go to the
runWithContext: method, and comment these two lines:

```
[context refreshObject:actor mergeChanges:NO];
```

```
[context refreshObject:studio mergeChanges:NO];
```

Launch the app, and rerun the test. On our machine, it takes about 1.3 seconds.

Now, create a new class called PreFetchFaultingTest, and implement the
PerformanceTest protocol. This test will look similar to SinglyFiringFaultTest with two
important differences:

- The fetch prefetches the actors and studios.
- The actors and studios aren't turned back into faults.

Listing 7-15 shows the header file, and Listing 7-16 shows the implementation file.

Listing 7-15. *PreFetchFaultingTest.h*

```
#import <Foundation/Foundation.h>
#import "PerformanceTest.h"

@interface PreFetchFaultingTest : NSObject <PerformanceTest> {

}
```

```
@end
```

Listing 7-16. *PreFetchFaultingTest.m*

```objc
#import <CoreData/CoreData.h>
#import "PreFetchFaultingTest.h"

@implementation PreFetchFaultingTest

- (NSString *)name {
  return @"Pre-fetch Faulting Test";
}

- (NSString *)runWithContext:(NSManagedObjectContext *)context {
  NSString *result = @"Pre-fetch Fault Test Complete!";

  // Fetch all the movies
  NSFetchRequest *request = [[NSFetchRequest alloc] init];
  [request setEntity:[NSEntityDescription entityForName:@"Movie"➥
inManagedObjectContext:context]];

  // Pre-fetch the actors and studios
  [request setRelationshipKeyPathsForPrefetching:[NSArray arrayWithObjects:@"actors",➥
@"studios", nil]];

  NSArray *results = [context executeFetchRequest:request error:nil];
  [request release];

  // Loop through all the movies
  for (NSManagedObject *movie in results) {
    // Fire a fault just for this movie
    [movie valueForKey:@"name"];

    // Loop through all the actors for this movie
    for (NSManagedObject *actor in [movie valueForKey:@"actors"]) {
      // Get the name for this actor
      [actor valueForKey:@"name"];
    }

    // Loop through all the studios for this movie
    for (NSManagedObject *studio in [movie valueForKey:@"studios"]) {
      // Get the name for this studio
      [studio valueForKey:@"name"];
    }
  }
  return result;
}

@end
```

The line in bold sets up the prefetching. Build and run this test. Our results were about 0.4 seconds, which is about 70 percent faster than the 1.3 seconds the same test took without prefetching.

Caching

Regardless of target language or platform, most data persistence frameworks and libraries have an internal caching mechanism. Properly implemented caches provide opportunities for significant performance gains, especially for applications that need to retrieve the same data repeatedly. Core Data is no exception. The NSManagedObjectContext class serves as a built-in cache for the Core Data framework. When you retrieve an object from the backing persistent store, the context keeps a reference to it to track its changes. If you retrieve the object again, the context can give the caller the same object reference as it did in the first invocation.

The obvious trade-off that results from the use of caching is that, while improving performance, caching uses more memory. If no cache management scheme were in place to limit the memory usage of the cache, the cache could fill up with objects until the whole system collapses from lack of memory. To manage memory, the Core Data context has weak references to the managed objects it pulls out of the persistent store. This means that if the retain count of a managed object reaches zero because no other object has a reference to it, the managed object will be discarded. The exception to this rule is if the object has been modified in any way. In this case, the context keeps a strong reference (that is, sends a retain signal to the managed object) and keeps it until the context is either committed or rolled back, at which point it becomes a weak reference again.

> **Note:** The default retain behavior can be changed by passing YES to the setRetainsRegisteredObjects: of NSManagedObjectContext. By passing YES, the context will retain all registered objects. The default behavior retains registered objects only when they are inserted, updated, deleted, or locked.

In this section, we examine the difference between fetching objects from the persistent store or from the cache. We build a test that does the following:

1. Resets the managed object context to flush the cache

2. Retrieves all movies

3. Retrieves all actors for each movie

4. Displays the time it took to perform both retrievals

5. Retrieves all movies (this time the objects will be cached)

6. Retrieves all actors for each movie

7. Displays the time it took to perform both retrievals

To start, create a class called CacheTest, and add it to the Tests group in Xcode. We make sure that CacheTest implements the PerformanceTest protocol.

Listing 7-17. *CacheTest.h*

```
#import <Foundation/Foundation.h>
#import "PerformanceTest.h"

@interface CacheTest : NSObject <PerformanceTest> {
}

@end
```

Listing 7-18. *CacheTest.m*

```
#import "CacheTest.h"
#import "Actor.h"

@implementation CacheTest

- (NSString *)name {
  return @"Cache Test";
}

- (void)loadDataFromContext :(NSManagedObjectContext *)context {
  // Fetch all the movies and all actors
  NSFetchRequest *request = [[NSFetchRequest alloc] init];
  [request setEntity:[NSEntityDescription entityForName:@"Movie"➥
inManagedObjectContext:context]];

  NSArray *results = [context executeFetchRequest:request error:nil];
  [request release];

  // Fetch all the actors
  for(NSManagedObject *movie in results) {
    NSSet *actors = [movie valueForKey:@"actors"];
    for(Actor *actor in actors) {
      [actor valueForKey:@"name"];
    }
  }
}

// Pull all the movies and verify that each of their actor objects are pointing to the
same actors
- (NSString *)runWithContext:(NSManagedObjectContext *)context {
  NSMutableString *result = [NSMutableString string];

  [context reset];  // Clear all potentially cached objects

  NSDate *startTest1 = [NSDate date];
  [self loadDataFromContext: context];
  NSDate *endTest1 = [NSDate date];

  NSTimeInterval test1 = [endTest1 timeIntervalSinceDate:startTest1];
  [result appendFormat:@"Without cache: %.2f s\n", test1];
```

```
    NSDate *startTest2 = [NSDate date];
    [self loadDataFromContext: context];
    NSDate *endTest2 = [NSDate date];

    NSTimeInterval test2 = [endTest2 timeIntervalSinceDate:startTest2];
    [result appendFormat:@"With cache: %.2f s\n", test2];

    return result;
}

@end
```

Let's examine the runWithContext: method in Listing 7-18. It does the same thing twice: fetch all the movies and all the actors. The first time, the cache is explicitly cleared using [context reset]. The second time around, all the objects will be in the cache, and therefore the data will come back much faster. The loadDataFromContext: method is invoked to retrieve all the movies and then pulls every actor for each movie. We explicitly get the name property of the actors in order to force Core Data to load the property, firing a fault if necessary.

Build the application, and run the Cache Test test. The output of the application will look similar to Figure 7-7, with the cached version running significantly faster than the version without a cache.

Figure 7-7. *Measuring the difference between loading cached and noncached objects*

If we reset the cache between the first and second tests using [context reset], then the time to execute the second test would be about the same as the first test. This is because the objects would all have to be retrieved from the persistent store again.

Expiring

Any time an application uses a cache, the question of cache expiration arises: when should objects in the cache expire and be reloaded from the persistent store? The difficulty in determining the expiration interval comes from juggling the performance gain obtained by caching objects for long intervals versus the extra memory consumption that entails and the potential staleness of the cached data. This section examines the trade-offs of the two possibilities for expiring the cache and freeing some memory.

Memory Consumption

As more and more objects are put into the cache, the memory usage increases. Even if a managed object is entirely faulted, a quick call to `NSLog(@"%d", class_getInstanceSize(NSManagedObject.class))` will show that the allocated size of an unpopulated managed object is 48 bytes. This is because it holds references (that is, 4-byte pointers) to other objects such as the entity description, the context, and the object ID. Even without any actual data, a managed object occupies a minimum of 48 bytes. This is a best-case scenario because this approximation does not include the memory occupied by the unique object ID, which is populated. This means that if you have 100,000 managed objects in the cache, even faulted, you are using at least five megabytes of memory for things other than your data. If you start fetching data without faulting, then you can run into memory issues quickly.

The trick to this balancing act is to remove data from the cache when it's no longer needed or if you can afford to pay the price of retrieving the objects from the persistent store when you need them again.

Brute-Force Cache Expiration

If you don't care about losing all the managed objects, you can reset the context entirely. This is rarely the option you want to choose, but it is extremely efficient. `NSManagedObjectContext` has a reset method that will wipe the cache out in one swoop. Once you call `[managedObjectContext reset]`, your memory footprint will be dramatically smaller, but you will have to pay the price of going to the persistent store if you want to retrieve any objects again. Please also understand that, like with any other kind of mass destruction mechanism, there are serious side effects and collateral damage to resetting the cache in the middle of a running application. For example, any managed object that you were using prior to the reset is now invalid. If you try to do anything with them, your efforts will be met with runtime errors.

Expiring the Cache Through Faulting

Faulting is a more subtle option, as the section on faulting explains. You can fault any managed object by calling `[context refreshObject:managedObject mergeChanges:NO]`. After this method call, the object is faulted, and therefore the memory it occupies in the cache is minimized, although not zero. A non-negligible advantage of this strategy, however, is that when the managed object is turned into a fault, any managed object it has a reference to (through relationships) is released. If those related managed objects have no other references to them, then they will be removed from the cache, further reducing the memory footprint. Faulting managed objects in this manner helps prune the entire object graph.

Uniquing

Both business and technology like to turn nouns into verbs, and the pseudoword *uniquing* testifies to this weakness. It attempts to define the action of making something unique or ensuring uniqueness. Usage suggests not only that Apple didn't invent the term but also that it predates Core Data. Apple embraces the term in its Core Data documentation, however, raising fears that one day Apple will call the action of listening to music *iPodding*.

The technology industry uses the term *uniquing* in conjunction with memory objects versus their representation in a data store. The book *Core Java Data Objects* says, "Uniquing ensures that no matter how many times a persistent object is found, it has only one in-memory representation. All references to the same persistent object within the scope of the same `PersistenceManager` instance reference the same in-memory object."

Martin Fowler, in *Patterns of Enterprise Application Architecture*, gives it a less colorful, more descriptive, and more English-compliant name: identity map. He explains that an identity map "ensures that each object gets loaded only once by keeping every loaded object in a map." Whatever you call it or however you describe it, *uniquing* means that Core Data conserves memory use by ensuring the uniqueness of each object in memory and that no two memory instances of an object point to the same instance in the persistent store.

Consider, for example, the Shapes application from Chapter 5. Each `Shape` instance has a relationship with two `Canvas` instances. When you run the Shapes application and reference the two `Canvas` instances through any `Shape` instances, you always get the same two `Canvas` instances, as Figure 7-8 depicts. If Core Data didn't use uniquing, you could find yourself in the scenario shown in Figure 7-9, where each `Canvas` instance is represented in memory several times, once for each `Shape`, and each `Shape` instance is represented in memory several times, once for each `Canvas`.

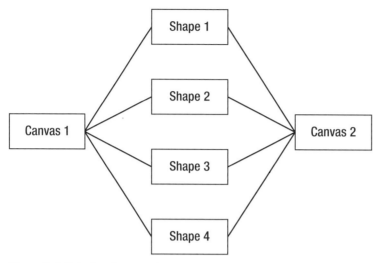

Figure 7-8. *Uniquing shapes and canvases*

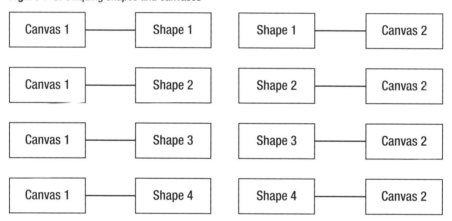

Figure 7-9. *Nonuniquing shapes and canvases*

Uniquing not only conserves memory but also eliminates data inconsistency issues. Think what could happen, for example, if Core Data didn't employ uniquing and the Shapes application had two memory instances of each shape (one for each canvas). Suppose that Canvas 1 changed the color of a shape to mauve and Canvas 2 changed the color of the shape to lime green. What color should the shape display? When the application stores the shape in the persistent store, what color should it save? You can imagine the data inconsistency bugs you'd have to track down if Core Data didn't maintain only one instance of each data object in memory.

Note that uniquing occurs within a single managed object context only, not across managed object contexts. The good news, however, is that Core Data's default behavior, which you can't change, is to unique. Uniquing comes free with Core Data.

To test uniquing, you'll create a test that fetches all the movies from the persistent store and then compares each of their related actors to each other movie's related actors. For the test to pass, the code must verify that only 200 Actor instances live in memory and that each movie points to the same 200 actors. To begin, create a new class called UniquingTest. UniquingTest.h should implement the PerformanceTest protocol and look like Listing 7-19.

Listing 7-19. *UniquingTest.h*

```
#import <Foundation/Foundation.h>
#import "PerformanceTest.h"

@interface UniquingTest : NSObject <PerformanceTest> {

}

@end
```

The implementation file, UniquingTest.m, fetches all the movies and iterates through them, pulling all the actors that relate to each one. The code sorts the actors so they're in a determined order so we can predictably compare instances. The first time through the loop (for the first movie), the code stores each of the actors in a reference array so that all subsequent loops have something to compare the actors against. Each subsequent loop, the code pulls the actors for the movie and compares them to the reference array. If just one actor doesn't match, the test fails. The code is shown in Listing 7-20.

Listing 7-20. *UniquingTest.m*

```
#import <CoreData/CoreData.h>
#import "UniquingTest.h"

@implementation UniquingTest

- (NSString *)name {
  return @"Uniquing test";
}

// Pull all the movies and verify that each of their actor objects are pointing to the➥
same actors

- (NSString *)runWithContext:(NSManagedObjectContext *)context {
  NSString *result = @"Uniquing test passed";

  // Array to hold the actors for comparison purposes
  NSMutableArray *referenceActors = nil;

  // Sorting for the actors
  NSSortDescriptor *sortDescriptor = [[NSSortDescriptor alloc] initWithKey:@"name"➥
ascending:YES];

  NSArray *sortDescriptors = [[NSArray alloc] initWithObjects:sortDescriptor, nil];
  [sortDescriptor release];

  // Fetch all the movies
  NSFetchRequest *request = [[NSFetchRequest alloc] init];
```

```
  [request setEntity:[NSEntityDescription entityForName:@"Movie"➥
inManagedObjectContext:context]];

  NSArray *results = [context executeFetchRequest:request error:nil];
  [request release];

  // Go through each movie
  for (NSManagedObject *movie in results) {
    // Get the actors
    NSSet *actors = [movie mutableSetValueForKey:@"actors"];
    NSArray *sortedActors = [actors sortedArrayUsingDescriptors:sortDescriptors];

    if (referenceActors == nil) {
      // First time through; store the references
      referenceActors = [[NSArray alloc] initWithArray:sortedActors];
    } else {
      for (int i = 0, n = [sortedActors count]; i < n; i++) {
        if ([sortedActors objectAtIndex:i] != [referenceActors objectAtIndex:i]) {
          result = [NSString stringWithFormat:@"Uniquing test failed; %@ != %@",➥
[sortedActors objectAtIndex:i], [referenceActors objectAtIndex:i]];

          break;
        }
      }
    }
  }
  [referenceActors release];
  [sortDescriptors release];
  return result;
}

@end
```

To run this test, open PerformanceTuningViewController.m, and add an instance of UniquingTest to the tests array and an import for UniquingTest.h. Running the test should show that each actor exists only once in memory and that Core Data has used uniquing to reduce your application's memory footprint. See Figure 7-10.

Figure 7-10. *The results of the uniquing test*

Improve Performance with Better Predicates

Despite the year in the movie title *2001: A Space Odyssey*, we are still far away from our machines having the intelligence to respond with things like "I'm sorry, Dave. I'm afraid I can't do that." As of the time of writing this book, programmers still have to do a lot of hand-holding to walk their machines through the process of doing what they are asked to do. This means that how you write your code determines how efficient it will be. You often have multiple ways to retrieve the same data, but the solution you use can significantly alter the performance of your application.

Using Faster Comparators

Generally speaking, string comparators perform slower than primitive comparators. When predicates are compounded using an OR operator, it is always more efficient to put the primitive comparators first because if they resolve to TRUE, then the rest of the comparators don't need to be evaluated. This is because "TRUE OR anything" is always true. A similar strategy can be used with AND-compounded predicates. In this case, if the first predicate fails, then the second will not be evaluated, because "FALSE AND anything" is always false.

To validate this, we add a new test to our performance test application. We call the new class PredicatePerformanceTest. Listing 7-21 shows the header file.

Listing 7-21. *PredicatePerformanceTest.h*

```
#import <Foundation/Foundation.h>
#import "PerformanceTest.h"

@interface PredicatePerformanceTest : NSObject <PerformanceTest> {

}

@end
```

This test consists of two fetch requests, which retrieve the same objects using a OR-compounded predicate. In the first test, the string comparator LIKE is used before the primitive comparator. In the second test, the comparators are permuted. We run each test 1,000 times in order to get significant timings in seconds, and each time through the loop, the cache is reset so that we keep a clean context. Listing 7-22 shows the implementation.

Listing 7-22. *PredicatePerformanceTest.m*

```
#import "PredicatePerformanceTest.h"

@implementation PredicatePerformanceTest
- (NSString *)name {
    return @"Predicate Performance Test";
}

- (NSString *)runWithContext:(NSManagedObjectContext *)context {
    NSMutableString *result = [NSMutableString string];

    NSFetchRequest *request;

    NSDate *startTest1 = [NSDate date];
    for(int i=0; i<1000; i++) {
        [context reset];
        request = [[NSFetchRequest alloc] init];
        [request setEntity:[NSEntityDescription entityForName:@"Movie"➥
inManagedObjectContext:context]];

        [request setPredicate:[NSPredicate predicateWithFormat:@"(name LIKE %@) OR (rating➥
< %d)", @"*c*or*", 5]];
```

```
    [context executeFetchRequest:request error:nil];
    [request release];
  }
  NSDate *endTest1 - [NSDate date];

  NSTimeInterval test1 = [endTest1 timeIntervalSinceDate:startTest1];
  [result appendFormat:@"Slow predicate: %.2f s\n", test1];

  NSDate *startTest2 = [NSDate date];
  for(int i=0; i<1000; i++) {
    [context reset];
    request = [[NSFetchRequest alloc] init];
    [request setEntity:[NSEntityDescription entityForName:@"Movie"➡
inManagedObjectContext:context]];

    [request setPredicate:[NSPredicate predicateWithFormat:@"(rating < %d) OR (name➡
like %@)", 5, @"*c*or*"]];
    [context executeFetchRequest:request error:nil];
    [request release];
  }
  NSDate *endTest2 = [NSDate date];

  NSTimeInterval test2 = [endTest2 timeIntervalSinceDate:startTest2];
  [result appendFormat:@"Fast predicate: %.2f s\n", test2];

  return result;
}

@end
```

To see the test in the user interface, open `PerformanceTuningViewController.m`, and add an instance of `PredicatePerformanceTest` to the `tests` array and an import for `PredicatePerformanceTest.h`.

Running the test will consistently show a significant timing difference between the two tests. Of course, the timings will differ depending on the performance of your machine, but here's an example run:

```
Slow predicate: 1.10s
Fast predicate: 0.84s
```

Using Subqueries

We saw in the previous chapter how to use subqueries to help simplify the code. In this section, we add a test to show the difference between using subqueries and retrieving related data manually. Consider an example in which we want to find all actors from a movie that match a certain criteria. To do this without using a subquery, we have to first fetch all the movies that match the criteria. We then have to iterate through each movie and extract the actors. We then go through the actors and add them to our result set, making sure we don't duplicate actors if they play in the multiple movies. The test is shown in Listing 7-23.

Listing 7-23. *Manually Subquerying*

```
NSMutableDictionary *actorsMap = [NSMutableDictionary dictionary];
request = [[NSFetchRequest alloc] init];
[request setEntity:[NSEntityDescription entityForName:@"Movie"➥
inManagedObjectContext:context]];

[request setPredicate:[NSPredicate predicateWithFormat:@"(rating < %d) OR (name LIKE➥
%@)", 5, @"*c*or*"]];

NSArray *movies = [context executeFetchRequest:request error:nil];
[request release];

for(NSManagedObject *movie in movies) {
  NSSet *actorSet = [movie valueForKey:@"actors"];
  for(NSManagedObject *actor in actorSet) {
    [actorsMap setValue:actor forKey:[[[actor objectID] URIRepresentation]➥
description]];

  }
}
```

In this implementation, the actorsMap dictionary contains all the actors. We keyed them by objectID in order to eliminate duplicates. The alternative to doing this is to use subqueries. Please refer to Chapter 6 for more information on building subqueries. In this case, the subquery looks like Listing 7-24.

Listing 7-24. *Using a Subquery for Better Performance*

```
request = [[NSFetchRequest alloc] init];
[request setEntity:[NSEntityDescription entityForName:@"Actor"➥
inManagedObjectContext:context]];

[request setPredicate:[NSPredicate predicateWithFormat:@"(SUBQUERY(movies, $x,➥
($x.rating < %d) OR ($x.name LIKE %@)).@count > 0)", 5, @"*c*or*"]];


NSArray *actors = [context executeFetchRequest:request error:nil];
[request release];
```

One of the major differences here is that we let the persistent store do all the work of retrieving the matching actors, which means that most of the results don't have to make it back up to the context layer of Core Data for us to post-process. With the subquery, we don't actually retrieve the movies, and the fetched request is set up to fetch actors directly. The manual option, on the other hand, has to fire faults to retrieve the actors after retrieving the movies.

To demonstrate this in a test, we create a new class in our project called SubqueryTest. The header file is shown in Listing 7-25.

Listing 7-25. *SubqueryTest.h*

```
#import <Foundation/Foundation.h>
#import "PerformanceTest.h"
```

```
@interface SubqueryTest : NSObject <PerformanceTest> {
}

@end
```

The tests are implemented in SubqueryTest.m, as illustrated in Listing 7-26.

Listing 7-26. *SubqueryTest.m*

```objc
#import "SubqueryTest.h"

@implementation SubqueryTest
- (NSString *)name {
  return @"Subquery Performance Test";
}

- (NSString *)runWithContext:(NSManagedObjectContext *)context {
  NSMutableString *result = [NSMutableString string];

  NSFetchRequest *request;

  int count = 0;

  [context reset];
  NSDate *startTest1 = [NSDate date];
  NSMutableDictionary *actorsMap = [NSMutableDictionary dictionary];
  request = [[NSFetchRequest alloc] init];
  [request setEntity:[NSEntityDescription entityForName:@"Movie"➥
inManagedObjectContext:context]];

  [request setPredicate:[NSPredicate predicateWithFormat:@"(rating < %d) OR (name LIKE➥
%@)", 5, @"*c*or*"]];
  NSArray *movies = [context executeFetchRequest:request error:nil];

  for(NSManagedObject *movie in movies) {
    NSSet *actorSet = [movie valueForKey:@"actors"];
    for(NSManagedObject *actor in actorSet) {
      [actorsMap setValue:actor forKey:[[[actor objectID] URIRepresentation]➥
description]];
    }
  }

  count = [actorsMap count];

  [request release];
  NSDate *endTest1 = [NSDate date];

  NSTimeInterval test1 = [endTest1 timeIntervalSinceDate:startTest1];
  [result appendFormat:@"No subquery: %.2f s\n", test1];
  [result appendFormat:@"Actors retrieved: %d\n", count];

  [context reset];
  NSDate *startTest2 = [NSDate date];
  request = [[NSFetchRequest alloc] init];
```

```
    [request setEntity:[NSEntityDescription entityForName:@"Actor"➥
inManagedObjectContext:context]];

    [request setPredicate:[NSPredicate predicateWithFormat:@"(SUBQUERY(movies, $x,➥
($x.rating < %d) OR ($x.name LIKE %@)).@count > 0)", 5, @"*c*or*"]];


    NSArray *actors = [context executeFetchRequest:request error:nil];
    count = [actors count];
    [request release];
    NSDate *endTest2 = [NSDate date];

    NSTimeInterval test2 = [endTest2 timeIntervalSinceDate:startTest2];
    [result appendFormat:@"Subquery: %.2f s\n", test2];
    [result appendFormat:@"Actors retrieved: %d\n", count];

    return result;
}

@end
```

Open `PerformanceTuningViewController.m`, and add an instance of `SubqueryTest` to the tests array in order to be able to run the test. The test results are unequivocal:

```
No subquery: 0.64 s
Actors retrieved: 200
Subquery: 0.14 s
Actors retrieved: 200
```

How you write your predicates can have a profound effect on the performance of your application. You should always be mindful of what you are asking Core Data to do and how you can accomplish the same results with more efficient predicates.

Analyzing Performance

Although thinking things through before writing code and understanding the implications of things such as faulting, prefetching, and memory usage usually nets you solid code that performs well, you often need a nonbiased, objective opinion on how your application is performing. The least biased and most objective opinion on your application's performance comes from the computer it's running on, so asking your computer to measure the results of your application's Core Data interaction provides essential insight for optimizing performance.

Apple provides a tool called Instruments that allows you to measure several facets of an application, including Core Data–related items. This section shows you how to use Instruments to measure the Core Data aspects of your application. We encourage you to explore the other measurements Instruments offers.

Launching Instruments

Although you can launch Instruments as you would any other application, Xcode provides a simpler way to launch it to run your application. From the Xcode menu, select **Run ➤ Run with Performance Tool**, and from the drop-down menu, select what you want to measure (Time Profiler, Leaks, et al.). Unfortunately, Core Data is grayed out, preventing you from selecting it. For some reason, Xcode enables the Core Data menu item only for Mac OS X applications, not iOS applications. You can still use Instruments, however, to measure your Core Data interactions in iOS applications. You just have to work a little harder.

Launch Instruments as you would launch any other application. It resides in /Developer/Applications alongside Xcode. A dialog appears asking you to choose a template, as shown in Figure 7-11. Select All under iOS Simulator on the left, Blank on the right, and click Choose. A blank Instruments window appears, as you requested, with a message asking you to drag instruments onto it from the library, as shown in Figure 7-12. Click the arrow beside Library to display the library. You'll see four Core Data-related instruments, as shown in Figure 7-13.

Figure 7-11. *Instruments asking you to choose a template*

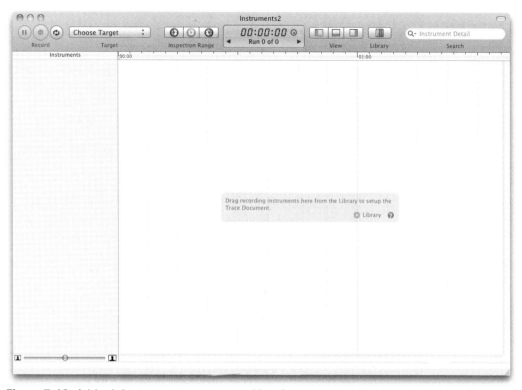

Figure 7-12. A blank Instruments screen waiting for you to add instruments from the Library

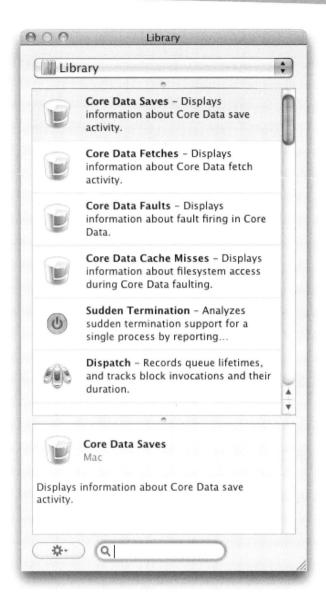

Figure 7-13. The Instruments library with the Core Data instruments displayed

Drag all four of these to the Instruments window. Go back to Xcode and launch the iOS application you want to measure—in this case, the PerformanceTuning application. Then, return to Instruments, click the Choose Target drop-down, and select **Attach to Process ➤ PerformanceTuning** (you may have to search a bit, depending on the number of processes you're currently running). See Figure 7-14.

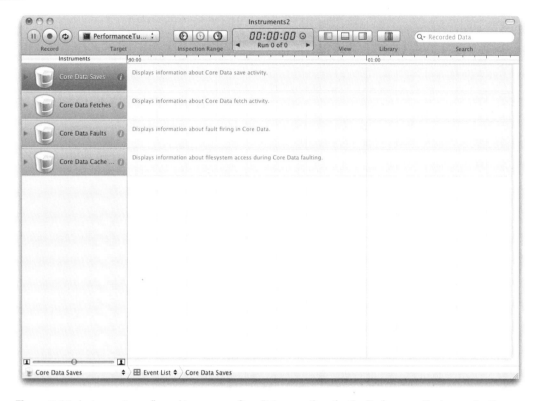

Figure 7-14. *Instruments configured to measure Core Data operations for the PerformanceTuning application*

Now, click the Record button in Instruments, and Instruments begins measuring your application's Core Data-related operations.

Understanding the Results

The Instruments window shows the Core Data measurements it's tracking:

- Core Data saves
- Core Data fetches
- Core Data faults
- Core Data cache misses

Run any of the tests in the PerformanceTuning application—say, the Pre-fetch Faulting Test—and wait for the test to complete. When the test finishes, click the Stop button in the upper left of Instruments to stop recording Core Data measurements. You can then review the results from your test to see information about saves, fetches, faults, and cache misses. You can save the results to the file system for further review by selecting **File ➤ Save As**... from the menu. You reopen them in Instruments using the standard **File ➤ Open**... menu item.

Figure 7-15 shows the Instruments window after running the Pre-fetch Faulting Test. You can see the fetch counts and fetch durations, which are in microseconds, for the Core Data fetches (you may have to jiggle the headers a bit to get everything to display). The code ran one fetch request against the Movie entity (Instruments lists the call for a fetch twice: once when the call starts and once when it finishes). The request, which took 417,326 microseconds, fetched 200 movies, which you can tell from the fetch entity, Movie, and the fetch count, 200.

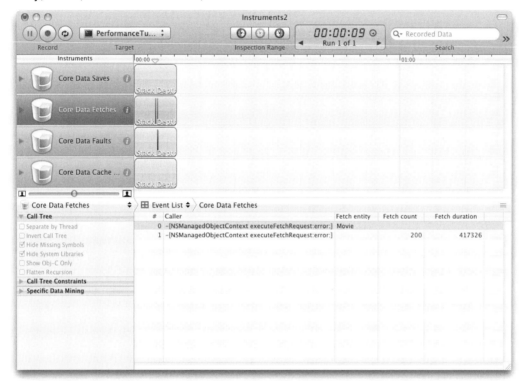

Figure 7-15. *Results from the Pre-fetch Faulting Test*

You can see the call tree for the fetch request by changing the drop-down in the middle of the window from Event List to Call Tree. You can reduce the navigation depth required to see the calls in your application's code by checking the box next to Hide System Libraries on the left of the window. Figure 7-16 shows the call tree for the fetch request. Using the call tree, you can determine which parts of your code are fetching data from your Core Data store.

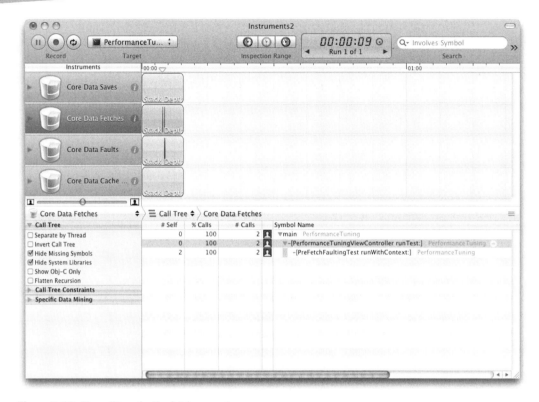

Figure 7-16. *The call tree for the fetch request*

This is just a taste of what Instruments can do for you to help you determine how your application is using Core Data and how it can lead you to places where Core Data performance is slow enough to warrant optimization efforts.

Summary

From uniquing to faulting to caching managed objects, Core Data performs a significant amount of data access performance optimization for you. These optimizations come free, without any extra effort on your part. You should be aware of the optimizations that Core Data provides, however, so that you make sure to work with, not against, them.

Not all Core Data performance gains come automatically, however. In this chapter, you learned how to use techniques such as prefetching and predicate optimization to squeeze all the performance from Core Data that you can for your applications. You also learned how to analyze your Core Data application using the Instruments application, so you can understand how your application is using Core Data and where the trouble spots are.

Other iOS programming books might do an excellent job showing you how to display a spinner and a "Please Wait" message when running long queries against your persistent store. This book shows you how to avoid the need for the spinner and "Please Wait" message entirely.

Chapter **8**

Versioning and Migrating Data

As you develop Core Data–based applications, you usually don't get your data model exactly right the first time. You start by creating a data model that seems to meet your application's data needs, but as you progress through the development of the application, you'll often find that your data model should change to serve your growing vision of what your application will do. During this stage of your application's life, changing your data model to match your new understanding of the application's data poses little cost: your application will no longer launch, crashing on startup with the message:

`The model used to open the store is incompatible with the one used to create the store`

You resolve this issue either by finding the database file on the file system and deleting it or by deleting your fledgling application from the iPhone Simulator or your device. Either way, the database file that uses your outdated schema disappears, along with data in the persistent store, and your application re-creates the database file the next time it launches. You'll probably do this several times during the development of your application.

Once you release your application, however, and people start using it, they will accumulate data they deem important in the persistent stores on their devices. Asking them to delete their data stores any time you want to release a new version of the application with a changed data model will drop your app instantly to one-star status, and the people commenting will decry Apple's rating system for not allowing ratings with zero or even negative stars.

Does that mean releasing your application freezes its data model, that the data model in the 1.0 version of your application is permanent? That you'd better get the first public version of the data model perfect, because you'll never be able to change it? Thankfully, no. Apple anticipated the need for improving Core Data models over the life of applications and built mechanisms for you to change data models and then migrate users' data to the new models, all without their intervention or even awareness. This chapter goes through the process of versioning your data models and migrating data across those versions, however complex the changes you've made to the model are.

Versioning

To take advantage of Core Data's support for versioning your data model and migrating data from version to version, you start by explicitly creating a new version of the data model. To illustrate how this works, we bring back the Shapes application from Chapter 5. In the original version of Shapes, we created a data model, which makes the model appear as shown in Figure 8-1.

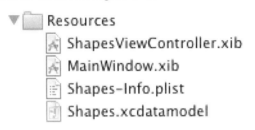

Figure 8-1. *The unversioned data model*

Shapes.xcdatamodel contains the model and is actually a directory on your file system. It contains files necessary to create the Core Data storage when your application runs. It's an unversioned data model, however. To turn it into a versioned data model, select Shapes.xcdatamodel and then, from the Xcode menu, select **Design ➤ Data Model ➤ Add Model Version**. Xcode creates a new directory on your file system called Shapes.xcdatamodeld (note the *d* at the end), moves the Shapes.xcdatamodel directory into it, and creates a new directory inside it called Shapes 2.xcdatamodel. See Figure 8-2. Each listing below Shapes.xcdatamodeld represents a version of your data model, and the green check mark denotes the version your application is currently using.

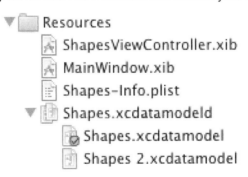

Figure 8-2. *The versioned data model*

You can see that your original data model, Shapes.xcdatamodel, is the current version. Before changing the current version from Shapes.xcdatamodel to Shapes 2.xcdatamodel, run the Shapes application and create a few shapes so you have data to migrate across versions. You need data in your database to test that the data migrations through this chapter work properly.

Now, suppose you want to add a new name attribute to the Shape entity. If you edit your current model and add a name attribute to the Shape entity, you will have the unpleasant surprise of seeing your application crash on startup. That's because the data stored in the data store does not match the Core Data data model. One option to alleviate this problem is to delete your existing data store. This is an acceptable option while you are developing your app, but if you already have customers using this app and you are working on an update, this will trigger the wrath of all your users. For a smoother experience, we strongly recommend versioning your model and using Core Data's migrations to preserve your users' data by migrating it from the old model to the new. Any changes you make to your data model go into the new version of the model, not any of the old ones. For us, this means that we'll add the name attribute to the Shape entity in the Shapes 2 data model.

To make this change, select the Shapes 2 data model, and then add a name attribute of type String to the Shape entity in the normal way. Figure 8-3 shows the Xcode window with the new version of the Core Data model and the name attribute added to the Shape entity.

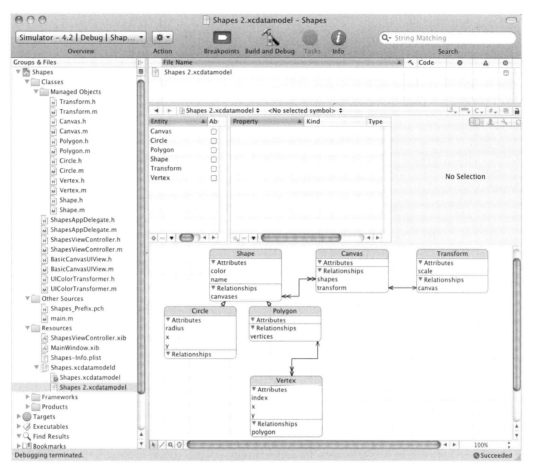

Figure 8-3. *The Xcode window with a second version of the model*

To change the current version of the model from Shapes to Shapes 2, make sure Shapes 2.xcdatamodel is selected and, from the menu, select **Design ➤ Data Model ➤ Set Current Version**. This moves the green check mark from Shapes.xcdatamodel to Shapes 2.xcdatamodel.

At this point, your application has a new current version of the data model, but it is not ready to run yet. You need to define a policy for migrating the data from the version of the model called Shapes to the one called Shapes 2. If you tried running the application now, you would get a crash because, just as if you had changed the first model, the data store does not match the current model. The application needs to be told how you want it to handle switching from the old model to the new one. The rest of the chapter discusses the various ways to do that.

Switching from Unversioned to Versioned

Switching from an unversioned model to a versioned model can leave some detritus in your application bundle that causes your application to crash. Jeff LaMarche discusses the issue, along with possible remedies, here: `http://iphonedevelopment.blogspot .com/2009/09/core-data-migration-problems.html`. Briefly, the problem is that your original, unversioned model lives in your application bundle in a file with a `.mom` extension. When you tell Xcode to version your model, it creates a directory with a `.momd` extension in the same directory as your original `.mom` file and creates your model files (`.mom` files), one for each version, in that directory. Depending on when you do a build or a clean, that original `.mom` file might still be sitting there when you attempt to launch your application.

If that original `.mom` file is still in the bundle when your application loads, it tries to load that model along with the versioned models and crashes the application with the message:

```
Can't merge models with two different entities named '<some entity name>'
```

To fix this is, you can implement code, as LaMarche demonstrates, to load the model only from the *.momd path, like this:

```
- (NSManagedObjectModel *)managedObjectModel {

  if (managedObjectModel != nil) {
    return managedObjectModel;
  }

  NSString *path = [[NSBundle mainBundle] pathForResource:@"Foo" ofType:@"momd"];
  NSURL *momURL = [NSURL fileURLWithPath:path];
  managedObjectModel = [[NSManagedObjectModel alloc] initWithContentsOfURL:momURL];

  return managedObjectModel;
}
```

Alternatively, you can try running **Build ➤ Clean** (or **Build ➤ Clean All Targets**) from the Xcode menu, which may or may not delete the file. Or, you can navigate to the directory on your file system where the application is being built (`~/Library/Application Support/iPhone Simulator/4.2/Applications/279D14B2-2680-4A45-9B79-BC3C514B663D/Shapes.app`, or something similar), where you'll find both the `.mom` file and the `.momd` directory, and delete the `.mom` file.

Lightweight Migrations

Once you have a versioned data model, you can take advantage of Core Data's support for migrations as you evolve your data model. Each time you create a new data model version, users' application data must migrate from the old data model to the new. For the migration to occur, Core Data must have rules to follow to know how to properly migrate the data. You create these rules using what's called a *mapping model*, and support for creating these is built in to Xcode. For certain straightforward cases, however, Core Data has enough smarts to figure out the mapping rules on its own without requiring you to create a mapping model. Called *lightweight migrations*, these cases represent the least work for you as a developer. Core Data does all the work and migrates the data.

For your migration to qualify as a lightweight migration, your changes must be confined to this narrow band:

- Add or remove a property (attribute or relationship)
- Make a nonoptional property optional
- Make an optional attribute nonoptional, as long as you provide a default value
- Add or remove an entity
- Rename a property
- Rename an entity

In addition to involving less work from you, a lightweight migration using a SQLite data store runs faster and uses less space than other migrations. Because Core Data can issue SQL statements to perform these migrations, it doesn't have to load all the data into memory in order to migrate it, and it doesn't have to move the data from one store to the other. Core Data simply uses SQL statements to alter the SQLite database in place. If feasible, you should aggressively try to confine your data model changes to those that lightweight migrations support. If not, the other sections in this chapter walk you through more complicated migrations.

Migrating a Simple Change

In the previous section, "Versioning," you created a new model version in the Shapes application called Shapes 2, and you added a new attribute called name to the Shape entity in the Shapes 2 model. The final step to performing a lightweight migration with that change is to tell the persistent store coordinator two things:

- It should migrate the model automatically.
- It should infer the mapping model.

You do that by passing those instructions in the options parameter of the persistent store coordinator's addPersistentStoreWithType: method. You first set up options, an NSDictionary, like this:

```
NSDictionary *options = [NSDictionary dictionaryWithObjectsAndKeys:[NSNumber➡
numberWithBool:YES], NSMigratePersistentStoresAutomaticallyOption, [NSNumber➡
numberWithBool:YES], NSInferMappingModelAutomaticallyOption, nil];
```

This code creates an instance of NSDictionary with two entries:

- One with the key of NSMigratePersistentStoresAutomaticallyOption, value of YES, which tells the persistent store coordinator to automatically migrate the data

- One with the key of NSInferMappingModelAutomaticallyOption, value of YES, which tells the persistent store coordinator to infer the mapping model

You then pass this options object, instead of nil, for the options parameter in the call to addPersistentStoreWithType:. Open the ShapesAppDelegate.m file and change the persistentStoreCoordinator method to look like this:

```
- (NSPersistentStoreCoordinator *)persistentStoreCoordinator {
  if (persistentStoreCoordinator_ != nil) {
    return persistentStoreCoordinator_;
  }

  NSString* dir = [NSSearchPathForDirectoriesInDomains(NSDocumentDirectory,➡
NSUserDomainMask, YES) lastObject];
  NSURL *storeURL = [NSURL fileURLWithPath: [dir stringByAppendingPathComponent:➡
@"Shapes.sqlite"]];
  NSDictionary *options = [NSDictionary dictionaryWithObjectsAndKeys:[NSNumber➡
numberWithBool:YES], NSMigratePersistentStoresAutomaticallyOption, [NSNumber➡
numberWithBool:YES], NSInferMappingModelAutomaticallyOption, nil];

  NSError *error = nil;
  persistentStoreCoordinator_ = [[NSPersistentStoreCoordinator alloc]➡
initWithManagedObjectModel:[self managedObjectModel]];
  if (![persistentStoreCoordinator_ addPersistentStoreWithType:NSSQLiteStoreType➡
configuration:nil URL:storeURL options:options error:&error]) {
    NSLog(@"Unresolved error %@, %@", error, [error userInfo]);
    abort();
  }
  return persistentStoreCoordinator_;
}
```

That's all you have to do to migrate the data. Build and run the application, open a Terminal, and navigate to the directory that contains the SQLite file for the Shapes application. You'll now find two files:

- Shapes.sqlite: The current database file

- Shapes~.sqlite : The old database file

Run the sqlite3 application on each file, in turn, and run the .schema command to see the definition for the ZSHAPE table. You can see that the Shapes.sqlite file has added a column for the name attribute: ZNAME VARCHAR.

Migrating More Complex Changes

As claimed earlier, lightweight migrations handle a few more cases other than adding an attribute. Create another new version of the model as you did in the "Versioning" section. Xcode will call this version Shapes 3. Do the following to the model:

- Add an entity called Ellipse that has four Float values: x, y, width, and height.

- Make the transform relationship of the Canvas entity optional.

Once again, build and run the Shapes application, and everything will start fine: the new data model will be applied to the SQLite data store, and the data will migrate appropriately. Of course, ellipses haven't magically been added to the random shape mix because you haven't added any code to create them, and we won't bother doing that because it doesn't further our understanding of model versioning and data migration, but if you look at the schema for your database, you'll see the table for ellipses:

```
CREATE TABLE ZELLIPSE ( Z_PK INTEGER PRIMARY KEY, Z_ENT INTEGER, Z_OPT INTEGER, ZHEIGHT
FLOAT, ZWIDTH FLOAT, ZX FLOAT, ZY FLOAT );
```

Renaming Entities and Properties

Lightweight migrations also support renaming entities and properties but require a little more effort from you. In addition to changing your model, you must specify the old name for the item whose name you changed. You can do this in one of two ways:

- In the Xcode data modeler

- In code

The Xcode data modeler is the simpler option. When you select an entity or property in the Xcode data modeler, general information about that entity or property shows in the panel to the right. If you select the third button at the top of the panel, which looks like a wrench, you go to the Configurations tab where you see a Versioning section. In that section, you see a field called Renaming Identifier. Put the old name of whatever you've changed into this field. See Figure 8-4.

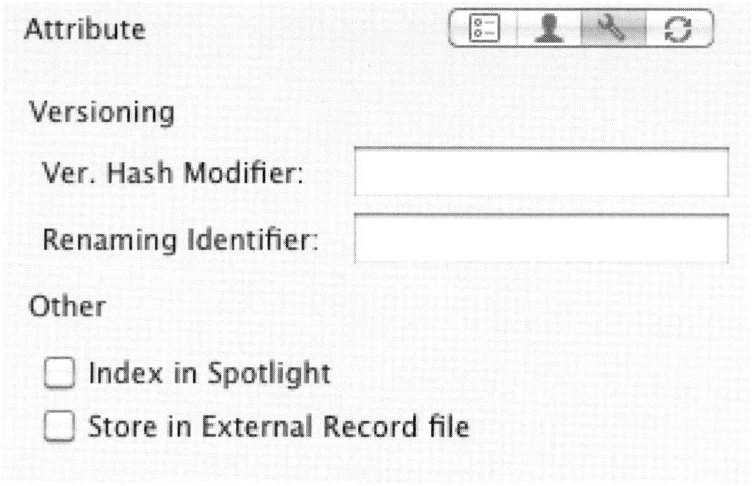

Attribute

Versioning

Ver. Hash Modifier:

Renaming Identifier:

Other

☐ Index in Spotlight

☐ Store in External Record file

Figure 8-4. *The Versioning section with the Renaming Identifier field*

If you insist on specifying the old name in code (or if you're still running under Leopard and have no field for Renaming Identifier), you'd make a call to the setRenamingIdentifier: method of NSEntityDescription or NSPropertyDescription, depending on what you've renamed, passing the old name for the entity or property. You do this after the model has loaded, but before the call to open the persistent store (addPersistentStoreWithType:). If, for example, you wanted to change the name of the Vertex entity to Point, you'd add this code before the call to addPersistentStoreWithType:

```
NSEntityDescription *point = [[managedObjectModel entitiesByName]➥
objectForKey:@"Point"];
[point setRenamingIdentifier:@"Vertex"];
```

Core Data takes care of migrating the data, but you still have the responsibility to update any code in your application that depends on the old name.

To see this in practice, create a new version of your data model. You should now be on version 4 (Shapes 4). In this version of the model, you'll rename the Vertex entity to Point. Go to your new model file, Shapes 4.xcdatamodel, and rename the Vertex entity to Point. Then, go to the Versioning section in the Configurations tab, and type the old name, **Vertex**, into the renaming identifier field so that Core Data will know how to migrate the existing data, as Figure 8-5 shows, and save this model.

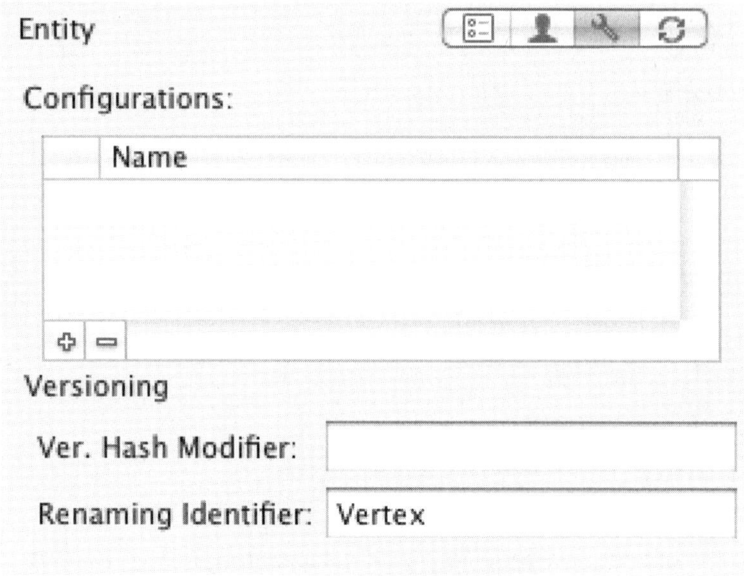

Entity

Configurations:

Name

➕ ➖

Versioning

Ver. Hash Modifier: [   ]

Renaming Identifier: [Vertex   ]

Figure 8-5. *Renaming Vertex to Point and specifying the renaming identifier*

Wait! Before running the application, remember that you're responsible for changing any code that relies on the old name, Vertex. You could change the custom managed object class name from Vertex to Point, change the relationship name in the Polygon entity from vertices to points, change any variable names appropriately, but we'll keep it simple here and change the one place the Shapes application refers to the Vertex entity name. You find it in Polygon.m in the call to [NSEntityDescription insertNewObjectForEntityForName]. It currently reads as follows:

```
Vertex *vertex = [NSEntityDescription insertNewObjectForEntityForName:@"Vertex"➥
inManagedObjectContext:context];
```

Change the entity name passed to the method from Vertex to Point so the line reads like this:

```
Vertex *vertex = [NSEntityDescription insertNewObjectForEntityForName:@"Point"➥
inManagedObjectContext:context];
```

You can now build and run the Shapes application, and all existing shapes, including polygons, should appear. You can open the SQLite database and confirm that the schema now has a ZPOINT table:

```
CREATE TABLE ZPOINT ( Z_PK INTEGER PRIMARY KEY, Z_ENT INTEGER, Z_OPT INTEGER, ZINDEX
INTEGER, ZPOLYGON INTEGER, ZX FLOAT, ZY FLOAT );
```

and no ZVERTEX table.

As you've seen, lightweight migrations are nearly effortless, at least for you. Core Data handles the difficult work of figuring out how to map and migrate the data from old model to new. When your model changes, however, don't fit within what lightweight migrations can handle, you must specify your own mapping model. This is the subject of the next section.

Creating a Mapping Model

When your data model changes exceed Core Data's ability to infer how to map data from the old model to the new, you can't use a lightweight migration to automatically migrate your data. Instead, you have to create what's called a *mapping model* to tell Core Data how to execute the migration. A mapping model is roughly analogous to a data model—whereas a data model contains entities and properties, a mapping model, which is of type NSMappingModel, has entity mappings (of type NSEntityMapping) and property mappings (of type NSPropertyMapping). The entity mappings do just what you'd expect them to do: they map a source entity to a target entity. The property mappings, as well, do what you'd think: map source properties to target properties. The mapping model uses these mappings, along with their associated types and policies, to perform the migration.

> **Note:** Apple's documentation and code use the terms *destination* and *target* interchangeably to refer to the new data model. In this chapter, we follow suit and use both *destination* and *target* interchangeably.

In a typical data migration, most entities and properties haven't changed from the old version to the new. For these cases, the entity mappings simply copy each entity from the source model to the target model. When you create a mapping model, you'll notice that Xcode generates these entity mappings, along with anything else it can infer from your model changes, and stores these mappings in the mapping model. These mappings represent how Core Data would have migrated your data in a lightweight migration. You have to create new mappings, or adjust the mappings Xcode generates, to change how your data migrates.

Understanding Entity Mappings

Each entity mapping, represented by an NSEntityMapping instance, contains three things:

- A source entity
- A destination entity
- A mapping type

When Core Data performs the migration, it uses the entity mapping to move the source to the destination, using the mapping type to determine how to do that. Table 8-1 lists the mapping types, their corresponding Core Data constants, and what they mean.

Table 8-1. *The Entity Mapping Types*

Type	Core Data Constant	Meaning
Add	NSAddEntityMappingType	The entity is new in the destination model—it doesn't exist in the source model—and should be added.
Remove	NSRemoveEntityMappingType	The entity doesn't exist in the destination model and should be removed.
Copy	NSCopyEntityMappingType	The entity exists in both the source and destination models unchanged and should be copied as is.
Transform	NSTransformEntityMappingType	The entity exists in both the source and destination models but with changes. The mapping tells Core Data how to migrate each source instance to a destination instance.
Custom	NSCustomEntityMappingType	The entity exists in both the source and destination models but with changes. The mapping tells Core Data how to migrate each source instance to a destination instance.

The Add, Remove, and Copy types don't generate much interest, because lightweight migrations handle these types of entity mappings. The Transform and Custom types, however, are what make this section of the book necessary. They tell Core Data that each source entity instance must be transformed, according to any specified rules, into an instance of the destination entity. We'll see an example of both a Transform and a Custom entity mapping type in this chapter. If you specify a value expression for one of the entity's properties, the entity mapping is of type Transform. If you specify a custom migration policy for the entity mapping, the entity mapping becomes a Custom type. As you work through this chapter, pay attention to the types the Core Data mapping modeler makes to your mapping model in response to changes you make.

To specify the rules for a Custom entity mapping type, you create a migration policy, which is a class you write that derives from NSEntityMigrationPolicy. You then set the class you create as the custom policy for the entity mapping in the Xcode mapping modeler.

Core Data runs your migration in three stages:

1. Create the objects in the destination model, including their attributes, based on the objects in the source model.

2. Create the relationships among the objects in the destination model.

3. Validate the data in the destination model and save it.

You can customize how Core Data performs these three steps through the Custom Policy. The NSEntityMigrationPolicy class has seven methods you can override to customize how Core Data will migrate data from the source entity to the target entity, though you'll rarely override all of them. These methods, listed in Apple's documentation for the NSEntityMigrationPolicy class, provide various places during the migration that you can override and change Core Data's migration behavior. You can override as few or as many of these methods as you'd like, though a custom migration policy that overrides none of the methods is pointless. Typically, you'll override createDestinationInstancesForSourceInstance: if you want to change how destination instances are created or how their attributes are populated with data. You'll override createRelationshipsForDestinationInstance: if you want to customize how relationships between the destination entity and other entities are created. Finally, you'll override performCustomValidationForEntityMapping: if you want to perform any custom validations during your migration.

The createDestinationInstancesForSourceInstance: method carries with it a caveat: if you don't call the superclass's implementation, which you probably won't because you're overriding this method to change the default behavior, you must call the migration manager's associateSourceInstance:withDestinationInstance: ➥ forEntityMapping: method to associate the source instance with the destination instance. Forgetting to do that will cause problems with your migration. We show you the proper way to call this method later in this chapter, with the Shapes application.

Understanding Property Mappings

A property mapping, like an entity mapping, tells Core Data how to migrate source to destination. A property mapping is an instance of NSPropertyMapping and contains three things:

- The name of the property in the source entity
- The name of the property in the destination entity
- A value expression that tells Core Data how to get from source to destination

To change the way a property mapping migrates data, you provide the value expression for the property mapping to use. Value expressions follow the same syntax as predicates and use six predefined keys to assist with retrieving values:

- $manager, which represents the migration manager
- $source, which represents the source entity
- $destination, which represents the destination entity
- $entityMapping, which represents the entity mapping
- $propertyMapping, which represents this property mapping
- $entityPolicy, which represents the entity migration policy

As you can see, these keys have names that make deducing their purposes easy. When you create a mapping model, you can explore the property mappings Xcode infers from your source and target data models to better understand what these keys mean and how they're used.

The simplest value expressions copy an attribute from the source entity to the destination entity. If you have a Person entity, for example, that has a name attribute and the Person entity hasn't changed between your old and your new model versions, the value expression for the name attribute in your PersonToPerson entity mapping would be as follows:

```
$source.name
```

You can also perform manipulations of source data using value expressions. Suppose, for example, that the same Person entity had an attribute called salary that stores each person's salary. In the new model, you want to give everyone 4 percent raises. Your value expression would look like this:

```
$source.salary*1.04
```

Since properties represent both attributes and relationships, property mappings represent mappings for both attributes and relationships. The typical value expression for a relationship calls a function, passing the migration manager, the destination instances, the entity mapping, and the name of the source relationship. For example, if our old data model had a relationship called staff in the Person entity that represented everyone who reported to this person and our new model has renamed this relationship to reports, the value expression for the reports property would look like this:

```
FUNCTION($manager, "destinationInstancesForEntityMappingNamed:sourceInstances:",
"PersonToPerson", $source.staff)
```

Notice that we use the $manager key to pass the migration manager, that we get the destination instances from the entity mapping for the source instances, that we pass the appropriate entity mapping (PersonToPerson), and that we pass the old relationship that we get from the $source key.

Creating a New Model Version That Requires a Mapping Model

Earlier in this chapter, you created an entity called Ellipse that had four attributes: x, y, width, and height. You didn't do anything with that entity, and it wasn't incorporated into the application. The time for Ellipse to shine has come, however, and you're going to incorporate it into the application. Acting on the idea that Circles are just Ellipses that have the same width and height, which may make mathematicians shudder but that fits nicely with the Shape application's code, you'll migrate all the Circle instances to the Ellipse entity and delete the Circle entity entirely.

You've also decided that you'd rather call the scale attribute of the Transform entity scalarValue. What's more, you've decided that the shapes that the application draws are too big and that the scales should be reduced 20 percent to 0.4 and 0.8, instead of the existing 0.5 and 1.0.

To perform this migration, you'll need to create a mapping model and a custom policy that will migrate each `Circle` instance to a corresponding `Ellipse` instance. The x and y values will copy across as is, and the `radius` value from the `Circle` will be copied to the `width` and `height` attributes of the `Ellipse`. This custom policy will attach to an entity mapping that's responsible for mapping `Circles` to `Ellipses`.

You'll also need to modify the property mapping for `scalarValue` to multiply each `scale` value by 0.8 as the data migrates.

To get started, create a new version of your data model—you should be up to version 5. In the new data model, delete the `Circle` entity. Next, go to the `Transform` entity, and change the name for the `scale` attribute to `scalarValue`. Change the parent entity for the `Ellipse` entity to `Shape`. Create or generate a custom class for the `Ellipse` entity, put it in the Managed Objects group, and then set the `Ellipse` entity in the data model (if necessary) to this class, as Figure 8-6 shows. Modify the `Ellipse` code according to Listings 8-1 and 8-2.

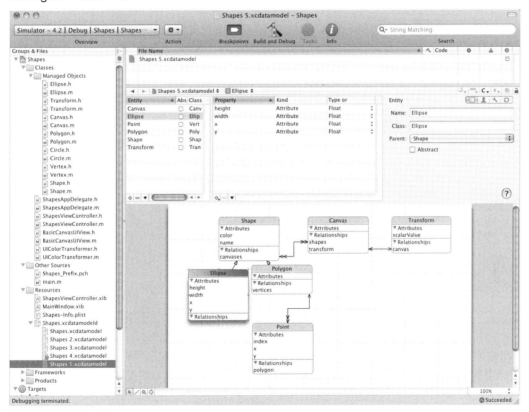

Figure 8-6. *The* `Ellipse` *entity set to the Ellipse class*

Listing 8-1. `Ellipse.h`

```
#import <CoreData/CoreData.h>
#import "Shape.h"
```

```
@interface Ellipse :  Shape
{
}

@property (nonatomic, retain) NSNumber * y;
@property (nonatomic, retain) NSNumber * x;
@property (nonatomic, retain) NSNumber * width;
@property (nonatomic, retain) NSNumber * height;

+ (Ellipse *)randomInstance:(CGPoint)origin inContext:(NSManagedObjectContext *)context;

@end
```

Listing 8-2. *Ellipse.m*

```
#import "Ellipse.h"

@implementation Ellipse

@dynamic y;
@dynamic x;
@dynamic width;
@dynamic height;

+ (Ellipse *)randomInstance:(CGPoint)origin inContext:(NSManagedObjectContext *)context
{
  Ellipse *ellipse = [NSEntityDescription insertNewObjectForEntityForName:@"Ellipse"➡
inManagedObjectContext:context];

  float width = 10 + (arc4random() % 90);
  float height = 10 + (arc4random() % 90);
  ellipse.x = [NSNumber numberWithFloat:origin.x];
  ellipse.y = [NSNumber numberWithFloat:origin.y];
  ellipse.width = [NSNumber numberWithFloat:width];
  ellipse.height = [NSNumber numberWithFloat:height];

  return ellipse;
}

@end
```

The Ellipse class looks suspiciously like the Circle class but with width and height properties instead of a single radius property. You now must update the Shapes application code in a few places to use Ellipse instead of Circle. In ShapesViewController.m, change the line:

```
#import "Circle.h"
```

to the following:

```
#import "Ellipse.h"
```

Then, in the createShapeAt: method, change the code that creates the shapes to create an Ellipse instead of a Circle for the case where the random value for type is 0:

```
if (type == 0) { // Ellipse
  shape = [Ellipse randomInstance:point inContext:self.managedObjectContext];
}
else {  // Polygon
  shape = [Polygon randomInstance:point inContext:self.managedObjectContext];
}
```

In BasicCanvasUIView.m, change the Circle.h import to instead import Ellipse.h, then find the line in the drawRect: method that looks like this:

```
if ([entityName compare:@"Circle"] == NSOrderedSame) {
```

The code inside the if condition draws a Circle, and you must change it to draw an Ellipse. The updated code looks like this:

```
if ([entityName compare:@"Ellipse"] == NSOrderedSame) {
  Ellipse *ellipse = (Ellipse *)shape;
  float x = [ellipse.x floatValue];
  float y = [ellipse.y floatValue];
  float width = [ellipse.width floatValue];
  float height = [ellipse.height floatValue];

  CGContextFillEllipseInRect(context, CGRectMake(x - (width / 2), y - (height / 2),➥
width, height));
}
```

That completes the code changes to use Ellipses instead of Circles. You now must make code changes to use the new name for the scale attribute of the Transform entity, scalarValue. In Transform.h, change the property name from scale to scalarValue. In Transform.m, change this line:

```
@dynamic scale;
```

to this:

```
@dynamic scalarValue;
```

and change this line:

```
transform.scale = [NSNumber numberWithFloat:scale];
```

to this:

```
transform.scalarValue = [NSNumber numberWithFloat:scale];
```

Open BasicCanvasUIView.m, and change the scale: method to look like this:

```
-(float)scale {
  NSManagedObject *transform = [canvas valueForKey:@"transform"];
  return [[transform valueForKey:@"scalarValue"] floatValue];
}
```

You also must change the code that initially creates the two Transform instances to use 0.4 and 0.8 for the scale, instead of 0.5 and 1.0. This code is in ShapesViewController.m, in the viewDidLoad: method, and looks like this:

```
// If there aren't any canvases, then we create them
Transform *transform1 = [Transform initWithScale:1 inContext:self.managedObjectContext];
canvas1 = [Canvas initWithTransform:transform1 inContext:self.managedObjectContext];
```

```
Transform *transform2 = [Transform initWithScale:0.5
inContext:self.managedObjectContext];
canvas2 = [Canvas initWithTransform:transform2 inContext:self.managedObjectContext];
```

Change it to this:

```
// If there aren't any canvases, then we create them
Transform *transform1 = [Transform initWithScale:0.8
inContext:self.managedObjectContext];
canvas1 = [Canvas initWithTransform:transform1 inContext:self.managedObjectContext];

Transform *transform2 = [Transform initWithScale:0.4
inContext:self.managedObjectContext];
canvas2 = [Canvas initWithTransform:transform2 inContext:self.managedObjectContext];
```

You have your new model, and you've updated the code to use it. You're ready to create a mapping model that will transform your Circles into Ellipses and reduce the scales by 20 percent. The next section walks you through creating the mapping model.

Creating a Mapping Model

To create a mapping model, go to Xcode's menu, and select **File ➤ New File….** In the ensuing dialog box, select Resource under iOS on the left, and select Mapping Model on the right, as shown in Figure 8-7. Click Next.

Figure 8-7. *Creating a new mapping model*

In the next dialog, save this mapping model as Model4to5.xcmappingmodel and click Next. The next dialog box, shown in Figure 8-8, asks you for the source data model and the destination data model. Select Shapes 4.xcdatamodel for the source and Shapes 5.xcdatamodel for the destination, as shown in Figure 8-9, and click Finish. You should now see Xcode with your mapping model created, including all the entity mappings and property mappings that Core Data could infer, as shown in Figure 8-10.

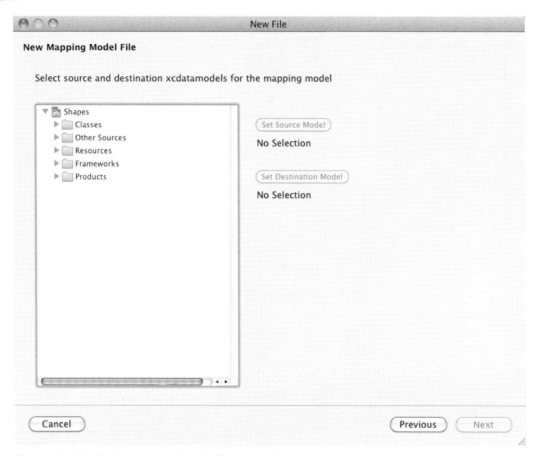

Figure 8-8. *Selecting the source and destination data models*

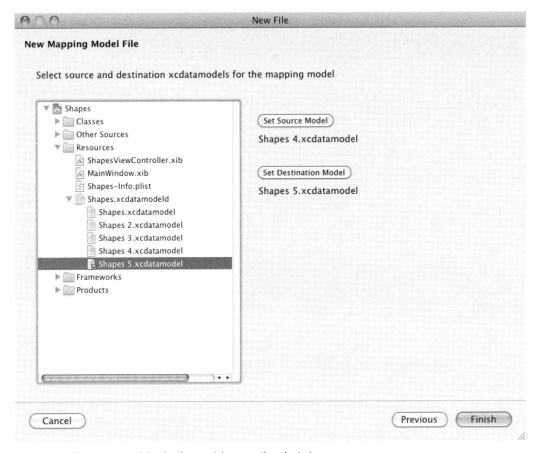

Figure 8-9. *The source and destination models correctly selected*

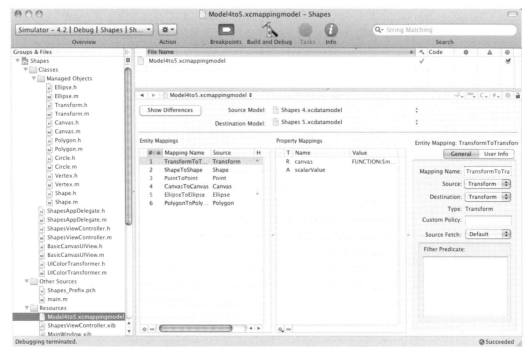

Figure 8-10. *Your new mapping model*

Creating a mapping model puts you in the same place you'd be with a lightweight migration, with mappings that Core Data can infer from your source and target data models. The next step is to customize the mapping model to migrate `Circles` to `Ellipses`. Start by creating the custom policy you'll use, which is a subclass of `NSEntityMigrationPolicy`. Create a new class called `CircleToEllipseMigrationPolicy`, and create a new group for it called Migration Mappings under `Classes`. The header file is simple, as shown in Listing 8-3.

Listing 8-3. *CircleToEllipseMigrationPolicy.h*

```
#import <Foundation/Foundation.h>
#import <CoreData/CoreData.h>

@interface CircleToEllipseMigrationPolicy : NSEntityMigrationPolicy {

}

@end
```

The implementation file, `CircleToEllipseMigrationPolicy.m`, overrides the `createDestinationInstancesForSourceInstance:` method. While performing the migration, Core Data will call this method each time it goes to create an `Ellipse` instance from a `Circle` instance. Keep in mind that both `Circle` and `Ellipse` inherit from the `Shape` entity, so you're responsible for handling any of `Shape`'s properties as well. In your implementation, you create an `Ellipse` instance; copy over the x, y, and `color` values from the `Circle` instance passed to this method; and then copy the `Circle`'s radius value to the Ellipse's width and height values. Finally, you tell the migration manager about the relationship between the source's Circle instance and the target's new Ellipse instance, which is an important step for the migration to occur properly. Listing 8-4 shows the implementation file.

Listing 8-4. *CircleToEllipseMigrationPolicy.m*

```
#import "CircleToEllipseMigrationPolicy.h"

@implementation CircleToEllipseMigrationPolicy

- (BOOL)createDestinationInstancesForSourceInstance:(NSManagedObject *)sInstance➥
entityMapping:(NSEntityMapping *)mapping manager:(NSMigrationManager *)manager➥
error:(NSError **)error {
  // Create the ellipse managed object
  NSManagedObject *ellipse = [NSEntityDescription➥
insertNewObjectForEntityForName:[mapping destinationEntityName]➥
inManagedObjectContext:[manager destinationContext]];

  // Copy the x, y, and color values from the Circle to the Ellipse
  [ellipse setValue:[sInstance valueForKey:@"x"] forKey:@"x"];
  [ellipse setValue:[sInstance valueForKey:@"y"] forKey:@"y"];
  [ellipse setValue:[sInstance valueForKey:@"color"] forKey:@"color"];

  // Copy the radius value from the Circle to the width and height of the Ellipse
  [ellipse setValue:[sInstance valueForKey:@"radius"] forKey:@"width"];
  [ellipse setValue:[sInstance valueForKey:@"radius"] forKey:@"height"];

  // Set up the association between the Circle and the Ellipse for the migration manager
  [manager associateSourceInstance:sInstance withDestinationInstance:ellipse➥
forEntityMapping:mapping];

  return YES;
}

@end
```

You might notice that we've ignored the name attribute of Shape. Normally, you would copy this property from the source to the target as well, but we've done nothing with the name attribute in the Shapes application. We never added it to the Shape custom class, and we haven't added any code that would fill that value, so we left it out here to illustrate a point: if you leave an attribute out of a mapping policy, that attribute won't be copied over and will be blank in the target entity.

Notice also that we didn't copy over the canvases relationships. The relationships are copied over by default in NSEntityMigrationPolicy's createRelationshipsForDestinationInstance: method. By not overriding that method, we get Core Data to copy those over for us.

Now, you're ready to create the entity mapping between Circle and Ellipse. With your mapping model (Model4to5.xcmappingmodel) selected, click the + button below the Entity Mappings section on the left. Name the new entity mapping CircleToEllipse and set its Source to Circle, its Destination to Ellipse, and its Custom Policy to CircleToEllipseMigrationPolicy. See Figure 8-11.

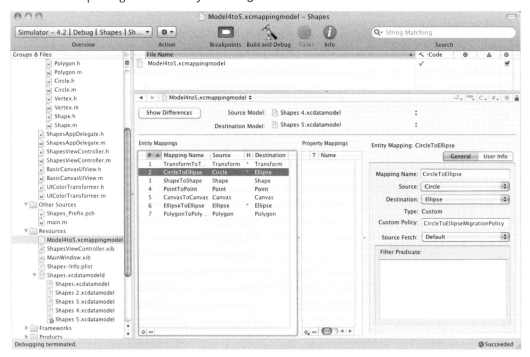

Figure 8-11. *Adding and configuring the CircleToEllipse entity mapping*

That takes care of mapping Circles to Ellipses. Next, you need to set up the property mapping for migrating the scale values of Transform to scalarValues at 80 percent of their original values. Select the TransformToTransform entity mapping in the mapping model, which displays its information, including its Property Mappings, as shown in Figure 8-12.

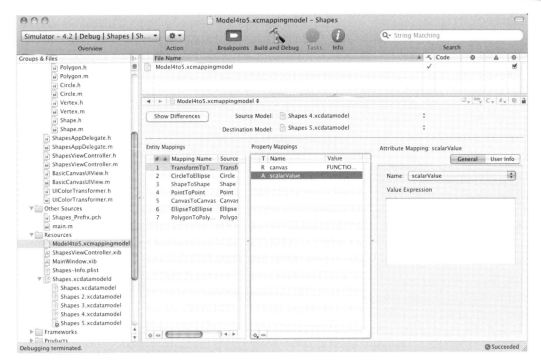

Figure 8-12. *The* `TransformToTransform` *mapping*

Select the `scalarValue` property mapping, and on the right side enter the following for the Value Expression setting:

`$source.scale*0.8`

This tells Core Data to take the value from the `scale` attribute from the source data model, multiply it by 0.8, and store the value in the `scalarValue` attribute of the target.

Your mapping model is ready to perform the migration. Just as with lightweight migrations, however, you need to add some code to the application delegate to tell Core Data to execute a migration. This is the subject of the next section.

Migrating Data

Creating the mapping model is essential to performing a migration that lightweight migrations can't handle, but you still must perform the actual migration. This section explains how to do that and then updates the code for the Shapes application to actually run the migration. By the end of this section, you will have a Shapes application that includes all the shapes it had before, including the circles, but now the circles are ellipses with the same width and height. As you tap the screen, you'll see at random ellipses being created. You also may notice that everything is 80 percent of the size it was before.

Telling Core Data to migrate from the old model to the new one using a mapping model you create is similar to how you tell Core Data to use a lightweight migration. As you learned earlier, the way to tell Core Data to perform a lightweight migration is to pass an options dictionary that contains YES for two keys:

- NSMigratePersistentStoresAutomaticallyOption
- NSInferMappingModelAutomaticallyOption

The first key tells Core Data to automatically migrate the data, and the second tells Core Data to infer the mapping model.

For a migration using a mapping model you created, you clearly want Core Data to still automatically perform the migration, so you still set the NSMigratePersistentStoresAutomaticallyOption to YES. Since you've created the mapping model, however, you don't want Core Data to infer anything; you want it to use your mapping model. Therefore, you set NSInferMappingModelAutomaticallyOption to NO, or you leave it out of the options dictionary entirely.

How, then, do you specify the mapping model for Core Data to use to perform the migration? Do you set it in the options dictionary? Do you pass it somehow to the persistent store coordinator's addPersistentStoreWithType: method? Do you set it into the persistent store coordinator? Into the managed object model? Into the context?

The answer, which seems a little shocking, is that you do nothing. Core Data will figure it out. It searches through your mapping models, finds one that's appropriate for migrating from the source to the destination, and uses it. This makes migrations almost criminally easy.

Running Your Migration

To run the migration of your Shapes data store, open the ShapesAppDelegate.m file, and remove the NSInferMappingModelAutomaticallyOption key from the options dictionary. This means you change this line:

```
NSDictionary *options = [NSDictionary dictionaryWithObjectsAndKeys:[NSNumber➡
numberWithBool:YES], NSMigratePersistentStoresAutomaticallyOption, [NSNumber➡
numberWithBool:YES], NSInferMappingModelAutomaticallyOption, nil];
```

to this:

```
NSDictionary *options = [NSDictionary dictionaryWithObjectsAndKeys:[NSNumber➡
numberWithBool:YES], NSMigratePersistentStoresAutomaticallyOption, nil];
```

That's seriously all you have to do to get Core Data to migrate your data using your mapping model, `Model4to5.xcmappingmodel`. Build and run the Shapes application, and you should see all the shapes you had in the database before you ran the migration, albeit shown at 80 percent of the size they were before. Go look at the SQLite database to confirm that the migration ran. You can see that the ZSHAPE table now has columns for ZWIDTH and ZHEIGHT, but none for ZRADIUS:

```
CREATE TABLE ZSHAPE ( Z_PK INTEGER PRIMARY KEY, Z_ENT INTEGER, Z_OPT INTEGER, ZHEIGHT
FLOAT, ZWIDTH FLOAT, ZX FLOAT, ZY FLOAT, ZNAME VARCHAR, ZCOLOR BLOB );
```

You can also fetch the values for ZSCALARVALUE (not ZSCALE) from the ZTRANSFORM table to verify that they're 20 percent smaller than the 0.5 and 1.0 that they used to be:

```
sqlite> select distinct zscalarvalue from ztransform;
0.4
0.8
```

Tap the screen of the Shapes application a few times to see some ellipses created, as shown in Figure 8-13.

Figure 8-13. *The Shapes application with ellipses*

Custom Migrations

In most data migration cases, using the default three-step migration process (create the destination objects, create the relationships, and validate and save) is sufficient. Data objects are created in the new data store from the previous version, then all relationships are created, and finally the data is validated and persisted. This scheme works well but greedily consumes memory because it creates and holds every object until the end of the migration, when everything is committed to the store. The migration manager has no mechanism for cleaning up the context because it operates through the data set and therefore objects accumulate without any possibility to clean them up. This could cause the migration to be impossible because of memory constraints. In some cases, however, when it is possible to split the data model into multiple object graphs, taking control of the migration process initialization can help alleviate this memory problem.

Imagine a case where you have a customer relationship management (CRM) application for iPad. This application contains a database of your customers and any communication you've had with them. Suppose that on top of the CRM database, your application keeps track of your inventory, so part of your data model contains a catalog. The two data sets aren't related in terms of data modeling. That is, there is no relationship between the CRM object graph and the catalog object graph. To migrate the data to the new data store, you would create two independent mapping models and treat them separately. Controlling the migration process at a finer level allows you to migrate the two parts of the data store independently.

Taking control of the migration process initialization means that you need to perform all the work that Core Data usually does for you. This means that you need to do the following:

- Make sure migration is actually needed
- Set up the migration manager
- Run your migration by splitting the model into independent parts

Making Sure Migration Is Needed

To validate that a model is compatible with the persistent store, you use the `isConfiguration:compatibleWithStoreMetadata:` method of the `NSManagedObjectModel` class before adding the persistent store to the coordinator. The data store metadata can be retrieved by querying the coordinator using the `metadataForPersistentStoreOfType:URL:error:` method.

```
NSDictionary *sourceMetadata = [NSPersistentStoreCoordinator➥
metadataForPersistentStoreOfType:sourceStoreType URL:sourceStoreURL error:&error];
NSManagedObjectModel *destinationModel = [persistentStoreCoordinator ➥
managedObjectModel];
BOOL isMigrationNeeded = [destinationModel isConfiguration:configuration➥
compatibleWithStoreMetadata:sourceMetadata];
```

If migration is not needed, then the persistent store can be registered with the coordinator as usual.

Setting Up the Migration Manager

Once it has been determined that migration is indeed needed, the next step is to set up the migration manager, which is a subclass of NSMigrationManager. To do that, you need to get a hold of the model that matches the current persistent store: the previous version of the model. This is the model you use as the source model of your migration process. The source model can be obtained using the mergedModelFromBundles:forStoreMetadata: method, which looks for a model in the application main bundle that matches the given metadata, like this:

```
NSManagedObjectModel *sourceModel = [NSManagedObjectModel➡
mergedModelFromBundles:bundlesForSourceModel forStoreMetadata:sourceMetadata];

MyApplicationMigrationManager *migrationManager = [[MyApplicationMigrationManager➡
alloc] initWithSourceModel:sourceModel destinationModel:destinationModel];
```

Running the Migration

In this last step, you need to find all the mapping models and tell the migration manager to do its job for each of them.

```
NSMappingModel *crmMappingModel = [[NSMappingModel alloc]
initWithContentsOfURL:crmMappingURL];
BOOL crmDone = [migrationManager migrateStoreFromURL:sourceStoreURL type:➡
sourceStoreType options:nil
                withMappingModel:crmMappingModel
                toDestinationURL:destinationStoreURL
                destinationType:destinationStoreType
                destinationOptions:nil
                error:&error];

NSMappingModel *catalogMappingModel = [[NSMappingModel alloc]➡
initWithContentsOfURL:catalogMappingURL];
BOOL catalogDone = [migrationManager migrateStoreFromURL:sourceStoreURL➡
type:sourceStoreType options:nil
                withMappingModel:catalogMappingModel
                toDestinationURL:destinationStoreURL
                destinationType:destinationStoreType
                destinationOptions:nil
                error:&error];
```

Note that the source and destination store URLs are the same since we are migrating data for the same persistent store. The migration, however, can be done in multiple passes as long as the object graphs are not related, hence offering an opportunity to keep the memory clean.

Summary

Although changing data models can be painful in other programming environments, Core Data makes changing your data models nearly painless. With its support for model versions, lightweight migrations, and mapping models for migrations that aren't lightweight, you can change your data models with impunity and let Core Data make sure your users' data stays intact.

As with any part of your application, however, make sure you test your migrations. Test them extensively. Test them even more than you test your application code. Users can handle an occasional application crash, but if they upgrade to the latest version of your application and lose their data in the process, your application and reputation may never recover.

Chapter 9

Using Core Data in Advanced Applications

You can build a lot of cool apps without using the material in this chapter. Before you slam this book closed, however, we recommend you keep reading. This chapter contains material that addresses some advanced Core Data topics that your particular applications may require, especially if securing user data is important to your application. You caught a glimpse of one of the topics, using NSFetchedResultsController, with the League Manager application in Chapter 3. Follow along with this chapter to put some advanced Core Data tools in your tool box.

In this chapter, we walk you through building an application that illustrates each of the topics we cover. You'll build the application incrementally and will be able to run the application at the end of each section so you can see that section's advanced feature working. Because each section builds on the previous ones, you shouldn't try to skip any sections.

The application you build in this chapter, called MyStash, stores both passwords and notes. By the time you're done building it, the passwords are all safely encrypted. The notes, by default, aren't encrypted, but you can choose to encrypt individual notes. The passwords and notes live in separate databases, though they share the same data model. When you're done, you can make a few tweaks to the code, add an enticing icon, and who knows? You may have an App Store hit on your hands!

Creating an Application for Note and Password Storage and Encryption

To begin creating the application that you'll work with throughout this chapter, create a new Xcode project called MyStash. Choose the Window-based Application template, as in Figure 9-1; uncheck Use Core Data for storage, and set Product to iPhone. Click

Choose…, and then save the project as **MyStash** wherever you save your development projects.

Figure 9-1. *Selecting the Window-based Application template*

You can build and run your application now to view a blank, white screen. You have neither data nor a means to view that data. We'll start by adding data to the application.

Setting Up the Data Model

Before you can add data, you need a data model, and before you add a data model, you need to add Core Data support to your application. Add the Core Data framework to the Frameworks folder, and then add your data model by selecting **File ➤ New File…**, select Resources on the left and Data Model on the right, and call it MyStash.xcdatamodel.

The MyStash data model will have two entities: one to hold notes and one to hold passwords for systems (such as web sites). Open the data model, and create an entity called Note and another called System. Add two attributes to the Note entity:

- title (type String)
- body (type String)

Add three attributes to the System entity:

- name (type String)
- userId (type String)
- password (type String)

Your data model should look like Figure 9-2.

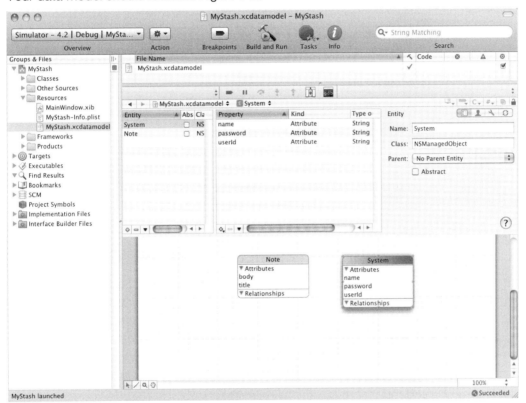

Figure 9-2. *The MyStash data model*

To finish adding support for the data model to the MyStash application, add a managed object context, a managed object model, and a persistent store coordinator to your application delegate, as you have many times throughout this book. Check Listings 9-1 and 9-2 for guidance.

Listing 9-1. *MyStashAppDelegate.h*

```
#import <UIKit/UIKit.h>
#import <CoreData/CoreData.h>

@interface MyStashAppDelegate : NSObject <UIApplicationDelegate> {
```

```
  UIWindow *window;

@private
  NSManagedObjectContext *managedObjectContext_;
  NSManagedObjectModel *managedObjectModel_;
  NSPersistentStoreCoordinator *persistentStoreCoordinator_;
}

@property (nonatomic, retain) IBOutlet UIWindow *window;
@property (nonatomic, retain, readonly) NSManagedObjectContext *managedObjectContext;
@property (nonatomic, retain, readonly) NSManagedObjectModel *managedObjectModel;
@property (nonatomic, retain, readonly) NSPersistentStoreCoordinator
*persistentStoreCoordinator;

- (NSString *)applicationDocumentsDirectory;

@end
```

Listing 9-2. *MyStashAppDelegate.m*

```
#import "MyStashAppDelegate.h"

@implementation MyStashAppDelegate

@synthesize window;

- (BOOL)application:(UIApplication *)application➡
didFinishLaunchingWithOptions:(NSDictionary *)launchOptions {

  [window makeKeyAndVisible];
  return YES;
}

- (void)dealloc {
  [window release];
  [super dealloc];
}

#pragma mark -
#pragma mark Core Data stack

- (NSManagedObjectModel *)managedObjectModel {
  if (managedObjectModel_ != nil) {
    return managedObjectModel_;
  }
  managedObjectModel_ = [[NSManagedObjectModel mergedModelFromBundles:nil] retain];
  return managedObjectModel_;
}

- (NSPersistentStoreCoordinator *)persistentStoreCoordinator {
  if (persistentStoreCoordinator_ != nil) {
    return persistentStoreCoordinator_;
  }

  NSString* dir = [NSSearchPathForDirectoriesInDomains(NSDocumentDirectory,➡
NSUserDomainMask, YES) lastObject];
```

```
   NSURL *storeURL = [NSURL fileURLWithPath: [dir stringByAppendingPathComponent:➡
@"MyStash.sqlite"]];


   NSError *error = nil;
   persistentStoreCoordinator_ = [[NSPersistentStoreCoordinator alloc]➡
initWithManagedObjectModel:[self managedObjectModel]];

   if (![persistentStoreCoordinator_ addPersistentStoreWithType:NSSQLiteStoreType➡
configuration:nil URL:storeURL options:nil error:&error]) {

      NSLog(@"Unresolved error %@, %@", error, [error userInfo]);
      abort();
   }
   return persistentStoreCoordinator_;
}

- (NSManagedObjectContext *)managedObjectContext {
   if (managedObjectContext_ != nil) {
     return managedObjectContext_;
   }

   NSPersistentStoreCoordinator *coordinator = [self persistentStoreCoordinator];
   if (coordinator != nil) {
     managedObjectContext_ = [[NSManagedObjectContext alloc] init];
     [managedObjectContext_ setPersistentStoreCoordinator:coordinator];
   }
   return managedObjectContext_;
}

#pragma mark -
#pragma mark Application's Documents directory

/**
 Returns the path to the application's Documents directory.
 */
- (NSString *)applicationDocumentsDirectory {
   return [NSSearchPathForDirectoriesInDomains(NSDocumentDirectory, NSUserDomainMask,➡
YES) lastObject];

}

@end
```

Once again, you can build and run the application, but all that happens is that you'll see a blank screen. In the next section, you add a rudimentary interface. Actually adding, editing, and deleting data, however, won't happen until the "Managing Table Views Using NSFetchedResultsController" section.

Setting Up the Tab Bar Controller

The MyStash application uses two tabs to swap between Notes view and Passwords view. This means you need to add a tab bar controller to the main window. Open MyStashAppDelegate.h, and add a UITabBarController instance to the interface:

```
UITabBarController *tabBarController;
```

Add a property as well, including the IBOutlet tag for Interface Builder:

```
@property (nonatomic, retain) IBOutlet UITabBarController *tabBarController;
```

Now, open the file MyStashAppDelegate.m, and add the tab bar controller to the @synthesize line:

```
@synthesize window, tabBarController;
```

In the application:didFinishLaunchingWithOptions: method, add the tab bar controller to the main window so that method now looks like this:

```
- (BOOL)application:(UIApplication *)application➡
didFinishLaunchingWithOptions:(NSDictionary *)launchOptions {
    [window addSubview:tabBarController.view];
    [window makeKeyAndVisible];
    return YES;
}
```

Release the tab bar controller in the dealloc: method:

```
- (void)dealloc {
    [tabBarController release];
    [window release];
    [super dealloc];
}
```

Now, open MainWindow.xib, and drag a tab bar controller to the MainWindow.xib window. With the tab bar controller selected, you should see a view with two tabs at the bottom. Select each, in turn, and press Delete. You should now see the view with a tab bar but no tabs, as in Figure 9-3. Right-click the tab bar controller to see the pop-up menu shown in Figure 9-4. Drag from the circle beside New Referencing Outlet, under Referencing Outlets, to My Stash App Delegate in the MainWindow.xib window, as in Figure 9-5. From the ensuing pop-up, select tabBarController.

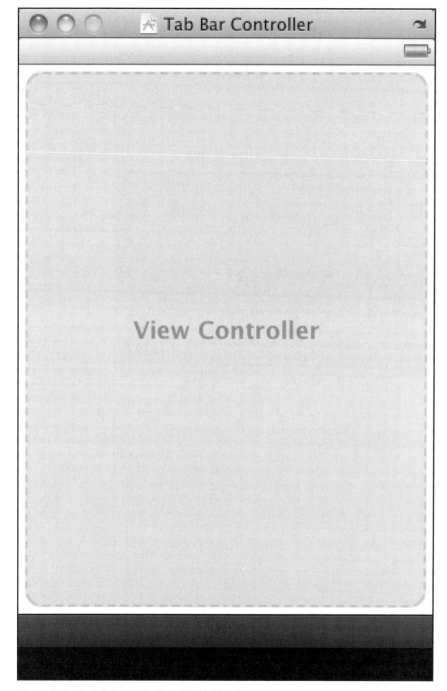

Figure 9-3. *The tab bar controller added to the view*

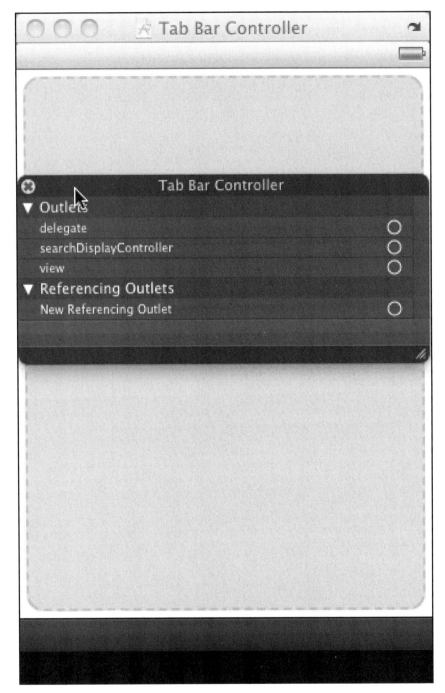

Figure 9-4. *Getting ready to connect the tab bar controller instance*

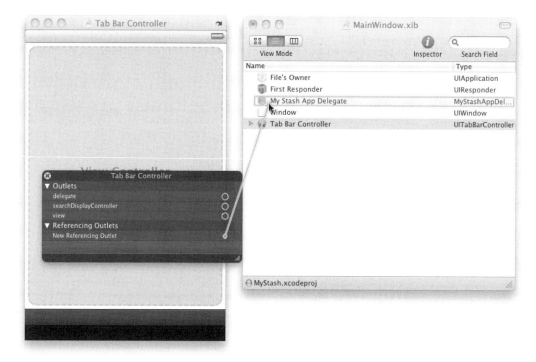

Figure 9-5. *Connecting the tab bar controller to the application delegate*

Adding the Tab

To add the tab for the Notes view, create a new UIViewController subclass called
NoteListViewController, checking only the box for "UITableViewController subclass"
(see Figure 9-6).

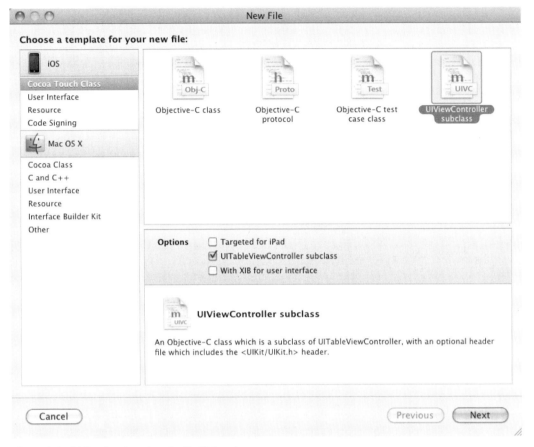

Figure 9-6. *Adding the view class for the Notes view*

Open NoteListViewController.m, and for now, find the two methods called numberOfSectionsInTableView: and tableView:numberOfRowsInSection:, and make them match this:

```
- (NSInteger)numberOfSectionsInTableView:(UITableView *)tableView {
    // Return the number of sections.
    return 1;
}

- (NSInteger)tableView:(UITableView *)tableView numberOfRowsInSection:(NSInteger)section
{
    // Return the number of rows in the section.
    return 1;
}
```

Add an initWithStyle: method, and in it, add a title and an image for the tab, like this:

```
- (id)initWithStyle:(UITableViewStyle)style {
    if ((self = [super initWithStyle:style])) {
        self.title = @"Notes";
        self.tabBarItem.image = [UIImage imageNamed:@"note"];
```

```
  }
  return self;
}
```

For the tab images, grab four files from the downloaded source code for this book:

- `note.png`
- `password.png`
- `note@2x.png`
- `password@2x.png`

Alternatively, you can create your own. The iPhone 4 versions (`*@2x.png`) should be about 60 pixels by 60 pixels, and the regular versions should be about 30 pixels by 30 pixels. Make them have a transparent background with a black image.

However you get the four images, add them to your Resources group, as in Figure 9-7.

Figure 9-7. *The tab images added to the project*

Now, add the Notes tab to the tab bar controller in the application delegate. Open `MyStashAppDelegate.m`, and add an import for the note list view:

```
#import "NoteListViewController.h"
```

Then, in the `application:didFinishLaunchingWithOptions:` method, create an instance of `NoteListViewController`, wrap it in an instance of `UINavigationController`, and add it to the tab bar controller. The updated method looks like this:

```
- (BOOL)application:(UIApplication *)application➡
didFinishLaunchingWithOptions:(NSDictionary *)launchOptions {
  NoteListViewController *noteListViewController = [[NoteListViewController alloc]➡
initWithStyle:UITableViewStylePlain];

  UINavigationController *navNoteController = [[[UINavigationController alloc]➡
initWithRootViewController:noteListViewController] autorelease];

  [noteListViewController release];

  [tabBarController setViewControllers:[NSArray arrayWithObjects:navNoteController,➡
nil]];

  [window addSubview:tabBarController.view];
  [window makeKeyAndVisible];
  return YES;
}
```

Now you can build and run the application, and you see the view has a single tab (the one for Notes), as shown in Figure 9-8.

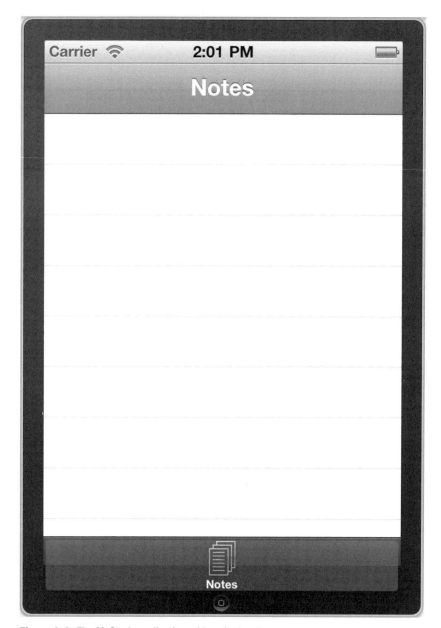

Figure 9-8. *The MyStash application with a single tab*

You still need the tab for passwords, so make another view controller, patterned after the one for notes. Once again, select "UIViewController subclass," check the box for "UITableViewController subclass," and call it PasswordListViewController.m. Open the PasswordListViewController.m file, and change the methods for returning the number of sections and the number of rows in a given section to these:

```
- (NSInteger)numberOfSectionsInTableView:(UITableView *)tableView {
  // Return the number of sections.
```

```
    return 1;
}

- (NSInteger)tableView:(UITableView *)tableView numberOfRowsInSection:(NSInteger)section
{
  // Return the number of rows in the section.
  return 1;
}
```

Add an `initWithStyle:` method, and use it to add a title and an icon for the tab:

```
- (id)initWithStyle:(UITableViewStyle)style {
  if ((self = [super initWithStyle:style])) {
    self.title = @"Passwords";
    self.tabBarItem.image = [UIImage imageNamed:@"password"];
  }
  return self;
}
```

Go back to the `MyStashAppDelegate.m` file and add an import for the password list view controller:

```
#import "PasswordListViewController.h"
```

In that same file, update the `application:didFinishLaunchingWithOptions:` method to add the Passwords tab to the tab bar controller:

```
- (BOOL)application:(UIApplication *)application➥
didFinishLaunchingWithOptions:(NSDictionary *)launchOptions {
  NoteListViewController *noteListViewController = [[NoteListViewController alloc]➥
initWithStyle:UITableViewStylePlain];

  UINavigationController *navNoteController = [[[UINavigationController alloc]➥
initWithRootViewController:noteListViewController] autorelease];

  [noteListViewController release];

  PasswordListViewController *passwordListViewController =➥
[[PasswordListViewController alloc] initWithStyle:UITableViewStylePlain];

  UINavigationController *navPasswordController = [[[UINavigationController alloc]➥
initWithRootViewController:passwordl istViewControllcr] autorelease];

  [passwordListViewController release];

  [tabBarController setViewControllers:[NSArray arrayWithObjects:navNoteController,➥
navPasswordController, nil]];

  [window addSubview:tabBarController.view];
  [window makeKeyAndVisible];
  return YES;
}
```

Now, when you build and run the MyStash application, you should see two tabs: one for notes and one for passwords, as Figure 9-9 shows. You now have the bare-bones MyStash application built, and you're ready to add the advanced features that the rest of the chapter walks you through.

Figure 9-9. *The MyStash application with two tabs*

Managing Table Views Using NSFetchedResultsController

Launch any nongame app on your iPhone, and chances are good that you'll find at least one table view. Apple made the table view an essential part of the iPhone interface and uses it to great advantage in Apple's own applications. Many, if not all, of the applications you develop will have table views, so anything you can learn to make using table views easier will benefit you.

In line with its legendary attention to detail, Apple includes a class with the Core Data framework that's designed to make Core Data work better with table views. Called NSFetchedResultsController, it eases the development tasks required to display data from a Core Data persistent store in a table view. This section explores how to use an NSFetchedResultsController and then incorporates it into the MyStash application to display the Notes and Passwords.

Understanding NSFetchedResultsController

The NSFetchedResultsController class works closely with UITableView instances to display data from a Core Data data model in a table view. It pulls managed objects from the persistent store, from the entity you specify, caching them to improve performance, and gives the data to the table view as necessary so that the table can show it. It also manages adding, removing, and moving rows in the table in response to data changes. You should probably use fetched results controllers any time you're working with Core Data and table views.

You create a fetched results controller with four parameters:

- A fetch request (NSFetchRequest instance)
- A managed object context
- A section name key path
- A cache name

Each of these parameters are explained in the following sections.

The Fetch Request

The fetch request is almost the same as any fetch request you've used throughout this book and in any of your Core Data development. It works with the entity in your data model that you specify and can optionally have a predicate (NSPredicate) to filter what it fetches. The one difference in this fetch request is that it must have at least one sort descriptor, or your application will crash with this message:

```
'NSInvalidArgumentException', reason: 'An instance of NSFetchedResultsController
requires a fetch request with sort descriptors'
```

This is because the fetched results controller works within the constraints of a table, which displays cells in a predictable order, so the fetched results controller must also have the data in a predictable order. A sort descriptor provides the mechanism required to help sort the data.

The Managed Object Context

This is a normal managed object context that holds the managed objects. Saving the context saves all the objects in it. You typically use your application's managed object context for this parameter.

The Section Name Key Path

Table views on iDevices are divided into sections, with a number of rows in each section. This structure is fundamental to the operation of table views, and every cell, or row, in the table corresponds to a given section and row within that section. A fetched results controller is optimized to work in that environment and can divide its data into sections to correspond to the table sections. The `sectionNameKeyPath` parameter specifies a key path into your Core Data model that divides the managed objects for the fetch request's entity into these sections.

Typically, you'd make this section name key path one of the properties of the entity this table displays. Suppose, for example, that the League Manager application used in several places in this book had a table view that listed all the players for all the teams, grouped by team. Each team, then, would be a section in the table, and each player would occupy a row in their team's section. The entity for the fetch request in this case would be the `Player` entity, and the section name key path would be the `team.name` property, which is the `name` attribute of the `Team` entity that's stored in the `Player`'s `team` relationship.

The Cache Name

The cache name parameter specifies a name for the cache that the fetched results controller uses to cache the managed objects it fetches and feeds to the table. In the 3.x versions of iOS, you were encouraged to make this cache name unique across fetch results controllers, but your application would still work if you shared the cache name with other fetch results controllers. As of iOS 4.0, this is no longer the case, and your fetch results controllers will behave unexpectedly if they share cache names.

Understanding NSFetchedResultsController Delegates

`NSFetchedResultsController` follows Apple's design patterns, using a delegate called `NSFetchedResultsControllerDelegate`, to implement key methods to make the table view and the fetched results controller work together. You typically make your table view's view controller the delegate for its fetched results controller. This delegate has a method for customizing the section names in your table, `controller:sectionIndexTitleForSectionName:`. The more interesting methods, however, are four that deal with changing the data displayed in the table:

- `controllerWillChangeContent:` is called when some content is about to change. This is a good place to tell your table view that you're about to make some changes so that it can initiate a sequence of changes through its `beginUpdates:` method.

- `controller:didChangeObject:atIndexPath:forChangeType:➥`
  `newIndexPath:` is called when a managed object changes (added, deleted, edited, or moved). In this method, you figure out what happened, and you add, move, delete, or refresh the content of the affected table rows accordingly.

- `controller:didChangeSection:atIndex:forChangeType:` is called when a section changes (added or deleted). In this method, you figure out whether a section was added or deleted and either insert or delete a section in the table.

- `controllerDidChangeContent:` is called when the changes are done. This is a good place to tell the table view that the changes initiated by the `beginUpdates:` method are complete by calling the `endUpdates:` method.

Implement these methods in your view controller, and when you create your fetched results controller, set its delegate to the view controller.

Using NSFetchedResultsController

During the execution of your Core Data–based, table view–based application, your fetched results controller becomes the liaison between your data and the table. The fetched results controller contains methods that return the data the table needs, according to section and row. This means that whether the table needs to display a cell, figure out which cell was tapped, determine how many rows are in a section, or any of the other pieces of data a table needs to display and function, the fetched results controller has the answers. Read on to the next section, "Incorporating NSFetchedResultsController into MyStash," to understand the details of how this works.

Incorporating NSFetchedResultsController into MyStash

If you run the MyStash application now, you see the expected tabs for notes and passwords. You can't add any notes or passwords, however, and you couldn't see them if you somehow added them. The next few sections will walk you through the following:

- Adding the `NSFetchedResultsController` to the list views (notes and passwords) so that notes and passwords display

- Adding support for deleting notes and passwords

- Adding support to add and edit passwords and notes

We'll make the changes for both notes and passwords simultaneously. You'll notice that the changes we make for both notes and passwords are similar, and even identical in many places, and you might wonder why we don't refactor much of the code into a common superclass. Such an approach would be valid, or even preferred, if we were developing this as a shipping application. Since the purpose of MyStash, however, is to instruct, we've chosen to keep the focus on how to implement

NSFetchedResultController into your table views, rather than how to refactor. After you have the application working, feel free to refactor.

To begin implementing NSFetchedResultsController into MyStash, open NoteListViewController.h, and import the header file for Core Data:

```
#import <CoreData/CoreData.h>
```

We'll have NoteListViewController act as the delegate for the NSFetchedResultsController we add, so make NoteListViewController implement the NSFetchedResultsControllerDelegate protocol:

```
@interface NoteListViewController : UITableViewController
<NSFetchedResultsControllerDelegate>
```

Add two members to the NoteListViewController interface: an NSFetchedResultsController and a managed object context that the NSFetchedResultsController will use:

```
NSFetchedResultsController *fetchedResultsController;
NSManagedObjectContext *managedObjectContext;
```

Add corresponding properties for those two members:

```
@property (nonatomic, retain) NSFetchedResultsController *fetchedResultsController;
@property (nonatomic, retain) NSManagedObjectContext *managedObjectContext;
```

Now, switch over to PasswordListViewController.h, and make the same changes. When you're done, it should match Listing 9-3.

Listing 9-3. *PasswordListViewController.h*

```
#import <UIKit/UIKit.h>
#import <CoreData/CoreData.h>

@interface PasswordListViewController : UITableViewController➡
<NSFetchedResultsControllerDelegate> {

  NSFetchedResultsController *fetchedResultsController;
  NSManagedObjectContext *managedObjectContext;
}
@property (nonatomic, retain) NSFetchedResultsController *fetchedResultsController;
@property (nonatomic, retain) NSManagedObjectContext *managedObjectContext;

@end
```

Open the implementation files, NoteListViewController.m and PasswordListViewController.m, and add the @synthesize directive to generate getters and setters for fetchedResultsController and managedObjectContext:

```
@synthesize fetchedResultsController, managedObjectContext;
```

You also need to release these members when these controllers are deallocated, so add calls to release in the dealloc: methods for each controller:

```
- (void)dealloc {
  [fetchedResultsController release];
  [managedObjectContext release];
```

```
    [super dealloc];
}
```

Creating the Fetched Results Controller

That was the easy part. Now it's time to set up your NSFetchedResultsController
instance. Do it in the accessor for the fetchedResultsController member. The
implementation will differ slightly between the notes controller and the passwords
controller, so start with the notes controller and add this:

```
#pragma mark -
#pragma mark Fetched results controller

- (NSFetchedResultsController *)fetchedResultsController {
  if (fetchedResultsController != nil) {
    return fetchedResultsController;
  }

  // Create the fetch request for the entity.
  NSFetchRequest *fetchRequest = [[NSFetchRequest alloc] init];
  NSEntityDescription *entity = [NSEntityDescription entityForName:@"Note"➥
inManagedObjectContext:self.managedObjectContext];

  [fetchRequest setEntity:entity];

  // Set the batch size
  [fetchRequest setFetchBatchSize:10];

  // Sort by note title, ascending
  NSSortDescriptor *sortDescriptor = [[NSSortDescriptor alloc] initWithKey:@"title"➥
ascending:YES];

  NSArray *sortDescriptors = [[NSArray alloc] initWithObjects:sortDescriptor, nil];
  [fetchRequest setSortDescriptors:sortDescriptors];

  // Create the fetched results controller using the
  // fetch request we just created, and with the managed
  // object context member, and set this controller to
  // be the delegate
  NSFetchedResultsController *aFetchedResultsController = [[NSFetchedResultsController➥
alloc] initWithFetchRequest:fetchRequest managedObjectContext:managedObjectContext➥
sectionNameKeyPath:nil cacheName:@"Note"];

  aFetchedResultsController.delegate = self;
  self.fetchedResultsController = aFetchedResultsController;

  // Clean up
  [aFetchedResultsController release];
  [fetchRequest release];
  [sortDescriptor release];
  [sortDescriptors release];

  // Fetch the results into the fetched results controller
      NSError *error = nil;
```

```
        if (![[self fetchedResultsController] performFetch:&error]) {
    NSLog(@"Unresolved error %@, %@", error, [error userInfo]);
    abort();
        }
  return fetchedResultsController;
}
```

This is a longish method, so let's go through it to make sure you understand it. The method starts by checking to see whether the `fetchedResultsController` instance has already been created. If it has, the method returns the member. If not, the method creates the `fetchedResultsController` instance before returning it.

If the method must create the `fetchedResultsController` member, it first creates a fetch request for the `Note` entity with a batch size of ten instances and sorts it by the `title` attribute. It then creates a fetched results controller instance and initializes it with the fetch request we just created, the managed object context member, and a unique cache name, `Note`, for this fetched results controller. Notice that we pass `nil` for the `sectionNameKeyPath` parameter, because we have no sections. The code then sets this controller as the delegate for the fetched results controller and then stores this variable into the `fetchedResultsController` member. After some cleanup, the code tells the `fetchedResultsController` member to fetch results before returning.

Add the same method to `PasswordListViewController.m`, changing both the entity name and the cache name from `Note` to `System` to match the data model. Also, change the attribute used for the sort descriptor from `title` to `name`.

Your controllers can now create their fetched results controllers, but they made a promise that they're not yet keeping, to implement the `NSFetchedResultsControllerDelegate` protocol. That's the topic of the next section.

Implementing the NSFetchedResultsControllerDelegate Protocol

You set your controllers (`NoteListViewController` and `PasswordListViewController`) as the delegates for their fetched result controller members, so you must implement the methods of that protocol. The good news is that your implementation of these methods for both controllers is identical, so you can add the following code, method by method, to `NoteListViewController.m`, and then copy and paste the whole thing to `PasswordListViewController.m`. Start by adding a #pragma directive to both controller's implementation files so you can find the protocol's methods easily in Xcode:

```
#pragma mark -
#pragma mark Fetched results controller delegate
```

The first method to implement, `controllerWillChangeContent:`, tells this controller's table view to start a series of updates:

```
- (void)controllerWillChangeContent:(NSFetchedResultsController *)controller {
  [self.tableView beginUpdates];
}
```

You bookend this with a corresponding call to end the updates when `controllerDidChangeContent:` is called:

```
- (void)controllerDidChangeContent:(NSFetchedResultsController *)controller {
  [self.tableView endUpdates];
}
```

Since neither the Notes view nor the Passwords view supports sections, you don't have to implement the controller:didChangeSection:atIndex:forChangeType:. If you did, though, a reasonable implementation looks like this:

```
- (void)controller:(NSFetchedResultsController *)controller didChangeSection:(id➡
<NSFetchedResultsSectionInfo>)sectionInfo
          atIndex:(NSUInteger)sectionIndex
forChangeType:(NSFetchedResultsChangeType)type {
  switch(type) {
    case NSFetchedResultsChangeInsert:
      [self.tableView insertSections:[NSIndexSet indexSetWithIndex:sectionIndex]➡
withRowAnimation:UITableViewRowAnimationFade];

      break;
    case NSFetchedResultsChangeDelete:
      [self.tableView deleteSections:[NSIndexSet indexSetWithIndex:sectionIndex]➡
withRowAnimation:UITableViewRowAnimationFade];

      break;
  }
}
```

We include it here for your reference, but you don't need to add it to the code.

The method you do need to add, however, is the controller:didChangeObject:atIndexPath:forChangeType:newIndexPath: method. This method is called any time a managed object that corresponds to this fetched results controller is changed. These changes include the following:

- When an object is added (inserted)

- When an object is deleted

- When an object is updated

- When an object is moved

Since we keep both notes and passwords in alphabetical order—notes by title and passwords by system name—and have only a single section in each view, allowing users to move the entries makes no sense, so we don't need code to support when an object is moved. We include it anyway, however, for reference purposes. If you later want to change the application to support moving the entries, you'll already have this part of the code in place. The full method, which goes in both NoteListViewController.m and PasswordListViewController.m, looks like this:

```
- (void)controller:(NSFetchedResultsController *)controller didChangeObject:(id)➡
      anObject atIndexPath:(NSIndexPath *)indexPath
forChangeType:(NSFetchedResultsChangeType)type
      newIndexPath:(NSIndexPath *)newIndexPath {
  UITableView *tableView = self.tableView;
  switch(type) {
    // An object has been added (inserted)
```

```
        case NSFetchedResultsChangeInsert:
            [tableView insertRowsAtIndexPaths:[NSArray arrayWithObject:newIndexPath]➥
withRowAnimation:UITableViewRowAnimationFade];

            break;
        // An object has been deleted
        case NSFetchedResultsChangeDelete:
            [tableView deleteRowsAtIndexPaths:[NSArray arrayWithObject:indexPath] ➥
withRowAnimation:UITableViewRowAnimationFade];

            break;
        // An object has been updated (edited)
        case NSFetchedResultsChangeUpdate:
            [self configureCell:[tableView cellForRowAtIndexPath:indexPath] ➥
atIndexPath:indexPath];

            break;
        // An object has been moved
        case NSFetchedResultsChangeMove:
            [tableView deleteRowsAtIndexPaths:[NSArray arrayWithObject:indexPath] ➥
withRowAnimation:UITableViewRowAnimationFade];

            [tableView insertRowsAtIndexPaths:[NSArray
arrayWithObject:newIndexPath]withRowAnimation:UITableViewRowAnimationFade]; ➥

            break;
    }
}
```

As you can see, this code gets a pointer to the UITableView instance that this controller controls and then branches according to the value of the NSFetchedResultsChangeType parameter called type to determine what has happened. If an object has been added (type is NSFetchedResultsChangeInsert), the code instructs the table view to make room for it. If an object is deleted (type is NSFetchedResultsChangeUpdate), the table view removes its row from the display. If an object has been edited, then a method in this controller that we haven't written yet is called. This method will be responsible for configuring a single table cell, and you'll reuse this method in the tableView:cellForRowAtIndexPath: method. Finally, if an object is moved (which won't happen in this application), the table view deletes the table row at the old location and adds a row at the new location.

You've written the code to create the fetched results controllers and respond to their protocol methods. The next step, the topic of the next section, is to incorporate the fetched results controllers into the table views.

Incorporating the Fetched Results Controllers into the Tables

The fetched results controllers have the data and configuration in place, so incorporating them into the tables for both the notes and the passwords is simple. Find the generated table view methods in NoteListViewController.m, and update them there first before copying over to PasswordListViewController.m.

The first method, numberOfSectionsInTableView:, always returns 1 to match the number of sections, one, in the table. In the interest of understanding how the fetched results controller works with the table, however, we return the count of sections in the fetched results controller, like this:

```
- (NSInteger)numberOfSectionsInTableView:(UITableView *)tableView {
    return [[self.fetchedResultsController sections] count];
}
```

The tableView:numberOfRowsInSection: method gets the NSFetchedResultsSectionInfo object from the fetched results controller that corresponds to the specified section. As its name suggests, this object contains information about the section, including the number of objects that belong to this section. This method returns that number of objects:

```
- (NSInteger)tableView:(UITableView *)tableView numberOfRowsInSection:(NSInteger)section
{
    id <NSFetchedResultsSectionInfo> sectionInfo = [[fetchedResultsController sections] ➥
objectAtIndex:section];

    return [sectionInfo numberOfObjects];
}
```

Returning a cell for a specified index path, which contains both section and row information, is the responsibility of the tableView:cellForRowAtIndexPath: method. This method gets an available cell of the right type, or creates one if no available cell exists, and then reuses the configureCell: method mentioned earlier that we haven't written yet. Here is the method for NoteListViewController.m:

```
- (UITableViewCell *)tableView:(UITableView *)tableView
cellForRowAtIndexPath:(NSIndexPath *)indexPath {
    static NSString *CellIdentifier = @"NoteCell";

    UITableViewCell *cell = [tableView dequeueReusableCellWithIdentifier:CellIdentifier];
    if (cell == nil) {
        cell = [[[UITableViewCell alloc] initWithStyle:UITableViewCellStyleDefault ➥
reuseIdentifier:CellIdentifier] autorelease];

    }
    [self configureCell:cell atIndexPath:indexPath];
    return cell;
}
```

For PasswordListViewController.m, change the value for CellIdentifier to PasswordCell:

```
static NSString *CellIdentifier = @"PasswordCell";
```

It's time to finally implement the configureCell: method for each controller. Start with NoteViewController.m, and add at the top, before the line that says @implementation NoteListViewController, a block of code that declares a private method on the NoteListViewController interface. That block of code looks like this:

```
@interface NoteListViewController()
- (void)configureCell:(UITableViewCell *)cell atIndexPath:(NSIndexPath *)indexPath;
@end
```

Inside the implementation, add an implementation of this method that configures the cell to display the note's text attribute. The interesting thing to note in this method is that you don't have to parse out the section and row from the passed index path. The fetched results controller knows how to work with an index path and uses the section and row indices it contains to return the correct managed object. Here is the method:

```
- (void)configureCell:(UITableViewCell *)cell atIndexPath:(NSIndexPath *)indexPath {
  NSManagedObject *note = [self.fetchedResultsController objectAtIndexPath:indexPath];
  cell.textLabel.text = [note valueForKey:@"title"];
}
```

These lines of code are similar but different for PasswordListViewController.m. They obviously declare the configureCell: method on the PasswordListViewController interface, not the NoteListViewController interface, and the configureCell: implementation displays the name attribute of the managed object. The lines look like this:

```
@interface PasswordListViewController()
- (void)configureCell:(UITableViewCell *)cell atIndexPath:(NSIndexPath *)indexPath;
@end

- (void)configureCell:(UITableViewCell *)cell atIndexPath:(NSIndexPath *)indexPath {
  NSManagedObject *system = [self.fetchedResultsController objectAtIndexPath:indexPath];
  cell.textLabel.text = [system valueForKey:@"name"];
}
```

The last method in the table view data source methods that you need to update is the tableView:commitEditingStyle:forRowAtIndexPath: method, which is called when a user moves or deletes a row. In the MyStash application, the users can't move either notes or passwords, but they can delete them. Your implementation should determine whether the user deleted a row and then ask the fetched results controller to delete the specified object from the managed object context. Since you've actually changed the data in the context, you should then save the context. The method, which is the same for both controllers, looks like this:

```
- (void)tableView:(UITableView *)tableView
commitEditingStyle:(UITableViewCellEditingStyle)editingStyle
forRowAtIndexPath:(NSIndexPath *)indexPath {
  if (editingStyle == UITableViewCellEditingStyleDelete) {
    // Delete the managed object for the given index path
    NSManagedObjectContext *context = [self.fetchedResultsController ➡
managedObjectContext];

    [context deleteObject:[self.fetchedResultsController objectAtIndexPath:indexPath]];

    // Save the context.
    [self saveContext];
  }
}
```

You also must declare and implement the saveContext: method, which looks like this:

```
- (void)saveContext {
  NSManagedObjectContext *context = [fetchedResultsController managedObjectContext];
  NSError *error = nil;
```

```
   if (![context save:&error]) {
     NSLog(@"Unresolved error %@, %@", error, [error userInfo]);
     abort();
   }
}
```

Later in this chapter, we discuss better ways of handling errors, but this method suffices for now.

To finish incorporating the fetched results controllers into the MyStash application, you must provide the managed object contexts for the two view controllers. Open MyStashAppDelegate.m, find the application:didFinishLaunchingWithOptions: method, and set each controller's managed object context member right after initializing it. The two lines to add are as follows:

```
noteListViewController.managedObjectContext = self.managedObjectContext;
. . .
passwordListViewController.managedObjectContext = self.managedObjectContext;
```

Creating the Interface for Adding and Editing Notes and Passwords

The MyStash application can now display and delete notes and passwords, but you can't yet add or edit any notes or passwords. This next part walks you through adding interfaces to add and edit notes and passwords. You'll create one modal for notes and a different modal for passwords, and MyStash will use the same modal for both adding and editing.

Start with the interface for adding and editing notes. Create a UIViewController subclass, and make sure only the "With XIB for user interface" option is selected. Save it as NoteViewController.m. This creates three files:

- NoteViewController.h
- NoteViewController.m
- NoteViewController.xib

Open NoteViewController.h. You'll add the following:

- A text field to allow users to enter the note's title.
- A text view to hold the body of the note.
- A pointer to the parent controller so you can ask the parent to save any new note.
- A managed object that represents the current note, so the user can edit an existing note. If the current note is nil, the code will create a new one.
- An initializer that receives the parent controller and the note object.

- A method that responds to the user dismissing the modal with the Save button.

- A method that responds to the user dismissing the modal with the Cancel button.

See Listing 9-4 for what `NoteListViewController.h` should look like.

Listing 9-4. *NoteViewController.h*

```
#import <UIKit/UIKit.h>
#import <CoreData/CoreData.h>

@class NoteListViewController;

@interface NoteViewController : UIViewController {
  IBOutlet UITextField *titleField;
  IBOutlet UITextView *body;
  NoteListViewController *parentController;
  NSManagedObject *note;
}
@property (nonatomic, retain) UITextField *titleField;
@property (nonatomic, retain) UITextView *body;
@property (nonatomic, retain) NoteListViewController *parentController;
@property (nonatomic, retain) NSManagedObject *note;

- (id)initWithParentController:(NoteListViewController *)aParentController➥
note:(NSManagedObject*)aNote;

- (IBAction)save:(id)sender;
- (IBAction)cancel:(id)sender;
@end
```

The implementation file for the note view, `NoteViewController.m`, can be seen in Listing 9-5. Note the following:

- The initialization method stores the parent `NoteListViewController` instance and the specified `NSManagedObject` instance.

- When the view loads and the `viewDidLoad:` method is called, the code checks whether the `note` managed object is `nil`. If it is, the code sets the body text to "Type text here . . ." so that users know what to do. If it's not `nil`, the code takes the values from the managed object and puts them into the user interface fields.

- The `save:` method checks again if it's editing an existing note or adding a new one. If it's editing an existing note, it updates the `note` managed object with the values the user entered and asks the parent controller to save the context. If it's creating a new note, it asks the parent controller to insert a new note object, passing the user-entered values. Either way, it then dismisses the modal.

- The `cancel:` method simply dismisses the modal, discarding any user input.

Listing 9-5. *NoteViewController.m*

```objc
#import "NoteViewController.h"
#import "NoteListViewController.h"

@implementation NoteViewController

@synthesize titleField, body, parentController, note;

- (id)initWithParentController:(NoteListViewController *)aParentController➥
note:(NSManagedObject *)aNote {

  if ((self = [super init])) {
    self.parentController = aParentController;
    self.note = aNote;
  }
  return self;
}

- (void)viewDidLoad {
  [super viewDidLoad];
  if (note != nil) {
    titleField.text = [note valueForKcy:@"title"];
    body.text = [note valueForKey:@"body"];
  } else {
    body.text = @"Type text here . . .";
  }
}

- (IBAction)save:(id)sender {
  if (parentController != nil) {
    if (note != nil) {
      [note setValue:titleField.text forKey:@"title"];
      [note setValue:body.text forKey:@"body"];
      [parentController saveContext];
    }
    else {
      [parentController insertNoteWithTitle:titleField.text body:body.text];
    }
  }
  [self dismissModalViewControllerAnimated:YES];
}

- (IBAction)cancel:(id)sender {
  [self dismissModalViewControllerAnimated:YES];
}

- (void)dealloc {
  [parentController release];
  [note release];
  [super dealloc];
}

@end
```

You next must create the actual user interface that the `NoteViewController` instance controls. Double-click the `NoteViewController.xib` file to open it in Interface Builder. Perform the following steps:

1. Drag a Navigation Bar onto the view, and align it with the top edge of the view. Change its title to **Note**.

2. Drag two Bar Button Items onto the navigation bar—one on the left and one on the right.

3. Change the labels on the two Bar Button items you just added—the one on the left to **Cancel** and the one on the right to **Save**.

4. Ctrl+drag from the Cancel Bar Button Item to the File's Owner icon and select `cancel:` from the pop-up menu.

5. Ctrl+drag from the Save Bar Button Item to the File's Owner icon and select `save:` from the pop-up menu.

6. Drag a Label onto the top left of the view, below the navigation bar, and change its text to **Title:**.

7. Drag a Text Field onto the view, to the right of the Title: label.

8. Drag a Text View onto the view, below the Title: label, and make it fill the rest of the view.

9. Ctrl+drag from the File's Owner icon to the text field, and select `titleField` from the pop-up menu.

10. Ctrl+drag from the File's Owner icon to the text view, and select body from the pop-up menu.

Figure 9-10 shows you what your view should look like when you're done. Make sure you follow all the previous steps, including wiring the buttons to the action methods you created (`save:` and `cancel:`) and the user interface components to the appropriate variables.

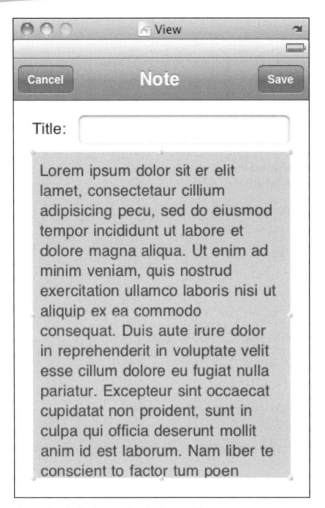

Figure 9-10. *Setting up the single note view*

All that's left for the MyStash application to be able to add and edit notes is to display this modal in response to two user actions from the note list view:

1. Tap the + button to add a new note.

2. Tap the note's title in the list to edit that note.

Open `NoteListViewController.h`, and add two method declarations: one to show the modal when the user clicks the + button and one to insert a new note:

```
- (void)showNoteView;
- (void)insertNoteWithTitle:(NSString *)title body:(NSString *)body;
```

Open `NoteListViewController.m`, import `NoteViewController.h`, and add definitions for those two methods. The first, `showNoteView:`, allocates an instance of `NoteViewController` and initializes it with the parent view controller and a `nil` note so

that a new note will be created. The second, `insertNoteWithTitle:`, is the method that
`NoteViewController` calls when the user saves a new note:

```
- (void)showNoteView {
  NoteViewController *noteViewController = [[NoteViewController alloc]➥
initWithParentController:self note:nil];

  [self presentModalViewController:noteViewController animated:YES];
  [noteViewController release];
}

- (void)insertNoteWithTitle:(NSString *)title body:(NSString *)body {
  NSManagedObjectContext *context = [fetchedResultsController managedObjectContext];
  NSEntityDescription *entity = [[fetchedResultsController fetchRequest] entity];
  NSManagedObject *newNote = [NSEntityDescription➥
insertNewObjectForEntityForName:[entity name] inManagedObjectContext:context];

  [newNote setValue:title forKey:@"title"];
  [newNote setValue:body forKey:@"body"];

  [self saveContext];
}
```

Now, you need to add the + button and the Edit button to the note list interface. Go to
the `viewDidLoad:` method, and add the Edit button on the left and the + button on the
right. Wire the + button to the `showNoteView` action:

```
- (void)viewDidLoad {
  [super viewDidLoad];

  // Set up the edit and add buttons.
  self.navigationItem.leftBarButtonItem = self.editButtonItem;

  UIBarButtonItem *addButton = [[UIBarButtonItem alloc]➥
initWithBarButtonSystemItem:UIBarButtonSystemItemAdd target:self➥
action:@selector(showNoteView)];

  self.navigationItem.rightBarButtonItem = addButton;
  [addButton release];
}
```

All that remains is to add support for editing a note. When the user taps an existing note,
the `tableView:didSelectRowAtIndexPath:` method is called. In that method, grab the
note that corresponds to the `indexPath` parameter, and then allocate and initialize a
`NoteViewController` instance. This time, you pass the `note` managed object so that the
existing note is edited. The method looks like this:

```
- (void)tableView:(UITableView *)tableView didSelectRowAtIndexPath:(NSIndexPath➥
*)indexPath {
  NSManagedObject *note = [[self fetchedResultsController] objectAtIndexPath:indexPath];

  NoteViewController *noteViewController = [[NoteViewController alloc]➥
initWithParentController:self note:note];

  [self presentModalViewController:noteViewController animated:YES];
```

```
    [noteViewController release];
}
```

Build and run the application. You will see a blank screen, as before, but now you can click the + button to add a note. If you do, you'll see the screen shown in Figure 9-11. Type in a note, and click Save. Your new note should appear in the list view, as Figure 9-12 shows.

Figure 9-11. *A new blank note*

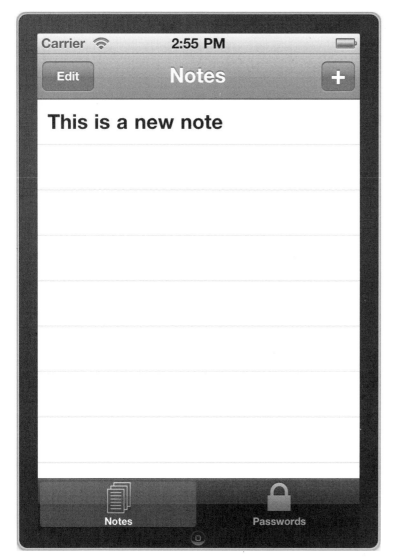

Figure 9-12. *The note list view with a note added*

You can tap the note, and it will appear for you to edit. You can edit it and save the changes, or you can cancel and no changes will be saved. From the notes list view, you can tap the Edit button to delete any notes, as Figure 9-13 shows. Tap the Done button to leave edit mode.

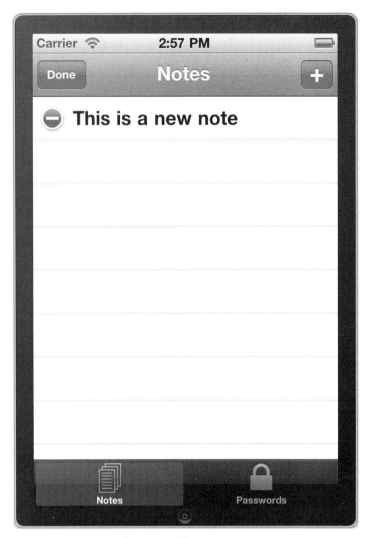

Figure 9-13. *The notes list view in edit mode*

To complete this phase of the MyStash application, you must create the interface for adding and editing passwords. Again, create a new UIViewController subclass with an XIB for the user interface and call it PasswordViewController. The code looks very much like the code for the NoteViewController, but with different fields that are appropriate to the System entity in the data model. You can find the code in Listings 9-6 and 9-7.

Listing 9-6. *PasswordViewController.h*

```
#import <UIKit/UIKit.h>
#import <CoreData/CoreData.h>

@class PasswordListViewController;

@interface PasswordViewController : UIViewController {
```

```
  IBOutlet UITextField *name;
  IBOutlet UITextField *userId;
  IBOutlet UITextField *password;
  PasswordListViewController *parentController;
  NSManagedObject *system;
}
@property (nonatomic, retain) UITextField *name;
@property (nonatomic, retain) UITextField *userId;
@property (nonatomic, retain) UITextField *password;
@property (nonatomic, retain) PasswordListViewController *parentController;
@property (nonatomic, retain) NSManagedObject *system;

- (id)initWithParentController:(PasswordListViewController *)aParentController➡
system:(NSManagedObject *)aSystem;

- (IBAction)save:(id)sender;
- (IBAction)cancel:(id)sender;

@end
```

Listing 9-7. *PasswordViewController.m*

```
#import "PasswordViewController.h"
#import "PasswordListViewController.h"

@implementation PasswordViewController

@synthesize name, userId, password, parentController, system;

- (id)initWithParentController:(PasswordListViewController *)aParentController➡
system:(NSManagedObject *)aSystem {

  if ((self = [super init])) {
    self.parentController = aParentController;
    self.system = aSystem;
  }
  return self;
}

- (void)viewDidLoad {
  [super viewDidLoad];
  if (system != nil) {
    name.text = [system valueForKey:@"name"];
    userId.text = [system valueForKey:@"userId"];
    password.text = [system valueForKey:@"password"];
  }
}

- (IBAction)save:(id)sender {
  if (parentController != nil) {
    if (system != nil) {
      [system setValue:name.text forKey:@"name"];
      [system setValue:userId.text forKey:@"userId"];
      [system setValue:password.text forKey:@"password"];
      [parentController saveContext];
    } else {
```

```
        [parentController insertPasswordWithName:name.text userId:userId.text➡
password:password.text];

    }
}
    [self dismissModalViewControllerAnimated:YES];
}

- (IBAction)cancel:(id)sender {
    [self dismissModalViewControllerAnimated:YES];
}

- (void)didReceiveMemoryWarning {
    [super didReceiveMemoryWarning];
}

- (void)viewDidUnload {
    [super viewDidUnload];
}

- (void)dealloc {
    [parentController release];
    [system release];
    [super dealloc];
}

@end
```

The user interface for the password view looks similar to, but different from, the note view. The steps to follow, then, are similar to the ones you followed for the note view. Open PasswordViewController.xib and follow these steps:

1. Drag a Navigation Bar onto the view, and align it with the top edge of the view. Change its title to **Password**.

2. Drag two Bar Button Items onto the navigation bar—one on the left and one on the right.

3. Change the labels on the two Bar Button items you just added—the one on the left to **Cancel** and the one on the right to **Save**.

4. Ctrl+drag from the Cancel Bar Button Item to the File's Owner icon and select cancel: from the pop-up menu.

5. Ctrl+drag from the Save Bar Button Item to the File's Owner icon, and select save: from the pop-up menu.

6. Drag a Label onto the top left of the view, below the navigation bar, and change its text to **System:**.

7. Drag a Text Field onto the view, below the System: label, and make it span the width of the view.

8. Drag another Label onto the view, below the text field you just added, and change its text to **User ID:**.

9. Drag a Text Field onto the view, below the User ID: label, and make it span the width of the view.

10. Drag another Label onto the view, below the text field you just added, and change its text to **Password:**.

11. Drag a Text Field onto the view, below the Password: label, and make it span the width of the view.

12. Ctrl+drag from the File's Owner icon to the text field below System: , and select name from the pop-up menu.

13. Ctrl+drag from the File's Owner icon to the text field below User ID:, and select userId from the pop-up menu.

14. Ctrl+drag from the File's Owner icon to the text field below Password:, and select password from the pop-up menu.

When you finish, the view should look like Figure 9-14.

Figure 9-14. *The configured password view*

The remaining steps are to update the `PasswordListViewController` class, as you did `NoteListViewController`, to show the password modal when adding or editing a password. Open `PasswordListViewController.h`, and add these two method declarations:

```
- (void)showPasswordView;
- (void)insertPasswordWithName:(NSString *)name userId:(NSString *)userId➟
password:(NSString *)password;
```

In `PasswordListViewController.m`, import `PasswordViewController.h`, and add this code:

```
- (void)showPasswordView {
  PasswordViewController *passwordViewController = [[PasswordViewController alloc] ➟
initWithParentController:self system:nil];

  [self presentModalViewController:passwordViewController animated:YES];
  [passwordViewController release];
}
```

```objc
- (void)insertPasswordWithName:(NSString *)name userId:(NSString *)userId➥
password:(NSString *)password {

  NSManagedObjectContext *context = [fetchedResultsController managedObjectContext];
  NSEntityDescription *entity = [[fetchedResultsController fetchRequest] entity];
  NSManagedObject *newPassword = [NSEntityDescription➥
insertNewObjectForEntityForName:[entity name] inManagedObjectContext:context];


  [newPassword setValue:name forKey:@"name"];
  [newPassword setValue:userId forKey:@"userId"];
  [newPassword setValue:password forKey:@"password"];

  [self saveContext];
}
```

Change the `viewDidLoad:` method to this:

```objc
- (void)viewDidLoad {
  [super viewDidLoad];

  self.navigationItem.leftBarButtonItem = self.editButtonItem;

  UIBarButtonItem *addButton = [[UIBarButtonItem alloc]➥
initWithBarButtonSystemItem:UIBarButtonSystemItemAdd target:self➥
action:@selector(showPasswordView)];

  self.navigationItem.rightBarButtonItem = addButton;
  [addButton release];
}
```

Finally, update the `tableView:didSelectRowAtIndexPath:` method:

```objc
- (void)tableView:(UITableView *)tableView didSelectRowAtIndexPath:(NSIndexPath➥
*)indexPath {
  NSManagedObject *system = [[self fetchedResultsController]➥
objectAtIndexPath:indexPath];


  PasswordViewController *passwordViewController = [[PasswordViewController alloc]➥
initWithParentController:self system:system];

  [self presentModalViewController:passwordViewController animated:YES];
  [passwordViewController release];
}
```

This phase of the MyStash application is now complete. You can add, edit, and delete notes and passwords. Build and run the application now and add a new password. When you tap the + button on the Passwords tab, you should see the modal for adding a new password, as Figure 9-15 shows. Add a few passwords, and you should see them appear in the list view, as depicted in Figure 9-16.

Figure 9-15. *Entering a new password*

Figure 9-16. *The password list view with three entries*

All the notes and passwords you create in the MyStash application live in the same persistent store. Read the next section to understand how to spread these data across multiple persistent stores.

Splitting Data Across Multiple Persistent Stores

Up to this point in the book, we have always associated a data model with a single persistent store. You may have cases, however, that would benefit from splitting the model into multiple stores. When multiple persistent stores are involved, Core Data is able to dispatch the entities to persist to the proper store and rebuild object graphs spawning across multiple stores. The role of the NSPersistentStoreCoordinator is to manage the multiple stores and make them appear to the Core Data API user as if they were a single store.

The MyStash data model contains both notes and passwords. When you run the MyStash application, all notes and passwords are stored in the MyStash.sqlite persistent store. Suppose, though, that you want to split the persistent store into two so that notes are stored in the Notes.sqlite persistent store and passwords go into the Passwords.sqlite persistent store. Figure 9-17 illustrates the split, showing where each type of managed object is persisted.

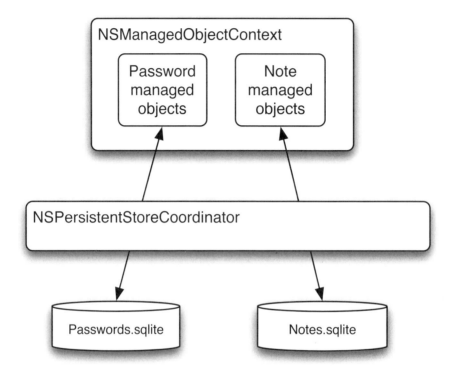

Figure 9-17. *Persistent store split*

Using Model Configurations

A Core Data model defines entities and their relationships in order to specify how data should be laid out, but it can also stipulate where the data should be written. To specify where data should be written, Core Data uses what's called *configurations*. Each entity can be associated with one or more configurations, and when a persistent store is created for a configuration, only the entities linked to that configuration are included in the persistence operation. In our example, we create two configurations. The first one will contain notes, and the second will store passwords.

In Xcode, open the MyStash.xcdatamodel model. Select the Note entity in the Entity pane, and the click the Configurations tab (the wrench icon) on the far right. This displays the list of configurations, as shown in Figure 9-18. Initially, only the default configuration exists, which contains both the Note and the System entities and isn't listed. Click the + button below the configuration list and add a configuration called **Notes**. Repeat the process to create another configuration called **Passwords**.

The Notes configuration currently has no associated entities. To add the Note entity to the associated list of entities, select the Notes entity, and then check the box beside the Notes configuration, as shown in Figure 9-19. To add the System entity to the Passwords configuration, select the System entity, and check the box beside the Passwords configuration, as shown in Figure 9-20.

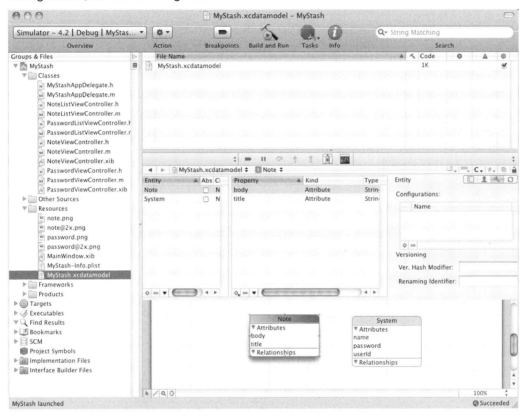

Figure 9-18. *The empty list of configurations*

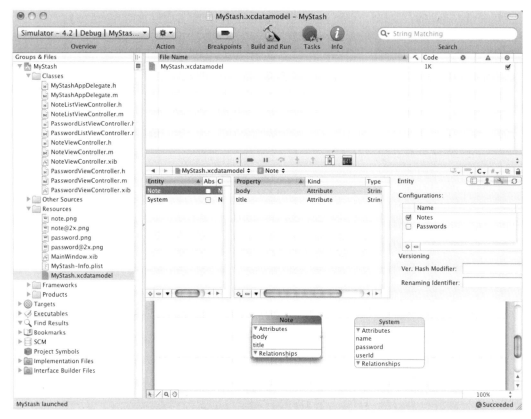

Figure 9-19. *The* Note *entity added to the* Notes *configuration*

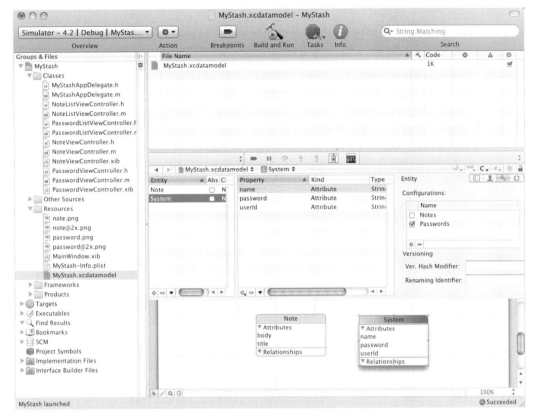

Figure 9-20. *The* System *entity added to the* Passwords *configuration*

You have now prepared your model for the persistent store split. All that is left to do is to create the persistent stores using the new configurations. For this, open MyStashAppDelegate.m, and change the persistentStoreCoordinator: method as shown here:

```
- (NSPersistentStoreCoordinator *)persistentStoreCoordinator {

  if (persistentStoreCoordinator_ != nil) {
    return persistentStoreCoordinator_;
  }

  persistentStoreCoordinator_ = [[NSPersistentStoreCoordinator alloc]➥
initWithManagedObjectModel:[self managedObjectModel]];

  {
    NSURL *passwordStoreURL = [NSURL fileURLWithPath: [[self ➥
applicationDocumentsDirectory] stringByAppendingPathComponent: @"Passwords.sqlite"]];

    NSError *error = nil;
```

```
    if (![persistentStoreCoordinator_ addPersistentStoreWithType:NSSQLiteStoreType➡
configuration:@"Passwords" URL:passwordStoreURL options:nil error:&error]) {

        NSLog(@"Unresolved error with password store %@, %@", error, [error userInfo]);
        abort();
    }
  }

  {
    NSURL *notesStoreURL = [NSURL fileURLWithPath: [[self ➡
applicationDocumentsDirectory] stringByAppendingPathComponent: @"Notes.sqlite"]];

    NSError *error = nil;
    if (![persistentStoreCoordinator_ addPersistentStoreWithType:NSSQLiteStoreType➡
configuration:@"Notes" URL:notesStoreURL options:nil error:&error]) {

        NSLog(@"Unresolved error with notes store %@, %@", error, [error userInfo]);
        abort();
    }
  }

  return persistentStoreCoordinator_;
}
```

Instead of creating a single store, we created two persistent stores in an almost identical manner. The only difference is that we explicitly named the configuration for the store to use, instead of passing `nil` for the configuration parameter. For `Passwords.sqlite`, we use the `Passwords` configuration, while the `Notes.sqlite` persistent store uses the `Notes` configuration.

This is a good time to take a deserved break and launch the application. Add a new note as well as a new password entry to verify that it works. To your dismay, you will find that your excitement is short lived because you won't notice any difference. But rejoice because this is exactly what we were aiming for: a change in the underlying persistent store structure shouldn't affect the rest of the MyStash application. Be content that the app still works even though you've completely changed how data is stored. To see the difference, we need to pop the hood open and take a look at the SQLite databases. Open a Terminal window, and go find your data stores using the following command:

```
find ~/Library/Application\ Support/iPhone\ Simulator/ -name "*.sqlite"
```

You will see your two new databases listed there, `Notes.sqlite` and `Passwords.sqlite`. If you open the `Notes.sqlite` database and run the `.schema` command, you will see the entire model, but although you can see that the note has been saved correctly, the `System` table does not contain any data.

```
sqlite> .schema
CREATE TABLE ZNOTE ( Z_PK INTEGER PRIMARY KEY, Z_ENT INTEGER, Z_OPT INTEGER, ZBODY
VARCHAR, ZTITLE VARCHAR );
CREATE TABLE ZSYSTEM ( Z_PK INTEGER PRIMARY KEY, Z_ENT INTEGER, Z_OPT INTEGER, ZUSERID
VARCHAR, ZNAME VARCHAR, ZPASSWORD VARCHAR );
CREATE TABLE Z_METADATA (Z_VERSION INTEGER PRIMARY KEY, Z_UUID VARCHAR(255), Z_PLIST
BLOB);
```

```
CREATE TABLE Z_PRIMARYKEY (Z_ENT INTEGER PRIMARY KEY, Z_NAME VARCHAR, Z_SUPER INTEGER,
Z_MAX INTEGER);
sqlite> select * from ZNOTE;
1|1|1|Type text here . . .|Note1
sqlite> select * from ZSYSTEM;
sqlite> .q
```

Now do the same procedure on the `Passwords.sqlite` database, and the opposite is true. The table for the `System` entity is populated but not the `Note`.

```
sqlite> .schema
CREATE TABLE ZNOTE ( Z_PK INTEGER PRIMARY KEY, Z_ENT INTEGER, Z_OPT INTEGER, ZBODY
VARCHAR, ZTITLE VARCHAR );
CREATE TABLE ZSYSTEM ( Z_PK INTEGER PRIMARY KEY, Z_ENT INTEGER, Z_OPT INTEGER, ZUSERID
VARCHAR, ZNAME VARCHAR, ZPASSWORD VARCHAR );
CREATE TABLE Z_METADATA (Z_VERSION INTEGER PRIMARY KEY, Z_UUID VARCHAR(255), Z_PLIST
BLOB);
CREATE TABLE Z_PRIMARYKEY (Z_ENT INTEGER PRIMARY KEY, Z_NAME VARCHAR, Z_SUPER INTEGER,
Z_MAX INTEGER);
sqlite> select * from ZNOTE;
sqlite> select * from ZSYSTEM;
1|2|1|User1|System1|Password1
```

You have successfully split your data model into two persistent stores. The next section explains a situation in which this might be useful.

Adding Encryption

Data encryption is a big deal for any application that requires storage of sensitive information. Core Data does not do much to help you with this task, but it doesn't stand in your way either. Securing data follows two schools of thought, and you may choose to adhere to either one based on your own needs and requirements. These two schools are either to encrypt the entire database file or to just encrypt selected fields within your data store. The next sections explain both options.

Persistent Store Encryption Using Data Protection

One of the security options that were deployed with the iPhone 3GS is hardware-level disk encryption. Apple calls it *data protection*. When enabled, it encrypts a portion of your disk when the device is locked and is automatically decrypted when the device is unlocked.

For data protection to work, it must be manually enabled. Keep in mind that this is hardware-level disk encryption and therefore it works only on the device itself, not on the iPhone Simulator. To enable it, open the iPhone settings, and navigate to **Settings ➤ General ➤ Passcode Lock**. Enable the passcode if not enabled yet. The bottom of the page will display "Data protection is enabled," as illustrated in Figure 9-21, if everything is properly set up.

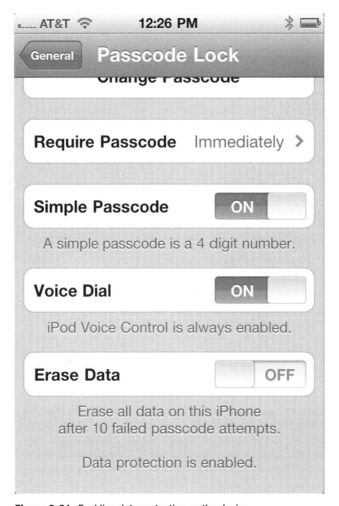

Figure 9-21. *Enabling data protection on the device*

From a programming standpoint, the work involved in encrypting your database is surprisingly simple. When creating the persistent store, we simply need to set the right attribute on the database file and let iOS do the rest. Open MyStashAppDelegate.m, and change the implementation of the persistentStoreCoordinator: to add the proper file attribute, as shown here. In this example, we are only going encrypt the password database.

```
- (NSPersistentStoreCoordinator *)persistentStoreCoordinator {

  if (persistentStoreCoordinator_ != nil) {
    return persistentStoreCoordinator_;
  }

  persistentStoreCoordinator_ = [[NSPersistentStoreCoordinator alloc]➡
initWithManagedObjectModel:[self managedObjectModel]];
```

```objectivec
{
    NSURL *passwordStoreURL = [NSURL fileURLWithPath: [[self➡
applicationDocumentsDirectory] stringByAppendingPathComponent: @"Passwords.sqlite"]];

    NSError *error = nil;
    if (![persistentStoreCoordinator_ addPersistentStoreWithType:NSSQLiteStoreType➡
configuration:@"Passwords" URL:passwordStoreURL options:nil error:&error]) {

        NSLog(@"Unresolved error with password store %@, %@", error, [error userInfo]);
        abort();
    }

    NSDictionary *fileAttributes = [NSDictionary➡
dictionaryWithObject:NSFileProtectionComplete forKey:NSFileProtectionKey];

    if(![[NSFileManager defaultManager] setAttributes:fileAttributes➡
ofItemAtPath:[passwordStoreURL path] error: &error]) {

        NSLog(@"Unresolved error with password store encryption %@, %@", error, [error➡
userInfo]);

        abort();
    }
}

{
    NSURL *notesStoreURL = [NSURL fileURLWithPath: [[self ➡
applicationDocumentsDirectory] stringByAppendingPathComponent: @"Notes.sqlite"]];

    NSError *error = nil;
    if (![persistentStoreCoordinator_ addPersistentStoreWithType:NSSQLiteStoreType➡
configuration:@"Notes" URL:notesStoreURL options:nil error:&error]) {

        NSLog(@"Unresolved error with notes store %@, %@", error, [error userInfo]);
        abort();
    }
}

    return persistentStoreCoordinator_;
}
```

When you run your application on a device that has data protection enabled, the
Passwords.sqlite database file will be automatically encrypted when the device is
locked. This method is cheap to implement, but you should be sure to understand that
once the device is unlocked, the file is automatically decrypted so the database is as
secure as the phone. If someone can guess the passcode, the database will be
accessible, especially if the phone is jailbroken (that is, root access is available). Another
inconvenience with this method is that for very large databases, the time it takes to
unlock and start your application might be rather large since a huge file will need to be
decrypted before it can be used.

Data Encryption

The other alternative to data security is to encrypt the data as you put it in the database. This is a case when you encrypt only what you want to secure. Let's assume that we want to be able to secure notes in the database. To support encrypted data, we modify the data model to use `Binary data` instead of `String` as the data type for the body attribute of the `Note` entity.

To make the programming easier, we create a `Note` class that extends `NSManagedObject`. Generate the `Note.h` and `Note.m` files to properly configure the object based on the `Note` entity using the same procedure shown in Chapter 5, "Working with Data Objects." Figure 9-22 shows the new setup.

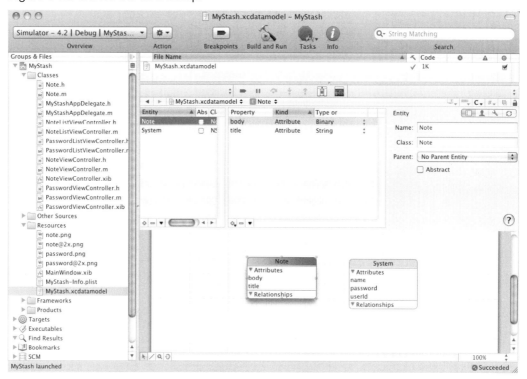

Figure 9-22. *The body attribute with binary data type*

Listings 9-8 and 9-9 show the `Note.h` and `Note.m` files.

Listing 9-8. *Note.h*

```
#import <CoreData/CoreData.h>


@interface Note :   NSManagedObject
{
}

@property (nonatomic, retain) NSString * title;
```

```
@property (nonatomic, retain) NSData * body;

@end
```

Listing 9-9. *Note.m*

```
#import "Note.h"


@implementation Note

@dynamic title;
@dynamic body;

@end
```

Using Encryption

iOS comes with an encryption library. To make encryption easier, we add a new category to the NSData class. In Xcode, create a new class, and call it NSData+Encryption. Since encryption algorithms lie outside the scope of this book, we simply give you the source code for NSData+Encryption.h in Listing 9-10 and NSData+Encryption.m in Listing 9-11. The basic principle is that this category adds two methods to the NSData class that will allow us to obtain an encrypted and decrypted version of its binary content.

Listing 9-10. *NSData+Encryption.h*

```
#import <Foundation/Foundation.h>

@interface NSData (Encryption)
- (NSData *)encryptWithKey:(NSString *)key;
- (NSData *)decryptWithKey:(NSString *)key;
@end
```

Listing 9-11. *NSData+Encryption.m*

```
#import <CommonCrypto/CommonCryptor.h>
#import "NSData+Encryption.h"

@implementation NSData (Encryption)

- (NSData *)transpose:(NSString *)_key forOperation:(int)operation {
    // Make sure the key is big enough or else add zeros
    char key[kCCKeySizeAES256+1];
    bzero(key, sizeof(key));

        // Populate the key into the character array
        [_key getCString:key maxLength:sizeof(key) encoding:NSUTF8StringEncoding];

        size_t allocatedSize = self.length + kCCBlockSizeAES128;
        void *output = malloc(allocatedSize);

        size_t actualSize = 0;
```

```
        CCCryptorStatus resultCode = CCCrypt(operation, kCCAlgorithmAES128,
kCCOptionPKCS7Padding,
                                    key, kCCKeySizeAES256, nil,
                                    self.bytes, self.length,
                                    output, allocatedSize, &actualSize);
        if (resultCode != kCCSuccess) {
    // Free the output buffer
    free(output);
    return nil;
    }

  return [NSData dataWithBytesNoCopy:output length:actualSize];
}

- (NSData *)encryptWithKey:(NSString *)key {
  return [self transpose:key forOperation:kCCEncrypt];
}

- (NSData *)decryptWithKey:(NSString *)key {
  return [self transpose:key forOperation:kCCDecrypt];
}

@end
```

Automatically Encrypting Fields

To provide automatic encryption and decryption, modify the Note object so that when new text is provided, it is automatically encrypted. Do this by adding a new attribute called text to the class and overriding its getter and setter to perform the encryption when necessary. Also, add a password attribute that will be used to temporarily store the password needed for encrypting and decrypting. The modified version of Note.h is shown in Listing 9-12.

Listing 9-12. *Note.h with New Attributes*

```
#import <Foundation/Foundation.h>
#import <CoreData/CoreData.h>

@interface Note : NSManagedObject {
  NSString* text;
  NSString* password;
}

@property (nonatomic, retain) NSString *title;
@property (nonatomic, retain) NSData *body;
@property (nonatomic, retain) NSString *text;
@property (nonatomic, retain) NSString *password;

@end
```

In Note.m, we add only a @synthesize directive for the password attribute since we will be providing our own implementation of the text attribute accessor methods. Make sure to import the new category, NSData+Encryption.h.

Begin with implementing the setText: method, as shown here:

```
-(void)setText:(NSString*)_text {
  text = [_text copy];

  if(text == nil) {
    self.body = nil;
    return;
  }

  NSData *data = [text dataUsingEncoding:NSUTF8StringEncoding];

  self.body = [data encryptWithKey:self.password];
}
```

This method simply takes the new text it is given and populates the body attribute using encryption. The getter for text does the opposite, as shown in the following snippet:

```
-(NSString*)text {
  if(text == nil) {
    NSData *data = self.body;
    if(data == nil) return nil;

    data = [data decryptWithKey:self.password];

    NSString *_text = [[NSString alloc] initWithData:data➡
encoding:NSUTF8StringEncoding];

    text = [_text copy];
    [_text release];
  }

  return text;
}
```

Of course, for all this to work, the user interface must access the text attribute instead of body. Before we can run the application again, we must modify the user interface code. Read the next section to understand what to change.

> **Note:** Since you have made a change to the data model without creating a new version of the model, you have to either delete the old SQLite files or simply reset the iPhone simulator. From the simulator menu, select **iPhone Simulator ➤ Reset Content and Settings**.

Changing the User Interface to Use the text Attribute

The first place to change is NoteListViewController.m. After importing Note.h, apply the following changes to the insertNoteWithTitle:body: method:

```
- (void)insertNoteWithTitle:(NSString *)title body:(NSString *)body {
  NSManagedObjectContext *context = [fetchedResultsController managedObjectContext];
  NSEntityDescription *entity = [[fetchedResultsController fetchRequest] entity];
```

```
  Note *newNote = [NSEntityDescription insertNewObjectForEntityForName:[entity name]➥
inManagedObjectContext:context];

  newNote.password = @"secret";
  newNote.title = title;
  newNote.text = body;

  [self saveContext];
}
```

Note how we stop using the body attribute of the Note entity and instead start using the
new text property of the Note class. We also create a password, which should obviously
be obtained from the user instead of being hard-coded. We leave this non-Core Data–
related task in your capable hands. You could, for example, have a different password
for each note in your own application. It is important, however, that you also apply this
password to any new note fetched from the data store, because passwords aren't
stored with the notes. This would really defy the purpose of encrypting. We make sure a
note can only make it to the user interface if it has its password set in the
configureCell:atIndexPath: method:

```
- (void)configureCell:(UITableViewCell *)cell atIndexPath:(NSIndexPath *)indexPath {
  Note *note = [self.fetchedResultsController objectAtIndexPath:indexPath];
  note.password = @"secret";
  cell.textLabel.text = note.title;
}
```

Edit NoteViewController to use the Note class instead of NSManagedObject.
NoteViewController.h is defined as shown in Listing 9-13.

Listing 9-13. *NoteViewController.h Using the* Note *Class*

```
#import <UIKit/UIKit.h>
#import <CoreData/CoreData.h>
#import "Note.h"

@class NoteListViewController;

@interface NoteViewController : UIViewController {
  IBOutlet UITextField *titleField;
  IBOutlet UITextView *body;
  NoteListViewController *parentController;
  Note *note;
}
@property (nonatomic, retain) UITextField *titleField;
@property (nonatomic, retain) UITextView *body;
@property (nonatomic, retain) NoteListViewController *parentController;
@property (nonatomic, retain) Note *note;

- (id)initWithParentController:(NoteListViewController *)aParentController➥
note:(Note*)aNote;

- (IBAction)save:(id)sender;
- (IBAction)cancel:(id)sender;

@end
```

Now make the appropriate changes in NoteViewController.m, starting with adjusting the newly modified signature for the init method:

```
- (id)initWithParentController:(NoteListViewController *)aParentController note:(Note➡
*)aNote {
  if ((self = [super init])) {
    self.parentController = aParentController;
    self.note = aNote;
  }
  return self;
}
```

Next, modify the viewDidLoad: method to utilize the text property instead of body:

```
- (void)viewDidLoad {
  [super viewDidLoad];
  if (note != nil) {
    titleField.text = note.title;
    body.text = note.text;
  } else {
    body.text = @"Type text here . . .";
  }
}
```

Make a similar change to the save: method:

```
- (IBAction)save:(id)sender {
  if (parentController != nil) {
    if (note != nil) {
      note.title = titleField.text;
      note.text = body.text;
      [parentController saveContext];
    }
    else {
      [parentController insertNoteWithTitle:titleField.text body:body.text];
    }
  }
  [self dismissModalViewControllerAnimated:YES];
}
```

The last change to make is back in NoteListViewController.m in order to deal with the recent API changes we have made. Edit the tableView:didSelectRowAtIndexPath: method to pass a Note object to the init: method:

```
- (void)tableView:(UITableView *)tableView didSelectRowAtIndexPath:(NSIndexPath➡
*)indexPath {
  Note *note = [[self fetchedResultsController] objectAtIndexPath:indexPath];

  NoteViewController *noteViewController = [[NoteViewController alloc]➡
initWithParentController:self note:note];

  [self presentModalViewController:noteViewController animated:YES];
  [noteViewController release];
}
```

Testing the Encryption

Unlike the previous section where we could not see the hardware-level encryption since it occurred only when the device was locked, with data encryption you can enjoy the peace of mind of verifying that your data is encrypted.

Launch the application and add a new note, as shown in Figure 9-23.

Figure 9-23. *Adding a new encrypted note*

We know you really enjoy running the MyStash app, but we need to ask you to put the toy down and take a look at the `Notes.sqlite` data store. Displaying the data in the table shows the encrypted data:

```
1|1|1|My encrypted note|?*YX}~?D□?.#?*?>?b?t
                        ?G
```

Of course, if you relaunch the application, the data will be decrypted properly before being displayed on the user interface. With this encryption strategy, you are in complete control of the data security. Regardless of whether the user has enabled data protection or not, the data is encrypted. If the device is stolen and unlocked, the data will still be encrypted.

Sending Notifications When Data Changes

On Mac OS X, Core Data provides UI bindings that allow you to link your data directly to your user interface. With iOS, however, Core Data currently offers no UI bindings, and the closest thing you have is the `NSFetchedResultsController`. When using that controller is not an option, you have to rely on your own coding, with some help from the Key-Value Observing (KVO) mechanism. Since `NSManagedObject` is Key-Value Coding (KVC) compliant, all the usual principles of KVO can be applied, and notifications can be fired on data modifications. The KVO model is very simple and decentralized, with only two objects at play: the observer and the observed. The observer must be registered with the observed object and the observed object is responsible for firing notifications when its data changes. Thanks to the default implementation of `NSManagedObject`, firing notifications is automatically handled for you.

To illustrate how to use notifications, we create an example in which an observer outputs an acknowledgment that it has received a change notification when the `name` attribute of the `System` entity is modified. For simplicity we output directly to the application console. In a real application, the KVO mechanism could be used to automatically update user interface elements.

Registering an Observer

To receive change notifications, the observer must be registered with the observed object using the `addObserver:forKeyPath:options:context:` method. The registration is valid for a given key path only, which means it is valid only for the named attribute or relationship. The advantage is that it gives you a very fine level of control over what notifications fire.

The options give you an even finer level of granularity by specifying what information you want to receive in your notifications. Table 9-1 shows the options, which can be combined with a bitwise OR.

Table 9-1. *The Notification Options*

Option	Description
NSKeyValueObservingOptionOld	The change dictionary will contain the old value under the lookup key NSKeyValueChangeOldKey.
NSKeyValueObservingOptionNew	The change dictionary will contain the new value under the lookup key NSKeyValueChangeNewKey.

In MyStash, we will add an observer for the System entities. Open
PasswordListViewController.m, and edit the configureCell:atIndexPath: method to
add the observer:

```
- (void)configureCell:(UITableViewCell *)cell atIndexPath:(NSIndexPath *)indexPath {
  NSManagedObject *system = [self.fetchedResultsController objectAtIndexPath:indexPath];
  cell.textLabel.text = [system valueForKey:@"name"];

  // Register this object for KVO
  [system addObserver:self forKeyPath:@"name"
          options:  NSKeyValueObservingOptionOld
                  | NSKeyValueObservingOptionNew context:nil];
}
```

In this case, we are registering the PasswordListViewController as an observer of the
name attribute that wants to receive the old and new values when the attribute for this
managed object is modified.

Receiving the Notifications

To receive notifications, the observer must provide an implementation for the
observeValueForKeyPath:ofObject:change:context: method. This is the method that is
called when a registered notification is fired. Since PasswordListViewController is the
observer, we add the method in PasswordListViewController.m:

```
- (void)observeValueForKeyPath:(NSString *)keyPath ofObject:(id)object
                    change:(NSDictionary *)change context:(void *)context {
  NSLog(@"Changed value for %@: %@ -> %@", keyPath,
      [change objectForKey:NSKeyValueChangeOldKey],
      [change objectForKey:NSKeyValueChangeNewKey]);
}
```

The change dictionary contains the modifications. Since we asked for both the old and
new values when we registered the observer, we can extract both values from the
dictionary.

Launch the application, and open the output console. Edit an existing password by
changing the system name, as shown in Figure 9-24:

Figure 9-24. *Changing the system name in MyStash*

You will see output in the console to show that the notification was received:

```
2010-12-17 16:58:28.751 MyStash[10305:207] Changed value for name: System1 -> System1New
```

Note that the change doesn't happen until you save the change and the context is saved.

The KVO mechanism provides you a simple way to respond to changes in your application's data.

Seeding Data

A question we hear often concerns how to distribute a persistent store that already contains some data. Many applications, for example, include a list of values for the user to pick from to categorize the data they enter, and developers need to populate the data store with those values. You can approach this problem in several ways, including creating a SQLite database yourself and distributing that with your application instead of allowing Core Data to create the database itself, but this approach has its drawbacks, especially if a future version of your application augments this list of values. You really shouldn't overwrite the user's database file with a new, otherwise blank one that has more values in its list.

What, then, is a simple approach that allows for future change? If you've been following along with the examples in this book, you've already preloaded data into your data stores many times. Think about all the applications in this book that don't have user interfaces and how you got data into those. That's right: you created managed objects in code and then saved the managed object context. If we extend this approach a bit with a version to identify the data that's been loaded, you can easily determine in code whether to add more values in the future. In this section, we show you how to seed data into a Core Data–created persistent store in a way that allows you to change the preseeded data in future versions of your application.

Adding Categories to Passwords

To demonstrate seeding a list of values in the data store, we'll add a category to the passwords in the MyStash application. Open the data model for MyStash, and add an entity named Category with a nonoptional attribute of type String called name. Add this new entity to the Passwords configuration. Add a to-many relationship called "systems" that has the System entity as its destination, and add an inverse relationship called "category" to the System entity.

To support versioning, add another entity called List with two attributes: a String called name and an Integer 16 called version. Add it to the Passwords configuration.

Your data model should look like Figure 9-25.

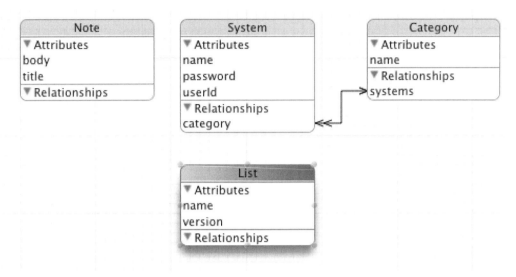

Figure 9-25. *The updated MyStash data model for seeding data*

Add three method declarations to MyStashAppDelegate.h: one to load the data, one to save the context, and a helper to create a Category managed object:

```
- (void)loadData;
- (void)saveContext;
- (NSManagedObject *)addCategoryWithName:(NSString *)name;
```

Add a call to the loadData: method in MyStashAppDelegate.m, in the application:didFinishLaunchingWithOptions: method, as the first line in that method.

Then, implement the method. It should do the following:

1. Fetch the version number for the "category" entry in the List entity, creating the entry if it doesn't exist.

2. Based on the version number, determine which category managed objects to create and create them.

3. Update the version number.

4. Save the managed object context.

The code for the loadData: method should look like this:

```
#pragma mark -
#pragma mark Seed Data

- (void)loadData {
  // Get the version object for "category"
  NSManagedObjectContext *context = [self managedObjectContext];
  NSFetchRequest *request = [[NSFetchRequest alloc] init];
  [request setEntity:[NSEntityDescription entityForName:@"List"➥
inManagedObjectContext:context]];
```

```
    [request setPredicate:[NSPredicate predicateWithFormat:@"name = 'category'"]];
    NSArray *results = [context executeFetchRequest:request error:nil];
    [request release];

    // Get the version number. If it doesn't exist, create it and set version to 0
    NSManagedObject *categoryVersion = nil;
    NSInteger version = 0;
    if ([results count] > 0) {
      categoryVersion = (NSManagedObject *)[results objectAtIndex:0];
      version = [(NSNumber *)[categoryVersion valueForKey:@"version"] intValue];
    } else {
      categoryVersion = [NSEntityDescription insertNewObjectForEntityForName:@"List"➥
inManagedObjectContext:context];

      [categoryVersion setValue:@"category" forKey:@"name"];
      [categoryVersion setValue:[NSNumber numberWithInt:0] forKey:@"version"];
    }

    // Create the categories to get to the latest version
    if (version < 1) {
      [self addCategoryWithName:@"Web Site"];
      [self addCategoryWithName:@"Desktop Software"];
    }

    // Update the version number and save the context
    [categoryVersion setValue:[NSNumber numberWithInt:1] forKey:@"version"];
    [self saveContext];
}
```

You can see that the code fetches the entry for "category" in the List entity and creates it if it doesn't exist. It pulls the version number for that entry to determine which version of the category list has been loaded. The first time you run this, the version will be set to zero. The code then adds the categories it should based on the version number and updates the version number to the latest so that subsequent runs won't append data that has already been loaded.

> **Note:** For the purpose of demonstrating the mechanism, we coded our seed data by hand. In a real application, you should consider pulling the lists from some text file or CSV file, for example.

The helper method for adding categories looks like this:

```
- (NSManagedObject *)addCategoryWithName:(NSString *)name {
  NSManagedObject *category = [NSEntityDescription➥
insertNewObjectForEntityForName:@"Category" inManagedObjectContext:[self➥
managedObjectContext]];

  [category setValue:name forKey:@"name"];
  return category;
}
```

And the method to save the context should look familiar:

```
- (void)saveContext {
  NSManagedObjectContext *context = [self managedObjectContext];
  NSError *error = nil;
  if (![context save:&error]) {
    NSLog(@"Unresolved error %@, %@", error, [error userInfo]);
    abort();
  }
}
```

Build and run the application, and then open Passwords.sqlite using sqlite3. If you run the .schema command, you'll see that the new tables for Category and List are present:

```
CREATE TABLE ZCATEGORY ( Z_PK INTEGER PRIMARY KEY, Z_ENT INTEGER, Z_OPT INTEGER, ZNAME
VARCHAR );
CREATE TABLE ZLIST ( Z_PK INTEGER PRIMARY KEY, Z_ENT INTEGER, Z_OPT INTEGER, ZVERSION
INTEGER, ZNAME VARCHAR );
```

The version number for the "category" list has been created:

```
sqlite> select zversion from zlist where zname='category';
1
```

Finally, the expected categories have been loaded:

```
sqlite> select * from zcategory;
1|1|1|Web Site
2|1|1|Desktop Software
```

You have successfully seeded your data store with category values. You can quit and rerun the application, and you'll notice that your versioning prevents these values from reloading and duplicating what's already been loaded.

Creating a New Version of Seeded Data

Suppose you want to add credit card PINs as a category. Adding a version to this code is simple. You simple add another if statement, guarded by the new version number, and change the version number that's written to the database. Here is the code for adding the entries for versions 1 and 2:

```
// Create the categories to get to the latest version
if (version < 1) {
  [self addCategoryWithName:@"Web Site"];
  [self addCategoryWithName:@"Desktop Software"];
}
if (version < 2) {
  [self addCategoryWithName:@"Credit Card PIN"];
}
```

Note that the code adds the entries cumulatively so that if you're running the application for the first time, you get the categories for both versions 1 and 2, but if you're already at version 1, the code loads only the values for version 2.

Finally, you update the version number in the data store to reflect the version currently loaded:

```
// Update the version number and save the context
```

```
[categoryVersion setValue:[NSNumber numberWithInt:2] forKey:@"version"];
[self saveContext];
```

We haven't updated the MyStash user interface to use the categories, but we leave that as an exercise for you.

Error Handling

When you ask Xcode to generate a Core Data application for you, it creates boilerplate code for every vital aspect of talking to your Core Data persistent store. This code is more than adequate for setting up your persistent store coordinator, your managed object context, and your managed object model. In fact, if you go back to a non–Core Data project and add Core Data support, you'll do well to drop in the same code, just as Xcode generates it, to manage Core Data interaction. The code is production ready.

That is, it is production ready except in one aspect: error handling.

The Xcode-generated code alerts you to this shortcoming with a comment that says this:

```
/*
  Replace this implementation with code to handle the error appropriately.

  abort() causes the application to generate a crash log and terminate. You should not
use this function in a shipping application, although it may be useful during
development. If it is not possible to recover from the error, display an alert panel
that instructs the user to quit the application by pressing the Home button.
*/
```

The Xcode-generated implementation logs the error and aborts the application, which is a decidedly unfriendly approach. All users see when this happens is your application abruptly disappearing, without any clue to why. Causing this to happen in a shipping application garners poor reviews and low sales.

Happily, however, you don't have to fall into this trap of logging and crashing. In this section, we explore strategies for handling errors in Core Data. No one strategy is the best, but this section should spark ideas for your specific applications and audiences and help you devise an error-handling strategy that makes sense.

We can divide errors in Core Data into two major categories:

- Errors in normal Core Data operations
- Validation errors

We discuss strategies for handling both types of errors, in turn.

Handling Core Data Operational Errors

All the examples in this book respond to any Core Data errors using the default, Xcode-generated error-handling code, dutifully outputting the error message to Xcode's console and aborting the application. This approach has two advantages:

■ It helps diagnose issues during development and debugging.

■ It's easy to implement.

These advantages help only you as developer, however, and do nothing good for the application users. Before you release an application that uses Core Data to the public, you should design and implement a better strategy for responding to errors. The good news is, the strategy needn't be large or difficult to implement, because your options for how to respond are limited. Although applications are all different, in most cases you won't be able to recover from a Core Data error and should probably follow Apple's advice, represented in the previous comment: display an alert and instruct the user to close the application. Doing this explains to users what happened and gives them control over when to terminate the app. It's not much control, but hey—it's better than just having the app disappear.

Virtually all Core Data operational errors should be caught during development, so careful testing of your app should prevent these scenarios. Dealing with them, however, is simple: just follow Apple's advice from the comment. To add error handling code to the MyStash application, declare a method in `MyStashAppDelegate.h` for showing the alert:

```
- (void)showCoreDataError;
```

Then, add the implementation to `MyStashAppDelegate.m`. You can quibble with the wording, but remember that error messages aren't a paean to the muses, and the longer the message, the less likely it will be read. Here's an implementation with a short and simple message, with only an extraneous exclamation to plead with the user to read it:

```
- (void)showCoreDataError {
  UIAlertView *alert = [[UIAlertView alloc] initWithTitle:@"Error!" message:@"MyStash➥
can't continue.\nPress the Home button to close MyStash." Delegate:nil➥
cancelButtonTitle:nil otherButtonTitles:@"OK", nil];

  [alert show];
  [alert release];
}
```

Now, change the `persistentStoreCoordinator` accessor method to use this new method instead of logging and aborting. The updated method should look like this, with the changed lines in bold:

```
- (NSPersistentStoreCoordinator *)persistentStoreCoordinator {

  if (persistentStoreCoordinator_ != nil) {
    return persistentStoreCoordinator_;
  }

  persistentStoreCoordinator_ = [[NSPersistentStoreCoordinator alloc]➥
initWithManagedObjectModel:[self managedObjectModel]];

  {
```

```
    NSURL *passwordStoreURL = [NSURL fileURLWithPath: [[self➥
applicationDocumentsDirectory] stringByAppendingPathComponent: @"Passwords.sqlite"]];


    NSError *error = nil;
    if (![persistentStoreCoordinator_ addPersistentStoreWithType:NSSQLiteStoreType➥
configuration:@"Passwords" URL:passwordStoreURL options:nil error:&error]) {
  [self showCoreDataError];
    }


    NSDictionary *fileAttributes = [NSDictionary➥
dictionaryWithObject:NSFileProtectionComplete forKey:NSFileProtectionKey];

    if(![[[NSFileManager defaultManager] setAttributes:fileAttributes➥
ofItemAtPath:[passwordStoreURL path] error: &error]) {
      [self showCoreDataError];
    }
  }

  {
    NSURL *notesStoreURL = [NSURL fileURLWithPath: [[self ➥
applicationDocumentsDirectory] stringByAppendingPathComponent: @"Notes.sqlite"]];


    NSError *error = nil;
    if (![persistentStoreCoordinator_ addPersistentStoreWithType:NSSQLiteStoreType➥
configuration:@"Notes" URL:notesStoreURL options:nil error:&error]) {
      [self showCoreDataError];
    }
  }

  return persistentStoreCoordinator_;
}
```

To force this error to display, run the MyStash application, and then close it. Go to the data model, add an attribute called foo to the Note entity, and then run the application again. The persistent store coordinator will be unable to open the data store, because the model no longer matches, and your new error message will display as in Figure 9-26.

Figure 9-26. *Handling a Core Data error*

That's probably the best you can do to handle unexpected errors. The next section, however, talks about handling expected errors: validation errors.

Handling Validation Errors

If you've configured any properties in your Core Data model with any validation parameters and you allow users to input values that don't automatically meet those validation parameters, you can expect to have validation errors. As you learned in Chapter 4, you can stipulate validation parameters on the properties of the entities in your data model. Validations ensure the integrity of your data; Core Data won't store anything you've proclaimed invalid into the persistent store. Just because you've created the validation rules, however, doesn't mean that users are aware of them, or even that they know that they can violate them. If you leave the Xcode-generated error handling in place, users won't know they've violated the validation rules even after they input invalid data. All that will happen is that your application will crash, logging a long stack trace that the users will never see. Users will be left bewildered with a crashing application, and they won't know why or how to prevent its occurrence. Instead of crashing when users enter invalid data, you should instead alert users and give them an opportunity to correct the data.

Validation on the database side can be a controversial topic, and for good reason. You can protect your data's integrity at its source by putting your validation rules in the data model, but you've probably made your coding tasks more difficult. Validation rules in your data model are one of those things that sound good in concept but prove less desirable in practice. Can you imagine, for example, using Oracle to do field validation on a web application? Yes, you can do it, but other approaches are probably simpler, more user-friendly, and architecturally superior. Validating user-entered values in code, or even designing user interfaces that prevent invalid entry altogether, make your job easier and users' experiences better.

Having said that, however, we'll go ahead and outline a possible strategy for handling validation errors. Don't say we didn't warn you, though.

Detecting that users have entered invalid data is simple: just inspect the NSError object that you pass to the managed object context's save: method if an error occurs. The NSError object contains the error code that caused the save: method to fail, and if that code matches one of the Core Data validation error codes shown in Table 9-2, you know that some part of the data you attempted to save was invalid. You can use NSError's userInfo dictionary to look up more information about what caused the error. Note that if multiple errors occurred, the error code is 1560, NSValidationMultipleErrorsError, and the userInfo dictionary holds the rest of the error codes in the key called NSDetailedErrorsKey.

Table 9-2. *Core Data Validation Errors*

Constant	Code	Description
NSManagedObjectValidationError	1550	Generic validation error
NSValidationMultipleErrorsError	1560	Generic message for error containing multiple validation errors
NSValidationMissingMandatoryPropertyError	1570	Nonoptional property with a nil value
NSValidationRelationshipLacksMinimumCountError	1580	To-many relationship with too few destination objects
NSValidationRelationshipExceedsMaximumCountError	1590	Bounded, to-many relationship with too many destination objects

(Continued)

Table 9-2. *Continued*

Constant	Code	Description
NSValidationRelationshipDeniedDeleteError	1600	Some relationship with NSDeleteRuleDeny is nonempty
NSValidationNumberTooLargeError	1610	Some numerical value is too large
NSValidationNumberTooSmallError	1620	Some numerical value is too small
NSValidationDateTooLateError	1630	Some date value is too late
NSValidationDateTooSoonError	1640	Some date value is too soon
NSValidationInvalidDateError	1650	Some date value fails to match date pattern
NSValidationStringTooLongError	1660	Some string value is too long
NSValidationStringTooShortError	1670	Some string value is too short
NSValidationStringPatternMatchingError	1680	Some string value fails to match some pattern

You can choose to implement an error-handling routine that's familiar with your data model and thus checks only for certain errors, or you can write a generic error handling routine that will handle any of the validation errors that occur. Though a generic routine scales better and should continue to work no matter the changes to your data model, a more specific error-handling routine may allow you to be more helpful to your users in your messaging and responses. Neither is the correct answer—the choice is yours for how you want to approach validation error handling.

To write a truly generic validation error handling routine would be a lot of work. One thing to consider is that the NSError object contains a lot of information about the error that occurred, but not necessarily enough information to tell the user why the validation failed. Imagine, for example, that we have an entity Foo with an attribute bar that must be at least five characters long. If the user enters **abc** for bar, we'll get an NSError message that tells us the error code (1670), the entity (Foo), the attribute (bar), and the value (abc) that failed validation. The NSError object doesn't tell us why abc is too short—it contains no information that bar requires at least five characters. To arrive at that, we'd have to ask the Foo entity for the NSPropertyDescription for the bar attribute, get the validation predicates for that property description, and walk through the predicates to see what the minimum length is for bar. It's a noble goal but tedious and usually overkill. This is one place where violating DRY and letting your code know something about the data model might be a better answer.

One other strange thing to consider when using validations in your data model is that they aren't enforced when you create a managed object; they're enforced only when you try to save the managed object context that the managed object lives in. This makes sense if you think it through, since creating a managed object and populating its properties happens in multiple steps. First you create the object in the context, and then you set its attributes and relationships. So, for example, if you were creating the managed object for the Foo entity in the previous paragraph, you'd write code like this:

```
NSManagedObject *foo = [NSEntityDescription insertNewObjectForEntityForName:@"Foo"➡
inManagedObjectContext:[self managedObjectContext]]; // foo is invalid at this point;➡
bar has fewer than five characters
[foo setValue:@"abcde" forKey:@"bar"];
```

The managed object foo is created and lives in the managed object context in an invalid state, but the managed object context ignores that. The next line of code makes the foo managed object valid, but that won't be validated until the managed object context is saved.

Handling Validation Errors in MyStash

In this section, you implement a validation error handling routine for the MyStash application. It's generic in that it doesn't have any knowledge of which attributes have validation rules set but specific in that it doesn't handle all the validation errors—just the ones that we know we set on the model. Before doing that, however, you need to add some validation rules to MyStash's data model. Make the following changes to the userId attribute of the System entity:

- Set Min Length to 3.
- Set Max Length to 10.
- Set the regular expression to allow only letters and numbers: [A-Za-z0-9]*.

The attribute fields should match Figure 9-27. Save the data model. Now you're ready to implement the validation error-handling routine.

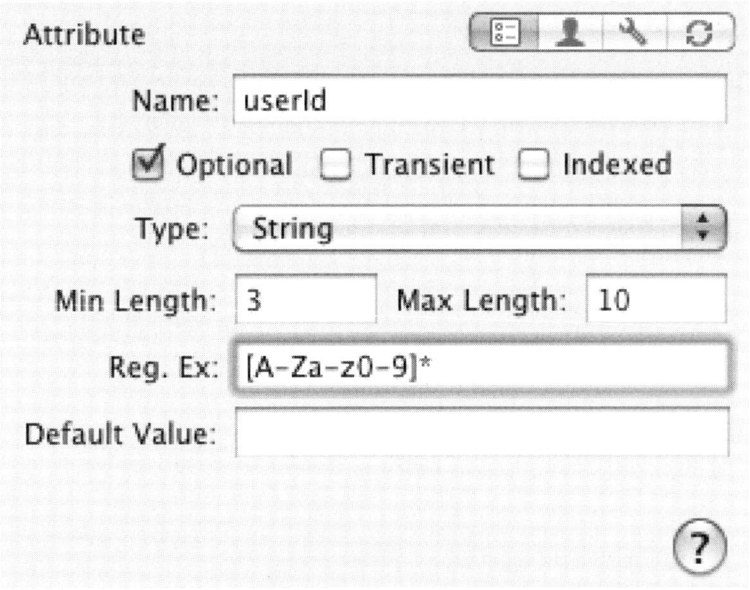

Figure 9-27. *Setting validations on the* userId *attribute of* System

Implementing the Validation Error Handling Routine

The validation error handling routine you write should accept a pointer to an NSError object and return an NSString that contains the error messages, separated by line feeds. Open PasswordListViewController.h, and declare the routine:

```
- (NSString *)validationErrorText:(NSError *)error;
```

The routine itself, which goes in PasswordListViewController.m, creates a mutable string to hold all the error messages. It then creates an array that holds all the errors, which can be multiple errors or a single error. It then iterates through all the errors, gets the property name that was in error, and, depending on the error code, forms a proper error message. Notice that some knowledge of the model (the minimum and maximum lengths, 3 and 10) is hard-coded, because the error objects don't have that information. The method should look like this:

```
#pragma mark -
#pragma mark Validation Error Handling

- (NSString *)validationErrorText:(NSError *)error {
  // Create a string to hold all the error messages
  NSMutableString *errorText = [NSMutableString stringWithCapacity:100];

  // Determine whether we're dealing with a single error or multiples, and put them ➡
all in an array

  NSArray *errors = [error code] == NSValidationMultipleErrorsError ? [[error ➡
userInfo] objectForKey:NSDetailedErrorsKey] : [NSArray arrayWithObject:error];
```

```
  // Iterate through the errors
  for (NSError *err in errors) {
    // Get the property that had a validation error
    NSString *propName = [[err userInfo] objectForKey:@"NSValidationErrorKey"];
    NSString *message;
    // Form an appropriate error message
    switch ([err code]) {
      case NSValidationMissingMandatoryPropertyError:
        message = [NSString stringWithFormat:@"%@ required", propName];
        break;
      case NSValidationStringTooShortError:
        message = [NSString stringWithFormat:@"%@ must be at least %d characters",➥
propName, 3];

        break;
      case NSValidationStringTooLongError:
        message = [NSString stringWithFormat:@"%@ can't be longer than %d characters",➥
propName, 10];

        break;
      case NSValidationStringPatternMatchingError:
        message = [NSString stringWithFormat:@"%@ can contain only letters and ➥
numbers", propName];

        break;
      default:
        message = @"Unknown error. Press Home button to halt.";
        break;
    }
    // Separate the error messages with line feeds
    if ([errorText length] > 0) {
      [errorText appendString:@"\n"];
    }
    [errorText appendString:message];
  }
  return errorText;
}
```

You have a fair amount of jiggling to do to the code to incorporate this routine into the application. Start in PasswordListViewController.h, and change the return types for two methods, for reasons that will become apparent in a few moments. Change insertPasswordWithName: to return an NSManagedObject*, and change saveContext: to return an NSString*, like this:

```
- (NSManagedObject *)insertPasswordWithName:(NSString *)name userId:(NSString *)userId➥
password:(NSString *)password;
- (NSString *)saveContext;
```

The reason insertPasswordWithName: must now return an NSManagedObject* is that you may have to delete the managed object this method creates. Consider the following sequence of events:

1. User taps + to create a new password.

2. User enters invalid data.

3. User taps Save. A new managed object is created in the context, but saving fails.

4. User dismisses the alert that complains of invalid data.

5. User taps Cancel.

If you don't have a handle to the newly created object so you can delete it, in this scenario the invalid object would still exist in the managed object context, and subsequent saves would fail without recourse. The updated `insertPasswordWithName:` method looks like this:

```
- (NSManagedObject *)insertPasswordWithName:(NSString *)name userId:(NSString *)userId➥
password:(NSString *)password {
  NSManagedObjectContext *context = [fetchedResultsController managedObjectContext];
  NSEntityDescription *entity = [[fetchedResultsController fetchRequest] entity];
  NSManagedObject *newPassword = [NSEntityDescription➥
insertNewObjectForEntityForName:[entity name] inManagedObjectContext:context];

  [newPassword setValue:name forKey:@"name"];
  [newPassword setValue:userId forKey:@"userId"];
  [newPassword setValue:password forKey:@"password"];

  return newPassword;
}
```

The `saveContext:` method will now return the error text if the save fails. Otherwise, it will return `nil`. It looks like this:

```
- (NSString *)saveContext {
  NSString *errorText = nil;
  NSManagedObjectContext *context = [fetchedResultsController managedObjectContext];
  NSError *error = nil;
  if (![context save:&error]) {
    errorText = [self validationErrorText:error];
  }
  return errorText;
}
```

The only thing that has to change in the `PasswordViewController` class is the implementation of the `save:` method. Remember how simple and clean it used to be? Well, it's simple no more. Users can now do things like edit an existing system entry, change some values so they're invalid, tap Save (which updates the values on the object), and then tap Cancel after dismissing the alert. You must change this method to undo any changes if a validation occurs, so save state before you make any changes so you can restore the state if any errors occur. If any errors occur, show the alert and don't dismiss the modal. The new method looks like this:

```
- (IBAction)save:(id)sender {
  NSString *errorText = nil;

  // Create variables to store pre-change state, so we can back out if validation ➥
errors occur
```

```objc
    NSManagedObject *tempSystem = nil;
    NSString *tempName = nil;
    NSString *tempUserId = nil;
    NSString *tempPassword = nil;

    if (parentController != nil) {
      if (system != nil) {
        // User is editing an existing system. Store its current values
        tempName = [NSString stringWithString:(NSString *)[system valueForKey:@"name"]];➥
        tempUserId = [NSString stringWithString:(NSString *)[system➥
valueForKey:@"userId"]];

        tempPassword = [NSString stringWithString:(NSString *)[system➥
valueForKey:@"password"]];


        // Update with the new values
        [system setValue:name.text forKey:@"name"];
        [system setValue:userId.text forKey:@"userId"];
        [system setValue:password.text forKey:@"password"];
      } else {
        // User is adding a new system. Create the new managed object but keep a pointer➥
to it

        tempSystem = [parentController insertPasswordWithName:name.text userId:userId.➥
text password:password.text];
      }
      // Save the context and gather any validation errors
      errorText = [parentController saveContext];
    }
    if (errorText != nil) {
      // Validation error occurred. Show an alert.
      UIAlertView *alert = [[UIAlertView alloc] initWithTitle:@"Error!" message:➥
errorText delegate:nil cancelButtonTitle:nil otherButtonTitles:@"OK", nil];

      [alert show];
      [alert release];

      // Because we had errors and the context didn't save, undo any changes this method➥
made

      if (tempSystem != nil) {
        // We added an object, so delete it
        [[parentController.fetchedResultsController managedObjectContext]➥
deleteObject:tempSystem];

      } else {
        // We edited an object, so restore it to how it was
        [system setValue:tempName forKey:@"name"];
        [system setValue:tempUserId forKey:@"userId"];
        [system setValue:tempPassword forKey:@"password"];
      }
    } else {
      // Successful save! Dismiss the modal only on success
      [self dismissModalViewControllerAnimated:YES];
    }
```

```
}
```

Whew! That was an awful lot of work to move validations to the data model. As you explore this way to do validations, you'll probably agree that designing better user interfaces (for example, enabling the Save button only when the userId field contains valid data) or validating values in code is a better approach.

If you run this application, tap to add a new password, and enter more than ten characters, including punctuation, in the User ID field, you'll see the fruits of your validation labor, as shown in Figure 9-28.

Figure 9-28. *Setting validations on the* userId *attribute of* System

Summary

In this chapter, you explored several advanced topics relating to Core Data. Some you'll most likely use, like the NSFetchedResultsController, in many of your applications. Some, like encryption, you might use only occasionally. You'll certainly use some sort of error handling strategy, although we hope you'll avoid the pain of model validations.

As you've worked through this book, you've learned how broad and deep Core Data is. You learned how much work Core Data does for you, and you learned what work you must do to properly interact with the Core Data framework. We hope you've enjoyed reading this book as much as we enjoyed writing it, and we look forward to hearing from you as you use Core Data in your applications!

Index

■S

You Need the Companion eBook

Your purchase of this book entitles you to buy the companion PDF-version eBook for only $10. Take the weightless companion with you anywhere.

We believe this Apress title will prove so indispensable that you'll want to carry it with you everywhere, which is why we are offering the companion eBook (in PDF format) for $10 to customers who purchase this book now. Convenient and fully searchable, the PDF version of any content-rich, page-heavy Apress book makes a valuable addition to your programming library. You can easily find and copy code—or perform examples by quickly toggling between instructions and the application. Even simultaneously tackling a donut, diet soda, and complex code becomes simplified with hands-free eBooks!

Once you purchase your book, getting the $10 companion eBook is simple:

❶ Visit **www.apress.com/promo/tendollars/**.

❷ Complete a basic registration form to receive a randomly generated question about this title.

❸ Answer the question correctly in 60 seconds, and you will receive a promotional code to redeem for the $10.00 eBook.

THE EXPERT'S VOICE™

233 Spring Street, New York, NY 10013

Offer valid through 8/11.